T0321771

Model-Based Design for Effective Control System Development

Wei Wu
Independent Researcher, USA

A volume in the Advances in
Systems Analysis, Software
Engineering, and High Performance
Computing (ASASEHPC) Book Series

www.igi-global.com

Published in the United States of America by
    IGI Global
    Information Science Reference (an imprint of IGI Global)
    701 E. Chocolate Avenue
    Hershey PA, USA 17033
    Tel: 717-533-8845
    Fax: 717-533-8661
    E-mail: cust@igi-global.com
    Web site: http://www.igi-global.com

Library of Congress Cataloging-in-Publication Data

Names: Wu, Wei (Control engineer), author.
Title: Model-based design for effective control system development / by Wei
    Wu.
Description: Hershey, PA : Information Science Reference, [2017] | Includes
    bibliographical references and index.
Identifiers: LCCN 2016058439| ISBN 9781522523031 (hardcover) | ISBN
    9781522523048 (ebook)
Subjects: LCSH: Automatic control--Design and construction. | Embedded
    computer systems--Design and construction. | Microcontrollers--Design and
    construction. | Manufacturing processes--Simulation methods.
Classification: LCC TJ213 .W876 2017 | DDC 629.8/9--dc23 LC record available at https://lccn.
loc.gov/2016058439

This book is published in the IGI Global book series Advances in Systems Analysis, Software Engineering, and High Performance Computing (ASASEHPC) (ISSN: 2327-3453; eISSN: 2327-3461)

British Cataloguing in Publication Data
A Cataloguing in Publication record for this book is available from the British Library.

All work contributed to this book is new, previously-unpublished material.
The views expressed in this book are those of the authors, but not necessarily of the publisher.

For electronic access to this publication, please contact: eresources@igi-global.com.

Advances in Systems Analysis, Software Engineering, and High Performance Computing (ASASEHPC) Book Series

ISSN:2327-3453
EISSN:2327-3461

Editor-in-Chief: Vijayan Sugumaran, Oakland University, USA

MISSION

The theory and practice of computing applications and distributed systems has emerged as one of the key areas of research driving innovations in business, engineering, and science. The fields of software engineering, systems analysis, and high performance computing offer a wide range of applications and solutions in solving computational problems for any modern organization.

The **Advances in Systems Analysis, Software Engineering, and High Performance Computing (ASASEHPC) Book Series** brings together research in the areas of distributed computing, systems and software engineering, high performance computing, and service science. This collection of publications is useful for academics, researchers, and practitioners seeking the latest practices and knowledge in this field.

COVERAGE

- Computer graphics
- Storage Systems
- Human-Computer Interaction
- Performance Modelling
- Software Engineering
- Network Management
- Parallel Architectures
- Metadata and Semantic Web
- Computer Networking
- Computer System Analysis

IGI Global is currently accepting manuscripts for publication within this series. To submit a proposal for a volume in this series, please contact our Acquisition Editors at Acquisitions@igi-global.com or visit: http://www.igi-global.com/publish/.

Titles in this Series

For a list of additional titles in this series, please visit:
http://www.igi-global.com/book-series/advances-systems-analysis-software-engineering/73689

Comparative Approaches to Using R and Python for Statistical Data Analysis
Rui Sarmento (University of Porto, Portugal) and Vera Costa (University of Porto, Portugal)
Information Science Reference • ©2017 • 197pp • H/C (ISBN: 9781683180166) • US $180.00

Developing Service-Oriented Applications Using the Windows Communication Foundation (WCF) Framework
Chirag Patel (Charotar University of Science and Technology, India)
Information Science Reference • ©2017 • 487pp • H/C (ISBN: 9781522519973) • US $200.00

Resource Management and Efficiency in Cloud Computing Environments
Ashok Kumar Turuk (National Institute of Technology Rourkela, India) Bibhudatta Sahoo
(National Institute of Technology Rourkela, India) and Sourav Kanti Addya (National Institute
of Technology Rourkela, India)
Information Science Reference • ©2017 • 352pp • H/C (ISBN: 9781522517214) • US $205.00

Handbook of Research on End-to-End Cloud Computing Architecture Design
Jianwen "Wendy" Chen (IBM, Australia) Yan Zhang (Western Sydney University, Australia)
and Ron Gottschalk (IBM, Australia)
Information Science Reference • ©2017 • 507pp • H/C (ISBN: 9781522507598) • US $325.00

Innovative Research and Applications in Next-Generation High Performance Computing
Qusay F. Hassan (Mansoura University, Egypt)
Information Science Reference • ©2016 • 488pp • H/C (ISBN: 9781522502876) • US $205.00

Developing Interoperable and Federated Cloud Architecture
Gabor Kecskemeti (University of Miskolc, Hungary) Attila Kertesz (University of Szeged,
Hungary) and Zsolt Nemeth (MTA SZTAKI, Hungary)
Information Science Reference • ©2016 • 398pp • H/C (ISBN: 9781522501534) • US $210.00

Managing Big Data in Cloud Computing Environments
Zongmin Ma (Nanjing University of Aeronautics and Astronautics, China)
Information Science Reference • ©2016 • 314pp • H/C (ISBN: 9781466698345) • US $195.00

For an enitre list of titles in this series, please visit:
http://www.igi-global.com/book-series/advances-systems-analysis-software-engineering/73689

www.igi-global.com

701 East Chocolate Avenue, Hershey, PA 17033, USA
Tel: 717-533-8845 x100 • Fax: 717-533-8661
E-Mail: cust@igi-global.com • www.igi-global.com

Table of Contents

Preface

Model based design uses a physical model of equipment or a process for system design, simulation, verification and validation against requirements throughout the product development cycle. The model based control design process comprises these steps: requirements specification, architecture design and controllability analysis, control algorithms design, automatic code generation, system integration and testing, and lab and field testing. Validation and verification is done early and often at different phases of the development cycle at the model level, the software level and the hardware level using the model-in-the-loop (MIL) simulation, the software-in-the-loop (SIL) simulation, and the hardware-in-the-loop (HIL) simulation technique respectively. By using a model of a product or process, simulation and testing are done earlier compared to the conventional design approach, where testing is done late in the development cycle on the real process, it thus saves the time and costs incurring during the lab testing and also catches design errors earlier in the development cycle, tremendously reducing the costs spent for fixing bugs. A system model including the model of the process under control and its environment, and the model of the controller can be used to verify that the control design meet all product requirements and the final product functions meet the customer needs. Using model based design tools, productivity is greatly improved by automatically generating production code from control algorithm models, automatically generating design documents from the models, and managing the models using a configuration management tool among a distributed design team.

Control systems exist in a lot of technical domains, different industries and all sorts of products, i.e. from navigation, to transportation, to appliances in homes, and consumer electronics. With the rapid technology advancements in hardware, computational power, and design tools, control systems become more and more complex with increasing number of functions and lines of code implementing these functions, their analysis and design become more challenging, especially for safety-critical products and large, complex embedded control systems. It is common that a large project team is distributed at different locations and organizational and cultural barriers make communications among team members difficult. Applying mode based design process to embedded control systems meets the current challenges and are being adopting by more and more companies and industries.

Model-based design is a model-centric approach to the development of control and other dynamic systems. Rather than relying on physical prototypes and textual specifications, model-based design uses a system level model throughout development. The model includes every component relevant to system behavior—algorithms, control logic, physical components, environment. Once the model is developed (elaborated), it becomes the source of many outputs, including reports and C code. Model-based design enables system-level and component-level design and simulation, automatic code generation, and continuous test and verification.

Model-based control design application can be flexible. Model-based design can support almost any organizational type, and it has been implemented successfully within many different development processes. How you implement it depends on the size, structure, and culture of your organization, as well as the systems being developed and the demands of your target market. You might choose to adopt model-based design enterprise-wide, transforming your entire development process; alternatively, you might apply it selectively to address a specific challenge, such as a workflow bottleneck, a sudden change in design requirements, or increased system complexity.

There are many books treating model-based design, but their application domains are mainly systems engineering and software engineering. Also there are numerous controls book, most of them very academic (focused on algorithms and not processes) and not directly useful for industrial engineers in the author's opinion. This book deals with the embedded controls system design integrated with the model-based design. Practical, industrial controls development process applying model based design techniques is presented in this book. Combining two topics: model-based design and embedded controls software development while focusing on practical techniques for solving industrial control problems, makes this book uniquely useful for engineers. It will help engineering teams in various industries set up the state-of-the-art design process for embedded controls development and apply practical controls techniques to improve development cycle, costs, efficiency, and product quality.

This book discusses how to design embedded control systems following the model based design process. The following steps and methods in the development cycle are included in the book: requirement definition, architecture design, controllability analysis, algorithm design, MIL/SIL/HIL simulation, verification and validation, documentation and configuration management. In the control algorithm design part, practical industrial design approaches are presented, together with real examples demonstrating their applications accumulated during the past fifteen years of the author's experiences from industrial projects and research.

This book is mainly for controls engineers, system engineers, embedded software engineers, test engineers, modeling engineers, and project managers in a broad range of industries such as automotive, aerospace, HVAC/R and process control, for controls software development; it can be used by undergraduate students and graduate students in the system and controls area of different engineering disciplines if they want to start a engineering career in the industry after their graduation. It can be used by corporations, e.g. for training purpose. Many large corporations have adopted and are adopting model-based design in product development. This book provides the practical knowledge of the model-based design process and methods that engineering teams can benefit. The readers of this book can directly apply these methods and processes or modify them to suit to their daily work, for example to develop new controls applications, upgrade an existing control system, improve development processes, etc. They will be able to do their job better, developing higher quality products with less time and costs. To benefit the most from this book, a reader is expected to have some knowledge of and experience in systems engineering, controls system, and modeling and computer simulation using tools such as MATLAB and Simulink/Stateflow.

It is the author's hope that readers of this book will become motivated in exploring further on mode-based design and practical control system design and developing more effective and efficient methods and processes for creating high quality controls systems to benefit their careers, their organizations, and welfare of the society at large.

Chapter 1
Model–Based Control Design

INTRODUCTION

Control applications are widespread and are still expanding into emerging areas. In aviation, control is used for guidance, navigation and control (GNC), for engine control, and for vehicle power and environmental control (temperature and pressure). In automotive, control is used for powertrain, suspension, traction, braking and steering. Control is widely applied in process industries: refineries, pulp and paper, and chemical processing. Control is also used in manufacturing machines, appliances, robotics, power generation and transmission, and transportation such as elevators, locomotives. More and more control is implemented in control application software on embedded control systems. Embedded control product development focus is shifting from hardware development to control software development. With ever increasing system complexity, control software development consumes more and more budget and time of product development projects, and the quality of the control software is becoming increasingly important to a product success in the market place.

Model-based control design is adopted by more and more companies and industries for developing embedded control systems. It applies systems engineering principles with the aid of modeling to control system development, ensuring the final product meeting customer needs and requirements through a rigorous design and testing process. In this chapter, we first give a brief introduction of systems engineering, then we talk about why we want to use

DOI: 10.4018/978-1-5225-2303-1.ch001

models and model-based design in embedded control system development. With new technologies and tasks introduced by model-based design, proper design and testing tools are required to efficiently implement a model-based design. Popular tools used in model-based design process are discussed, focusing on their usages. At the end, a model-based control design process is presented, with detailed description of each of it steps. This process can be applied directly to develop an embedded control system or it can be customized by the user to suit his/her project needs under realistic product development constraints.

SYSTEM ENGINEERING

Nowadays, more and more products with embedded control system appear in the markets and enter people's daily life. Aircraft can fly on autopilot and avoid collision; smart collision avoidance systems in automotive alert drivers to nearby vehicles and even take emergency evasive action. Control system implementation is moving from hardware to embedded software due to the enormous growth of the processing power of embedded microprocessor. For instance, today's modern cars contain dozens of microprocessors that may run 100millions lines of code for the purpose of delivering hundreds of functions to drivers and passengers. More often it is the software, rather than electronics, that makes a product stand out and determines the market winners. The inherent flexibility of software offers lots of opportunities to develop additional control functions, enabling manufacturers to create innovative products to meet customer expectations. By enabling seemingly boundless product functionality, software has taken center stage in all kinds of products, enabling many new kinds of interconnections between parts of the product and between the product and it environment. More connections create exponential increases in system complexity. This new development trend creates additional challenges for controls engineers.

There are many challenges for embedded control systems development. Expertise in multiple technical fields is needed, including electronics and software engineering. As software driven functionalities become the focal point, you have to get your hardware and software teams to work together really well. There are others issues controls engineers are facing today. More and more development teams are located in different places around the world; effectively managing distributed teams to ensure efficient, accurate and cooperative results becomes an issue. As customer demand for new control functions shortens the service life of even the best products, shrinking the product development life cycle to make sure you hit the market at the right time is a challenge. Changing customer needs, dynamic market conditions, and reprioritized corporate goals all cause the changes in product requirements. Adapting to ever-changing requirements presents a challenge to controls engineer. In some industries, for example aerospace industry, products are required to meet government regulatory and industry standards. Ensuring compliance of control products is also an issue to be addressed.

If you are unable to develop complex control products in a shorter cycle without compromising quality, you will lose revenue and market share. Large, complex control systems often have hundreds, even thousands, of unique requirements, making it difficult to maintain quality while shortening development cycles. Nearly one third of all devices produced today simply fail to meet the performance or functional requirements.

Model based design can be applied to developing large, complex (control) systems to meet a defined set of business and technical requirements. The aerospace, automotive and defense industries have been using model based design for a long time, and more and more other industries are adopting this approach to develop more complex, smart products, like appliances and HVAC (heating-ventilation-air-conditioning) equipment. Model based design is an application of systems engineering which aims to help you to manage complex product development and meet the product goals. Systems engineering has a few guiding principles, including the following:

- **Keep Your Eyes on the Prize:** Define the desired outcome of a project right from the start and don't stray away from your goal no matter how crazy things get.
- **Involve Key Stakeholders:** Get inputs from customers, engineers, managers, and others as you make decisions at various stages of the development process.
- **Break Down the Problem Into Manageable Chunks:** Decompose the system into smaller subsystems, and then divide each subsystem into hardware or software components. Managing the interfaces between components and subsystems ensures that they integrate successfully and ultimately deliver the required system capabilities.
- **Connect Requirements and Design:** Make sure that design decisions are justified by linking them back to specific technical and business requirements.

3

- **Test Early, Test Often:** Use models, prototypes, simulators, and any other ways to evaluate the system during the development cycle. Link requirements and tests and make sure tests prove that requirements are satisfied.

Over the past 20 or so years, experts in complex system design have developed and refined the systems engineering process, known as the V-model, which embodies the guiding principles (see Figure 1).

The V-model is a graphical representation of a series of steps for complex systems development. Travelling through the "V" from left to right, the process steps being executed are the following:

- **Concept of Operations (ConOps):** Identify and document key stakeholder needs, overall system capabilities, and performance measures for system validation at the end of the project.

Figure 1. The V-model for systems engineering process

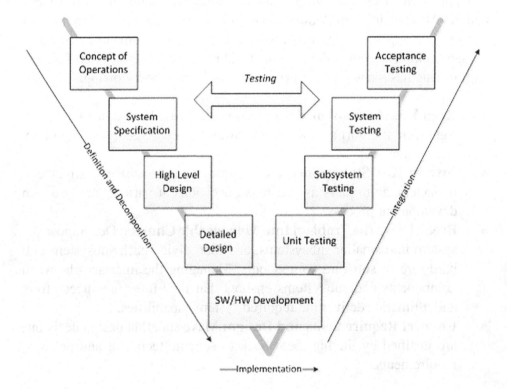

- **System Specification:** Define a set of verifiable system requirements that meet needs defined during ConOps.
- **High-Level Design:** Design a high-level system architecture that satisfies the system requirements and map out requirements for subsystems based on the system architecture.
- **Detailed Design:** Develop component-level requirements based on subsystems requirements.
- **Software/Hardware Development:** Select and procure the appropriate technology and develop the software and hardware to meet the component-level design specs.
- **Unit Testing:** Test each hardware and software component, verifying its functionality against the appropriate component requirements.
- **Subsystem Testing:** Integrate software and hardware components into subsystems. Test and verify each subsystem against subsystem-level requirements.
- **System Testing:** Integrating subsystems into system and test the entire system against system requirements. Verify that all interfaces have been properly implemented and all requirements and constraints have been satisfied.
- **Acceptance Testing:** Validate that the system developed achieves its intended goals.

Throughout the systems engineering process, you create and refine system documentation. At each step on the left side of the 'V", you create the requirements that drive the next step, as well as a test plan for verifying the implementation of the current level of decomposition. At each step on the right side of the "V", you create documentation to support system training, usage, maintenance, installation and testing. By linking all the steps on the left side of the "V" through requirement using requirement allocation and referring back to these requirements as you move up the right side of the "V", it is much more likely to maintain objectivity throughout the process and meet product goals at the end. These linkages provides for traceability in systems engineering.

WHY DO WE USE MODELS?

Model-based control design is centered on models or is model-centric. Why do we use models? Models are useful, especially when you are working on a complex system. If you can develop relatively inexpensive ways of designing, testing and verifying your system before you build it, you can save a lot of time and money. Models can be used to design, refine and test system throughout the development process.

System models allow you to capture complexity at many different levels, for example system, subsystem, and component levels. They enable you to explore the details of each of these levels independently and hide or expose details as appropriate. Models can be developed at different level of details, and it represents the relevant features and behaviors of the system under investigation. At each level of abstraction, the model can represent what you need to know about the system and hide extra details. There are various forms of models, graphical, symbolic (mathematical), and descriptive, etc. Physical or data driven system models used for computer simulation are often used in model-based control design.

Using models give you the following benefits. Models capture both the structure and behavior of a system, specifying relationships and interactions between system components. You can use models to predict behavior at various levels of abstraction, enabling to explore different architecture and design options early in the development cycle and perform trade studies to assess various design choices. You can develop executable models, allowing you to validate your design against requirements using through simulation before you build your system and running lab tests. You can view the details of a model from different perspectives (for example, architectural, logical, functional, physical, data, control, etc.), so you can address specific issues using the model. Models offer a lot of visibility into a system, providing a powerful focal point for discussion, mutual team understanding, and managing the development effort. Models offer a shared place to capture thoughts and design decisions, making it easier for the development team to collaborate. Most importantly, the system model provides a synchronization point across multiple engineering disciples involving in complex system development, offering a solution to the problem of coordinating hardware and software.

Systems by their nature consists of multiple levels, starting from the overall system at the highest level, and decomposing into subsystems, and subsystems decomposing then into components (only three levels are used here, sometimes subassemblies and parts are considered under the level of subsystems). The best way to model a system is to use a multi-step recursive process CURE, starting at the top, that consists of the following four stages:

- **Context:** Establish the boundaries of your system, identify people and systems with which your system interacts, and describe the interfaces. This contextual model defines the system and its surroundings.
- **Usage:** Describe the ways in which the system is used. Include who or what uses the system, and who or what the system uses. This is best done in specific, step-by-step, narrative-like stories of system usage, such as use cases. The same use cases become the basis for system testing later.
- **Realization:** Define structure and behavior models that together describe how each need of the system is achieved by the system through collaboration among components within the system architecture. Required behavior is realized in the components of the system.
- **Execution:** Execute the behavior models to demonstrate that your design satisfies the requirements. Simple, executable models, even at high levels of abstraction are a great and costing-saving way to discover bugs, miscommunications, missing or ambiguous requirements, and other schedule-busting issues early on.

In this layered modeling process, you start at the highest level of decomposition: the system level (the system itself). After establishing context and usage models, you define high level architecture and behavior models based on the system requirements. Then, you execute the models to demonstrate they indeed accomplish the system's intended uses. After you have completed the four steps for the system level, repeat the process for the next level of decomposition: the subsystem level. Continue to drill down through levels of decomposition, shifting your context, derive the requirements as you proceed to model at each subsequent level, until you reach the lowest level, the component level, where you specify the physical implementation of your design (for instance, electronics, software, or mechanical design). At each level, reach horizontally across the "V" and perform verification and validation using the models. Using executable models and other kinds of mathematical and design simulations to do as much verification as you can before reaching the implementation stage.

Modeling allows you to capture all of the details of your system design in an organized fashion, enabling you to visualize, understand, and assimilate the complexities of the system structure and behavior. It allows you to explore different architecture and design options, perform trade studies, and assess the impact of changes before you begin to build your system, thus driving down risk and development costs. Models provide context for reasoning about system concerns at various levels. You can use models to explore multiple views of a system so you can investigate big picture issues as easily as detailed design issues. Using industry-standard modeling languages and techniques reduces ambiguity and removes language barriers existing between members of diverse development teams, and provides a single master source for project development status and documentation. Improved collaboration and clear, precise documentation lead to greater efficiencies, shorter development cycles, and improved product quality.

WHY DO WE USE MODEL-BASED DESIGN?

In today's world of increasingly complex software-driven products, quality must become an integral part of the system development process for any hope of delivering products that are not only defect-free, but also demonstrate a fitness for purpose. Model-based design helps identify quality issues through validation and verification early in the development cycle, leading to improved chances for achieving quality goals.

The quality process starts when you start to design the system. You don't wait until the system is built to test it, good systems engineering practice exploits more sophisticated techniques for ensuring quality as the system is being built. As each component of the system (hardware or software) is built, it is tested by itself then integrated with others to form a subsystem. Next, the subsystem is tested by itself and then integrated with others to form the system, and then the system is tested. Finally, the whole system is tested along with its operating environment (within its context) to make sure the entire system fulfills it intended functions and uses in the real world. Before you test real components, subsystems, and the system, verification and validation can be performed on models through analysis and simulations for unit testing, subsystem testing, and system testing, bringing any problems to light early. The sooner you discover a defect, the cheaper it is to fix it. The cost of correcting defects increases dramatically throughout the development process: defects discovered after the product release can cost nearly 100 times more to fix than defects found during the requirement phase. By sticking to a rigorous testing process at each phase of the development process, you can drastically reduce the cost of fixing product defects by fixing it early.

Moving from document-centric to model-centric development process improves team collaboration and communication, eventually leading to improved productivity. Models at each level embody the design and are linked to requirements through bi-directional traceability, making it easier to ensure that the design meets the requirements. Design decisions are shared within the design team by using models: any changes to requirements leading to subsequent changes in the design are captured and reflected by the modified models. Models can be put under the management of a version control tool, making it possible for concurrent development. By using model as the source of reference, there is no miscommunication among large, distributed development teams because models are maintained in such a way that they always reflect up-to-date design and requirements. Modern model-based design tools have the capability of generating customizable design documents and requirements documents from the models, making documentation of the design easier and more efficient since it eliminates the copy-and-paste actions and the chance of missing the latest changes in design and requirements when creating documents.

Model-centric design approach links the requirements, design, testing, documentation, and production code seamlessly together using models. Quality is ensured by verification and validation using models at every stage of the design process. One of the biggest challenges in engineering complex embedded products is identifying defects earlier in the development process. Most defects are introduced during the design process, but not detected until the testing phase or, worse yet, after the product has made its way to the production or market. By testing often and testing early using executable models, model-based design is incredibly valuable in decreasing product defects. Various simulation techniques used for verification, model in the loop (MIL), software in the loop (SIL), hardware in the loop (HIL), and rapid control prototyping, can be applied to test the design based on models. Advanced model-based design tools also provide model checking against various industrial modeling standards to ensure the best and consistent model practices before generating production code from the models. Automatic code generation is another great benefit of using models. It saves costs and times of development and also improves quality. Various static code analysis techniques built into commercial model-based design tools can be applied to the model before generating code from it and the code generated from the model to improve model and code quality and coverage.

Focus of development of complex systems is shifting now from hardware to software. The majority of product innovations are realized by embedded systems and especially by software such as in the car industry. Costs of software development of complex systems are increasing rapidly, while hardware development costs remain constant or have small increases. In embedded system development, software design, implementation, and testing makes up more than 50% of the total man-hours, and approximately half of the research and development costs are taken up by software development. Today's software development is facing big challenges like shortened development times, higher quality requirements, and especially the growing complexity because of the rising number of functions and the increasing interactions between the functions. To master these challenges, software development paradigm is changed to model-based development. On the websites of model-based design tool vendors many success stories can be found, which report efficiency gains from up to 50% in the development, higher error reductions and a more rapid increase of maturity level of developed functions because of model-based development.

A model-based development process is specifically feasible in embedded domains like automotive software due to the fact that development in these domains is driven by two factors: on the one side the evolutionary develop of the systems, dealing with the iterated integration of new functions into a substantial amount of existing/legacy functionality from previous system versions; on the other side platform-independent development, substantially reducing the amount of reengineering/maintenance caused by fast changing hardware generations. As a result, a model-based approach is employed to enable a shift of focus of the development process on the early phases, supporting a function-based rather than a code-based engineering of embedded systems. A model-based approach, focusing on model of functionality as the most stable asset, promises considerable productivity increases, improvements in quality and cost savings.

On the other hand, the model-based development brings challenges since the use of model-based design results in a major process redesign. The introduction of model-based design influences established development processes, required resources and skills, thereby also the organizational structure. In addition, high investment costs for model-based design tools and for training of the employees for model-based design required skills are necessary. Costs and time of developing models can have big impact on a product development project as well. However, reuse of developed models for subsequent development pays off. One study shows that when having introduced model-based development, companies sometimes reported of huge productivity losses, because of immature tools and all companies reported of high costs for the process redesign from traditional to model-based development. The benefits of using models are seen in improving the understanding and communications among stakeholders.

MODEL-BASED DESIGN TOOL CHAIN

Tool support of model-based design is one of the key concerns from an industry adoption perspective. Model-based design process is different from the traditional development process, and it introduces a set of new technologies. Therefore it requires a new set of tools to aid in implementing these technologies and making model-based development process easier to execute and more efficient. Specific model-based design tool chains were developed as solutions for different companies. What tools to select and how to manage them to establish a highly efficient tool chain become centric for delivering the model-based design benefits and making model-based design projects successful.

Requirements still exist in textual form in Microsoft® Word or other documents. Requirement management tools such as IBM® Rational® DOORS® and DOORS Next Generation (DNG) are being widely adopted by companies in various industries. The widely adopted Systems Modeling Language (SysML) gives you a framework for modeling requirement. SysML enables you to create hierarchical requirements models that illustrate dependencies, classify requirements as original or derived, and capture design choice rationales. SysML requirements diagrams enable you to easily view the relationships and analyze the impact of changes to requirements on the system.

In system design, various general or domain-specific modeling languages are used for different needs. MATLAB/Simulink and Modelica are used as domain-specific modeling languages in a wide span of domains, while SCADE is mostly used for safety-critical systems and requires a strong background in rigorous design. Each language and its associated toolset provide good support for their own development process from modeling to implementation. However, a virtual integration using multiple languages and models can turn out to be complicated, ambiguous, and unpredictable.

Today, the model-based design tools developed by MathWorks and other tool vendors are widely adopted by corporations in various industries. Using MathWorks model-based development tools as examples, we introduce the type of tools needed for model-based design process, for instance modeling, verification, code generation, model checking, etc.

A typical system model is developed using Simulink block diagrams, Stateflow state machines and embedded MATLAB code. Embedded MATLAB is a subset of the MATLAB language that supports both simulation and C source code generation; it has grown to include most of operators and functions typically used for embedded deployment and real-time simulation. Together, they provide engineers with a highly flexible, multiple domain modeling environment for expressing system, software, and hardware designs.

In order for the model to be useful, it needs to execute or simulate. For simulation, Simulink (the graphical dynamic modeling environment) first requires that the model compile successfully per the model's diagnostic settings. Syntax and semantic checks are performed during the model compilation stage to check the model is well specified and complete. Subsequent run time analyses occur during the normal course of simulation such as array out-of-bounds and overflow checks.

Simulink model contains a hierarchy of components, capturing the complexity of real systems. Common components include subsystems, subsystems in libraries, and referenced models. The components can be virtual or non-virtual. Virtual components are graphical conveniences that do not impact simulation behavior. Non-virtual components impact simulation behavior because they are treated as atomic units and thus affect sorting and execution order. A related impact also occurs during code generation where C functions can be created for atomic subsystems yet virtual subsystems always produce in-line code.

Subsystems are part of the top level model they are placed in and cannot be changed independent of the parent model. Subsystems in libraries do exist in separate library models, however, they are not fully atomic or independent of the model they are placed in. Model reference allows the parent models to reference other models in separate model files through use of model blocks. A model block placed in parent model references a child model in a way that preserves the child model's interface.

The Real-Time Workshop Embedded Coder product should be used to generate code because it offers the greatest control of the code output options relating to efficiency, traceability, and verifiability. A code generation advisor for Real-Time Workshop Embedded Coder helps developers quickly establish settings based on criteria such as efficiency, traceability, or safety-precaution. In addition to generation of C code, now generation of C++, Verilog, and VHDL is supported, making it easy to target a variety of processors and hardware depending on the project's needs

Verifying the object code executing on the target against the model is necessary. Automated code verification using software-in-the-loop and process-in-the-loop testing is available with Simulink. Code generation verification APIs automates SIL and PIL using scripts for batch testing. Simulink Test™ provides a similar capability using graphical interface and automated reporting. Simulink Test™ provides tools for authoring, managing, and executing systematic, simulation-based tests of models, generated code, and simulated or physical hardware. It includes a Test Sequence block that lets you construct complex test sequences and assessments, and a test manager for managing and executing tests. Simulink Test enables functional, baseline, equivalence, and back-to-back testing, including software-in-the-loop (SIL), processor-in-the-loop (PIL), and real-time hardware-in-the-loop (HIL). You can apply pass and fail criteria that include absolute and relative tolerances, limits, logical checks, and temporal conditions. Setup and cleanup scripts help you automate or customize test execution. You can create nonintrusive test harnesses to test components in the system model or in a separate test model. You can store test cases and their results, creating a repository for reviewing and investigating failures. You can generate reports, archive and review test results, rerun failed tests, and debug the component or system under test. With Simulink Test and Simulink Verification and Validation™ toolbox, you can link test cases to requirements captured in Microsoft® Word, IBM® Rational® DOORS®, and other documents.

Using Model-based design, verification and validation occurs throughout development process. A number of new technologies have been introduced that assist with early model verification such as requirements traceability, model checking, model coverage, formal methods, and test case generation.

The Model Advisor with Simulink Verification and Validation™ checks models for areas that may impede the model's use in software environments. Some checks focus on simulation aspects, and others on code efficiency and a series of checks address certification standards such as DO-178B. There is also an API and graphical editor for adding custom, project–specific, checks.

Another important verification step is to develop and execute model tests based on requirements. Bidirectional linking between the model and requirements in documents, data bases, or requirements management tools such as DOORS is supported with the requirement management interface (RMI) in Simulink Verification and Validation. Requirements can appear in the generated code as comments with automated linking to and from the model. Requirements can also be linked to tests cases of the model.

With Simulink Design Verifier™ product, test cases can be automatically generated from the model based on desired model coverage criteria, such as MC/DC. Simulink Design Verifier can detect design error, for instance divide by zero, overflow, and dead logic. Simulink Design Verifier provides special blocks that help engineers perform formal proofs using formal methods to access the design logic and enhance its robustness.

Once the model has satisfied its requirement-based test and model structural test such as coverage, production code can be automatically generated from the model. Verification of the code with the model is performed using software-in-the-loop and processor-in-the-loop tests as previously mentioned.

Finally, in addition to the simulation based testing, it is important to analyze and verify your software using formal analysis, for example to show absence of certain run-time errors or to perform MISRA-C and JSF++ code checking. PolySpace code verification products enable this and support C, C++, and Ada source code.

Simulink Report Generator can automatically generate design and requirement documents from the model. It provides the capability for user to customize formats and contents of these reports. MATLAB also provides the capability to create local folder on developer computer for version control of the model or link to a server which runs version control management software such SVN for version control of models and other project files by creating a project within MATLAB.

MODEL-BASED CONTROL DESIGN PROCESS

The section focuses specifically on those steps associated with development of industrial embedded control systems including modeling, design, simulation, and verification and validation. Design of control systems covers control algorithms, control application software, and integrated embedded control system hardware. Model-based control design procedures are primarily associated with feedback control functions and corresponding control application software. Practical issues of control design include technical requirements, field service/support requirements, integration with existing system features, marketing needs, and regulation and certification. These issues can be better dealt with using model-based control design approach. In the development of real control applications, it is more than the control algorithm design, implementation and operational factors such as saturation, bumpless transfer, initialization, fault recovery, manual/auto mode and mode change, startup/shutdown, signal processing, user interface, etc. all affect the control system quality and user experience during its operation. Model-based design can help include these factors early in the design phase and analyze their effects on the overall system behavior and performance. Model-based design process can be applied to new product development, upgrading of legacy products, or reverse engineering of existing products. Model-based control design can be applied to the development of a whole control system, a subsystem of a control system, or a single control algorithm.

MODEL-BASED CONTROL DESIGN WORKFLOW

The Model-based control development process follows a standard design/verification systems engineering process like the one in the V model. The use of models of the system or equipment under control (the plant) as well as of the control laws and control logic is at the foundation of this process. The process is composed of nine steps here, and can be applied for the design of an entire control system or a part like a single control algorithm. The workflow graph of the process is laid out in Figure 2.

It is important to note that:

- Engineers with different roles and competencies participate and collaborate in the execution of the process such as systems engineer, product engineer, modeling engineer, testing engineer, and controls engineer. Control design is not exclusively the job of the controls engineer.

Figure 2. Model-based control design process

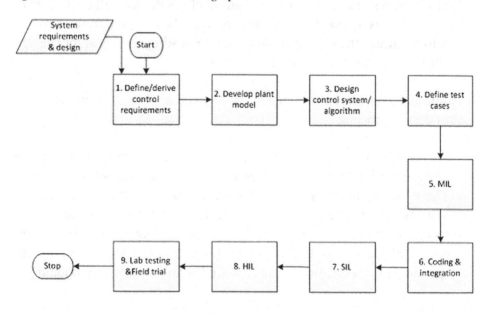

- The complete model-based design process is presented. However, the user can adopt the process by tailoring it to meet specific application needs, for example executing the process up to Step 5 of MIL testing, or up to Step 7 of SIL testing.
- Steps 1 to 5 are applied iteratively until the performance of the integrated control system or individual algorithm is satisfactory in terms of meeting control requirements.
- The process loop of Step 1-5 can be applied either for the design of a full control system or that of one or more control algorithms of a larger control system.
- Depending on the nature of the control development project, not all steps 1-5 may be executed within a single refinement iteration; and activities may occur in parallel for example step 1 and step 4.
- A series of formal verification steps together with model transformation and integration steps follow after Step 5. After the control models undergo formal Model-in-the-loop (MIL) verification, models are transformed into source code (automatic code generation is preferred than hand-written code). Code is again verified via SIL (at the unit level as well as at the integrated SW system level). Integration of software into the embedded platform follows. The integrated embedded hardware controller is tested via HIL before conducting final tests in the lab.
- All model-based verification steps use the plant (system under control) model as a substitute for the real physical system as well as models of the test cases to enable automated testing. The end goal of this process is to minimize the time spent in the lab for testing and to explore design alternatives early in the design process.

Additional considerations must be made when applying the model-based control design process:

- As mentioned above, a dynamic model of the system under control (the physical plant model) is used in lieu of the actual physical system. The dynamic model is an abstraction of the real physical system. It must be developed with a prescribed level of fidelity so that control requirements can be verified. This imposes that an initial concept design of the system under control has been made based on domain-specific (e.g. mechanical or electrical) design analysis and modeling.

- Verification is conducted by performing a series of tests involving closed loop simulations to check against verifiable requirements. The closed loop model is run in test cases that represent system real operation conditions or use cases. The test outputs are reviewed using agreed upon criteria to determine pass or fail of a test.
- Test generator and test monitor are models which derive from requirements through a formalization process, where requirements initially expressed in textual form are rewritten as logical expressions and then modeled in Simulink. See Chapter 7 for details on this topic.

Step 1: Define/Derive Control Requirements

Control systems, like any other systems of a product that have to be designed, require of specifying and properly managing requirements. Control requirements as derived from system requirements specifications define what the control system is expected to do, where the control system is part of the whole system. During this step, engineers also define the control problem, e.g. what inputs and outputs are available for control, what are the operational constraints and performance targets. Requirements are available in standard requirement documents, such as the SRD (for the top level system), SSRD (for subsystems including controls), and the SRS (software requirement specification for a control algorithm).

Controls requirements derive both from system requirements (e.g. product functionality, energy consumption and safety) within a defined range of operating conditions and component constraints to ensure proper system behavior and performance. Three categories of requirements are generally defined:

1. The first task of the control system is to ensure that the system and key components are protected. In other words, the system must be kept within its operational range.
2. The second task is generally that of meeting the functional requirements.
3. Last, the control system should operate to optimize the system efficiency in all conditions.

Other requirements including non-functional requirements are then specified depending on the specific system and operating conditions. Two important aspects to consider are:

- The definition of the system's operational range in terms of desired set point ranges and external environmental conditions.
- The specification of the system sensors and actuators to which the control system will interface. Requirements that aim at preserving the health of the actuators may exist, including rate of change, and on-off cycling limitations. Requirements on the measurement devices include resolution, range, sensitivity and dynamic characteristics.

It should be emphasized here that requirements definition should always be completely separated from implementation and design decisions. In other words, requirements tell what the control system should do (e.g. keeping a temperature at a desired set point), not what it should be (e.g. a PI control algorithm). Mixing requirements and implementation often leads to missing out on finding the best possible design.

As the control system is decomposed according to different functions, specific requirements may be developed for those functions. A hierarchy of requirements is typically created with the requirements on the component control algorithms at the bottom. Procedures and guidelines on how to capture, structure, and document requirements are discussed in Chapter 2.

Step 2: Develop Plant Dynamic Model

The availability of a dynamic model of the system under control is at the core of model-based design and verification. Dynamic models are developed in a modeling environment such as MathWorks Simulink and Stateflow. Specific details on how to create and validate a dynamic model are described next.

Define Model Specifications

The dynamic model of the physical plant serves the purposes of design, verification and validation of the control system. In the model specification phase, engineers must define model requirements, i.e. what the relevant physics to be modeled is and to what level of precision. This definition process begins with an evaluation of the control requirements. When specifying model requirements, the modeling engineer will have to ensure that the right level of abstraction is adopted. If the model is too simple, relevant physical phenomena which impact dynamic response could be omitted, possibly leading to the wrong control design. Conversely, if the model is too detailed, unnecessary effort, time and resources would be used without substantial design benefits.

1. Selection of Relevant Physics

Starting from control requirements, the product and modeling engineer will evaluate and decide what physical phenomena are relevant to the control problem to be designed. As anticipated, this decision is a tradeoff between accuracy, simulation speed and modeling effort. In fact:

- Complex models with a very high level of detail might not be necessary. Such models are usually harder to interpret and to analyze. They are usually not as numerically robust as simpler models. Another factor, against making models too complex, is that the added complexity usually leads to longer simulation times.
- Oversimplifying a model might make the model not representative and less useful. Nonlinear behavior of interest might not be captured satisfactorily, or physical phenomena occurring within the frequency range of the controller to be designed might be represented with excessive error.

2. Steady State Precision

Accuracy metrics for steady state must be defined. Once again, these depend on the control requirements. If, for example, it is required that the indoor temperature of a room is maintained within 1.0°C of a desired set point, the model will have to be accurate to that level of precision at steady state. However, if the control system must meet the above condition only within 0°C and 40°C, then the model will not need to be as precise outside of those bounds. In conclusion, static precision of key system variables is defined in terms of error at steady state and the range for which the precision is required.

3. Dynamic Precision

Dynamic precision is associated with the ability of the model to represent correctly transients at the right timescales and accuracy. This aspect is critical as the control system regulates the system dynamics, and control design relies on knowing the systems dynamic behavior with sufficient precision. Time domain metrics (raise time, settling time, overshoot, etc.) are used to define the dynamic precision of a model around selected operation conditions. However, it is often useful to make reference to precision metrics expressed in the frequency domain, i.e. model precision in terms of magnitude and phase errors of the transfer function of a linearized model up to a certain frequency. The maximum frequency for which precision metrics are defined depends on what are the relevant timescales associated with the physical plant and control objectives.

Precision of models will depend also on the use of the model (e.g. for design or verification purpose) in relation to control requirements. A more precise model capturing phenomena for a larger frequency band might be required for algorithm design, as one would like to make sure that the designed controller is able to reject high frequency disturbances. Conversely, a more simplified model representing phenomena at the timescales of the designed control system could be used for testing purposes, enabling faster execution of tests and real time computation when needed (e.g. for Hardware In the Loop testing). Different models could be used to design and test different control functions at different stages of the development process.

Create Dynamic Model

Once modeling requirements are defined, a dynamic model of the physical plant can be created. A system model enables to simulate the dynamic behavior of the system by specifying critical inputs and computing corresponding outputs. As anticipated, the modeling engineer should capture all the relevant physical phenomena to represent the system to the accuracy defined by the model requirements. This should include important behavior that is at times neglected, i.e. sensor precision, actuator dynamics, disturbances induced by the outside environment (thermal, electrical, etc.).

Model accuracy is linked with model complexity and computational speed. As the number of equations and nonlinear relations increase, so are the complexity and the computational speed. Computational time also depends on the duration of simulations (from seconds to hours to days depending on the timescales of interest). As computational time has a direct impact on the duration of the design and verification phase, it is important to meet computational speed requirements dictated by the project. Speed is typically defined as a multiplying factor of real time operation of the physical plant (e.g. 6x real time execution speed).

1. Real Time Model

A particular application of the dynamic plant model is for Hardware in the Loop (HIL) real time execution on a real time computing system. In this case, the model computational time must be less than the sample time of the real time system including the physical plant model. For models whose execution is slower than real time, "speeding" and simplification techniques are used to make models more computationally efficient. In some cases, faster model execution will result in degraded accuracy. It is important that accuracy requirements to enable HIL testing are met for the model to be viable.

Validate Dynamic Model

Experimental data from a prototype physical plant or field data, when available, is used for both calibration and validation of the model. The validation process ensures that model requirements are met and that the model can be used with confidence for control algorithm design and testing throughout the model-based development process.

Experimental data should be obtained via tests specifically designed for the purpose of dynamic model calibration and validation. A validation test plan should be developed, including instrumentation and data acquisition (sampling) requirements. When the execution of validation tests on the physical plant is not possible, then data already available for other testing purposes, from similar products or other reference models should be collected. Validation and the level of confidence on the model will depend on the nature of data available. The modeling engineer and the control algorithm engineers should be able to evaluate the risks associated with using a partially validated model.

Calibration and validation based on experimental data are conducted to ensure that the required levels of both static and dynamic precision are achieved.

1. Steady State Validation

A good match with experimental data at steady state is required to ensure that steady state (static) precision requirements are met. Often times, a lack of good steady state validation will go together with bad dynamic accuracy. Often, and unfortunately, steady state data is the only available data for validation.

Required accuracy is defined by the model requirements, and validation tests should be conducted to identify whether model requirements are met for all relevant conditions in the system operating envelope. Sometimes it is possible to validate component models separately before conducting system level validation. In this case, it is typical to observe that the accuracy of individual component models is often higher than that of the system model assembled from those components.

Experimental data points used for model validation should be obtained by performing an experimental test plan. The test plan would use DoE (Design of Experiments) to ensure that the minimum set of relevant points, including the corner points of the operational envelope, are included in the validation. Additional test points should be selected based on engineering judgment (most typical conditions, conditions where highly nonlinear behvaior is expected, and conditions where the system constraints may become active or where system components may perform at their limit of performance).

2. Dynamic Validation

Validating the dynamics of a model is conducted by comparing time series obtained from dynamic tests on the physical plant and from simulations with the dynamic model. A system's dynamic (transient) response is conducted with the plant and the model without feedback controls in operation. A change to the control actuators or disturbance variable is made, and the response of critical system parameters is recorded until a steady state condition is reached. A typical dynamic tests aims at looking at the *step response* of the system, where one input variable to the model is changed suddenly in magnitude by a finite amount.

The following should be considered when planning for dynamic tests:

- Definition of the amplitude of actuator step changes: amplitude needs to be large enough to observe a response from the system, but small enough to not leave the normal operation conditions of the plant or exciting nonlinear behaviour.
- It should also be investigated if the dynamic response of the system differs significantly (other than the sign) if the change of the actuator is negative or positive.
- Adequate sampling time should be used for dynamic testing, at least 10x the frequency of the dynamic phenomena being captured.
- As dynamic tests are more time consuming to perform in a lab environment it is in most cases not feasible to get measurement data with the same measurement grid density as for steady state data. In this case the corner points of the DoE should be prioritized and any additional test points should be chosen based on engineering judgment.

When dynamic responses from experimental tests and model simulations are compared, either time domain or frequency domain metrics can be used to evaluate precision. For example, the settling time error (time from when the step change is introduced to the time when the system settles at steady state within specified error band) or the rise time are time domain metrics often used. Comparison of frequency domain metrics (using Bode plots) is a more powerful method of dynamic model validation. Comparison of magnitude and phase Bode plots shows model precision within a specified frequency band within which the control system will operate.

During the validation process, the modeling engineer will also make sure that the model adequately represents relevant dynamic behavior which requires control engineers to pay particular attention to. These behaviors may include:

- Inverse response (non-minimum phase response).
- Pure time delays.
- Underamped higher order dynamics (oscillating or resonant behavior).
- Integrating response (e.g. reservoirs).

Step 3: Design Control System or Control Algorithms

In this step, alternative control architectures and algorithms can be modeled and simulated in closed loop with a model of the physical plant based on the control system requirements and derived component algorithm requirements. As a result of this step, the control architecture and algorithms are designed. This process step is discussed in detail in Chapter 3 on control architecture design, and Chapter 4 on control algorithm design. This step includes tasks such as controllability analysis (ensuring that a feasible control exists), controls architecting and algorithm design.

Controllability Analysis

Before any algorithm design begins, control requirements must be discussed and analyzed by the design team to ensure that all use cases and behaviors were addressed. No control modeling activity is yet involved in this phase. However, a dynamic model of the physical plant is used by the control algorithm engineer to perform dynamic controllability analysis (see Chapter 3 for details). Results of the controllability analysis are shared and requirements modified as needed. With controllability analysis we refer to the general problem of determining whether control requirements can be achievable for specified physical plant within specified operating conditions. This is a much broader definition than the controllability usually found in control theory textbooks.

The following steps are typically followed:

1. A few operation conditions where the analysis has to be conducted are selected. These can correspond to different conditions in which the system will operate within the operational envelope.
2. A set of simplified models for each selected operation conditions, typically a linearized FOTD (first order with time delay) model, is obtained by using available system identification tools such as that in MATLAB on step responses obtained from simulation run of the model.
3. Controllability analysis techniques are employed to verify whether the control requirements can be met using identified models.

In Chapter 3 several controllability analysis tools are presented to answer the following questions:

- How well can the plant be controlled? Is it a difficult control problem? Indeed, does there even exist a controller which meets the required performance objectives?
- What control structure should be used? What variables should we measure, what variables should we manipulate, and how are these variables can be paired together?
- How might the physical plant be changed to improve control? Should any components in the plant be changed to improve the control performance? For example, one may increase the size of a buffer tank to reduce the effects of disturbance in process control, or one may find the speed of response of a control valve is important for achieving acceptable control.

The tools presented are:

- Rules of controllability for single-input, single-ouput (SISO) plants: evaluation of model parameters and comparison with control requirements.
- Rules of controllability for multi-input, multi-ouput (MIMO) plants: evaluation of coupled effects that control input variables have on all controlled output variables, and tools to decouple them to form SISO pairing between inputs and outputs.

Controllability analysis will tell the control engineer how hard the control problem will be. When critical situations are observed during open loop controllability analysis (non-minimum phase behavior, oscillating underdamped, significantly long time delays, highly coupled MIMO systems) the control engineer should consult with other control engineering experts to ensure that proper techniques (sometimes more advanced techniques not directly discussed in this book) are used.

Control System Architecture Design

Based on the revised requirements and the results of controllability analysis, the control algorithm engineer will use the physical plant model and simplified models obtained via the system identification tools to architect and then design the control system. Two fundamental steps are undertaken:

- Control architecture definition: the identification of the control system structure, including selection of controlled variables, manipulated variables, measurements, the adoption of SISO or MIMO arcthiectures, decoupling and compensation schemes, suprvisory controls, control operational modes and their transitions.
- Control algorithm design: the selection of the controller type based on the selected architecture (e.g. PI or PID, on-off) and tuning of its parameters to obtain the desired performance.

The definition of control system architecture is a critical step towards meeting control requirements. Architecting a control system includes the definition of:

1. The definition of the operational modes, or discrete states of the system, and the transition among them, i.e. the conditions that, if verified, would trigger the control system to switch modes.
2. The definition and connection of the control algorithm schemes (components) and interactions (relationships). This includes, for each operational mode, sensor-actuator coupling for SISO schemes, staging sequences for on-off and multi-stage actuators for example fans, valves.
3. Where applicable, the creation of a hierarchy of control structure, from "low level" local loops to supervisory and coordinating algorithms.

The definition of the control system architecture is rarely conducted from scratch, unless some completely new functionality must be added to the control, the physical plant uses a different technology or it underwent a major redesign, or much more stringent requirements have been set. Even in that case, the knowledge of the physical plant and controllability analysis should offer precious information on how to proceed. The control architecture of a previous generation product is often a good starting point if control requirements haven't been changing significantly from the previous product. The existing architecture can be used as design baseline on which the new one will be developed. Of course, it is assumed that the existing architecture has produced reliable controls which meet requirements.

The control engineer will decide what control architecture is best suited to meet the requirements. Based on the results from controllability analysis a decentralized or centralized solution will be selected, and control schemes for each operational mode established. Modeling of the architecture in MATLAB/Simulink and simulation after having completed the control algorithm design and tuning phase will help to evaluate whether the chosen architecture is appropriate or re-architecting is needed.

Control Algorithm Design

Control design includes, for a specified control architecture, the specification of control algorithms of each control function and their tuning. For example, once it has been established that the compressor speed will be used to control the leaving water temperature of a chiller, the SISO controller will be selected (e.g. a PI, a PID, a lead lag scheme, a gain scheduling controller, a feed-forward compensation controller…) and the protection logic will be also created and refined. A model of the control algorithm will be therefore developed and its behavior will be examined through simulation. MATLAB Simulink and Stateflow are the common tools used to model the continuous time and logic behavior of control algorithms. Graphical control models using block diagram representation is quite intuitive and makes readability and interpretation easier than using program code. Proper modeling guidelines should be followed to ensure readability, reuse, and readiness for code generation from models.

Chapter 4 illustrates in detail the recommended approaches for industrial control system design and algorithm selection. It does not describe more advanced control design techniques and algorithms, like multivariable, robust, optimal, adaptive controls. These advanced control techniques are not used widely for industry control systems.

Standard control algorithms such as PID controllers have tuning parameters which affect the closed loop behavior of the system under control. As tuning greatly affects performance and the ability to meet control requirements, it is a key task of the control design step. Trial and error approaches should be avoided and the application of analytical methods for tuning should be instead applied. Chapter 4 presents standard tuning methods for PI and PID controllers that are suitable and have proven to work well for different applications. Tuning techniques are usually based on observation of the step response in open loop, calculation of plant dynamic parameters from the step response, calculation of the PI/PID controller parameters based on given tuning rules of the chosen tuning method.

Controller tuning is an iterative process part of the design – tuning – evaluate cycle. Approximate tuning parameters might be used during early design cycles for those parameters that cannot be easily determined using analytical rules. Parameter fine tuning and optimization can be conducted during the later design stages. Controller tuning may need to be conducted again when the plant model is refined or modified.

A summary of the procedure for tuning a PI controller is presented. The tuning process for PI controllers can be broken down to the following steps:

- Perform multiple step tests on the physical plant model: Step resposnes should be obtained at different operating conditions covering the operating envelope. If responses differ greatly, then gain scheduling of the PI parameters should be considered.
- Identify simplified FOTD transfer function models from the step responses by using one of the standard system identification tools.
- Determine the control parameters by using the tuning rules of the selected tuning approach.
- Select sampling time, filter time constants and anti-windup tracking time constants.

Step 4: Define Test Cases

Once requirements are finalized and the control architecture and control algorithms are designed and evaluated from the early design iterations, a rigorous and formal verification to ensure that the algorithm meets the requirements is executed. This first verification ensures that the algorithms indeed meets control requirements and prompts modifications to the algorithms as required. In order to enable formal verification and to enable automated processing, requirements in natural language must be transformed into executable test models, called a test monitor, which enables to tell if a test has passed or failed. Each test case model is composed by a use case model, called test generator, and a monitor. A use case model includes the input signals to the closed loop system (disturbances from the environment, operator action on the system's set points or settings), and performance parameters (like amplitude or time limits, error bounds, modes, etc.) used to evaluate the pass or fail of a requirement. The actual implementation of test generators and test monitors depends on the automated verification step (MIL, SIL, or HIL) and the modeling and simulation technology used.

Step 5: Model-in-the-Loop Test – Ensure Control Design Meet Control Requirements

Control algorithm verification (model in the loop or MIL) is the first step of the model-based testing process and is first used to verify the functionality of control algorithms relative to component level control requirements. For each test case designed at the previous step, a test case model is built which comprises of four components: the use case model, test monitor, control algorithm model, and the plant model. The test case model is then executed through simulation. At the end of this step, it is expected that all tests pass, or accepted justification and assessment of risk is provided for those which do not pass. When control algorithms are integrated into the control subsystem, the same MIL testing is repeated using the appropriately designed test cases against the set of control system level requirements. Based on the test results, some redesign of the control architecture or control algorithms may be needed, or requirement refinement is performed.

Step 6: Code Generation and Software Integration

Code generation is a necessary step towards implementation of functions and other services for embedded software driven product development. For Simulink control algorithm models tested via MIL, it is recommended to use the capability of Simulink to generate production code from models for embedded systems. If automated generation is used for code production, the process will include steps to ensure that the code produced automatically for control algorithms is compatible with the selected software architecture. Software code for other functionalities other than controls could still be developed manually, depending on the application.

Automated coding consists of three main activities:

1. Preparation of the model to be suitable for automated code generation. Certain modeling decisions affect the quality of the code generated. Modeling guidelines for automatic code generation should be followed. Certain tools can be applied to the model before generating the code to ensure the quality of the code generated from the model. Simulink Model Advisor can be applied to check the model against various modeling standards and custom modeling rules. Simulink Design Verifier can be applied to detect errors such as overflow, divide by zero, array index out of bounds, or analyze the structural coverage of the model.
2. Mapping of the control model inputs and outputs to the variables of the software module where the algorithm will be plugged in.
3. Configuration and use of the Simulink Embedded Coder to generate code. Evaluation of the code and reconfiguration of the model or the Embedded Coder parameters as needed.

Automatically generated or manually developed code is then integrated with the rest of the application software. The application software's architecture can be either new or a legacy architecture. In both cases automated code generation can be considered as a viable technology because it saves times, improve quality, and provide traceability to model and to requirements.

Step 7: Software-in-the-Loop – Verify Control Software Meets Control Requirements

Embedded control systems based on microprocessor or microcontroller technology are systems that include both hardware platform and software platform and application software running on the platforms. Application software implements a host of functions, including control functions.

Software testing and verification has multiple purposes and is conducted at different levels. When control algorithm models have been tested with MIL, then SIL verification is implemented to ensure that control code integrated within the application software architecture was implemented in a way that did not affect the capability of the control system to meet the same control requirements used in MIL test. SIL test should not be used to verify the algorithm functionality unless the functionality was not already tested with MIL. SIL test can be used for testing new control software integrated with legacy software.

Step 8: Hardware-in-the-Loop – Verify That the Embedded Controller System Meets Control Requirements

Application SW is fully integrated with software drivers and services (lower software architecture layer), and the integration has also been tested and verified to meet functional and nonfunctional specifications for example using SIL. Eventually software/hardware integration occurs, leading to a fully functional embedded system comprising of software ported to the target hardware platform. This process is dependent on the architecture (both SW and HW) selected.

Verification of the integrated embedded system is conducted to:

- Ensuring that services, drivers, communication operate correctly as specified;
- Ensuring that the implementation of the control system on HW platform did not introduce problems that would prevent the control system to meet its functional requirements.

For control functions, verification of most requirements can only be conducted in closed-loop when the control system is connected to the physical plant. HIL verification uses a model of the physical plant in lieu of laboratory test using a physical plant to do the testing early in the development cycle. HIL simulation is run in real time with the physical plant model running on a real time computer. To meet the real time requirement, the plant model may need to be modified for example simplified to make the calculation time less than the closed-loop sample time.

Step 9: Lab Testing – Confirm That the Actual System Meets Control Requirements

The control system is ready for a final test in the lab through connection to the actual equipment. The same system level tests performed during the previous verification stages should be performed to ensure that the control requirements are met. Failing tests at this stage would reveal unanticipated behavior that the model could not capture or uncertainty the controller designed did not account for. Test failures may lead to either rework of the control design or re-evaluation and modification of control system requirements.

Field trials may be conducted following the lab testing, they might reveal problems that were not expected or discovered during the requirement analysis, controller design and testing phases.

CONCLUSION

In the chapter, we discuss the challenges faced by complex embedded control systems developers and the needs for a model-based design approach. The model-based control design is introduced within the context of the systems engineering. Shifting to model-based design brings many advantages including improved product quality and improved productivity. However, applying model-based design requires a different set of skills, tools, and processes, also initial investments for developing models. These factors need to be considered when adopting model-based design. Sometimes, organization changes are needed to implement model-based design. A model-based control design workflow is presented among with each of it steps. In the subsequent chapters, these design steps will be discussed in greater detail.

Chapter 2
Requirements

INTRODUCTION

Model based controls system development starts from product requirements. The highest level and most abstract product requirements originate from the customer needs and the marketing analysis. The organized and analyzed customer needs are translated into the technical system requirements through applying functional analysis to start the product development: what functions the product needs to provide to meet the customer and market needs. The customer and market needs to be satisfied by the product are chosen on the other side based on the company's resource, product development cycle, product line development plan, and marketing strategies.

After the system level requirements are decided, the control subsystem level requirements need to be defined to begin the control system development. For embedded control systems, which is focused in this book, the overall control functions are implemented in software running on a hardware computing platform within the product, the controls software, as part of the overall product application software which also includes other software modules such as graphical user interface, and network communications, etc. So control subsystem requirements are in effect the requirements on the controls software.

Requirement flow down first starts from the system level to the subsystem level. From the product structure perspective, the controls subsystem is comprised of all elements (hardware, software and firmware) involved in providing and supporting the dynamic behaviors and functions of a product

DOI: 10.4018/978-1-5225-2303-1.ch002

defined by the system level requirements. For example for a vapor compression cycle air conditioning system, the control subsystem includes the compressor, evaporator, condenser, indoor and outdoor fans, measurement sensors such as pressure and temperature sensors, controller board and the embedded controls software. In general, the control system hardware includes the physical system under control (called the plant in controls term), actuation and sensing devices. In the air conditioning example, the plant is the assembly of the compressor, evaporator, condenser and pipes connecting them; assume the evaporator is equipped with a thermal expansion valve for superheat control at the compressor inlet and the compressor is controlled by a variable frequency speed drive, then the compressor variable frequency speed drive is the actuator which regulates the compressor speed; if fan speeds are adjustable instead of being fixed, then the various fan drives are actuators for changing the fan speeds too; pressure and temperature sensors installed at various locations in the system are the sensing devices for measuring controlled variables, for example the supply air temperature, and for monitoring internal variables for safe operation, for example the compressor suction superheat to prevent compressor from flooding. Based on the product structure design, the control subsystem components are identified along with its dynamic behaviors and interdependencies. The control subsystem requirements are collected, derived and then separated from the product system requirements, which describe the controlled system behaviors and performance for intended use cases. At this point, the interfaces between the control software and the rest of the application software needs to be thoughtfully defined based on the overall software application structure, for example the way in which the data is managed and shared among different modules of the application software.

The requirement flow down from system to control subsystem is further followed by the flow down of the requirements from control subsystem to control algorithm for an individual control function. At this level, control subsystem component behavior and performance are defined and quantified, for example how the compressor shall be controlled and how the evaporator fan shall be controlled to provide a specific cooling function with certain performance requirements. The decomposition of subsystem level controls into component level controls is supported by the control architecture design, and is focused around functions that the control subsystem as a whole needs to provide. For example, there could be different modes for cooling, such as mechanical cooling, free cooling (using outdoor cold air), and mixed mechanical and free cooling, they could be implemented as individual states of a state machine in the controller. In each mode, a control algorithm is required to provide the specific cooling function. At the control algorithm level, requirements for each control algorithm are defined, which includes requirements on the control performance indexes such as the gain margin, the phase margin, and the bandwidth frequency. When breaking down the control subsystem into component control algorithms according to the control architecture design, the interfaces between control algorithms should be clearly defined and need to be consistent, so the individual algorithms designed separately can be integrated into the control subsystem without any conflicts.

At each step of requirement flow down, requirement analysis and decomposition can be assisted by using models of the product. At the control subsystem level, based on the product design, control structure design can start using a plant model, such as the controllability analysis and pairing of the inputs and outputs for decoupled control. This step can discover missing requirements and can also identify infeasible requirements which cannot be met by the current product design. The latter situation requires modifying the existing product design, for example the response time of a selected sensor is not short enough or the flow rate of a valve is not large enough. On the other side, modeling requirements are also driven by the controls requirements. The level of accuracy is not always the higher the better because resources are always limited. The level of accuracy of the plant model needs to meet the level required by the controls requirements. Also, the physical phenomena needed to be captured in the model are determined by the product requirements and functions.

In this chapter, assuming the customer needs are identified through marketing analysis and translated into the system requirements, we start with discussion of developing the control software requirements and the control algorithm requirements. Requirements documents contents at the subsystem and component level are discussed respectively. Finally, the modeling requirements for plant model are addressed.

DEVELOPING CONTROLS REQUIREMENTS

This chapter describes the process for developing requirements for the control of dynamic product behaviors. In this context, "control" is used to describe the management of dynamic behaviors of the system through the application of processing logic and control loops (feedback, feedforward etc.). Although there can be mechanical or electronic ways to control systems, we focus on controls that are implemented using the embedded controls software. Controls software, being part of the overall application software, is generally in the subsystem level of the product structure amongst other subsystems of the product.

Controls software can be further broken down at the component level into individual "control algorithms" which may manage a specific function, mode or piece of equipment. The internal structure (identification of control algorithms and their relationships) of the controls software is described by the "controls architecture". The controls architecture represents a white box view of the controls software. Product controls are developed using the model-based design approach that utilizes dynamic simulation modeling tools (such as the MATLAB/Simulink tool chain). The focus here is on the characteristics and flowdown of requirements unique to controls software and control algorithms.

Controls Requirement Development Process

Requirement development involves engineers with different roles at different stages during the product development cycle. Requirements are the results of collaboration of the members of the product engineering team and have impacts on the tasks these engineers will perform. Participants involved in requirement development can include:

- **Product System Engineer:** Responsible for the engineering and development of the product to be controlled. Expertise includes systems engineering and design, requirements management and modeling. Product system engineer is responsible for defining product behavior and constraints.
- **Modeling Engineer:** Responsible for the development of the product dynamic model (plant model) used to derive more detailed requirements, determine requirement feasibility, and conduct control design.
- **Controls Engineer:** Responsible for the definition of the controls architecture and control algorithm design. The control algorithm engineer works with the product system engineer and the verification engineer on the definition, analysis and formalization of controls requirements. Controls engineer flows down the controls requirements to individual control algorithms based upon the controls architecture design. Controls engineer then works with the software engineer and

the modelling engineer to document the control algorithm's design and implementation.

- **Software Engineer:** Responsible for implementing the control algorithms designed by the controls engineer as code (it is recommended to use automated code generation when applicable) and integrating it with the overall software architecture.
- **Embedded Systems Engineer:** Responsible for the integration of hardware and software into the embedded computer platform (product controller). The computer platform (i.e. embedded system) owned by the embedded system engineer is an integrated system that fulfills additional functions beyond the feedback controls (e.g. user interface, alarming, connectivity with third party systems, data logging, etc.).
- **Verification Engineer:** Responsible for verifying that the control design meets the requirements. The verification engineer defines test cases, performs testing and verification via MIL, SIL, and HIL tests, and verifies the controls system and control algorithms requirements.

In order to start this requirements development process for controls workflow it is assumed that:

- The system requirements have been defined capturing expected dynamic product-level behaviors;
- The product system architecture has been defined and shows the relationships between major subsystems(including the control subsystem), and components (including sensors and actuators);
- Initial selection of critical components has been performed (or alternatives have been identified); and
- The initial overall software architecture (including control software) design is complete or maturing.

The product's controls are meant to manage the system in a certain manner over a range of conditions, referred to as the operating or design space. Beyond the overall system's requirements, the controls-specific behavior is defined in the subsystem-level controls software requirements and the component-level control algorithm requirements. The requirements flow down from the system level requirements is shown below in Figure 1.

To ensure that requirements are "feasible" at each level, the architecture design and concept design occur concurrently at each level as requirements are discovered and refined. Within each level's box in Figure 1, there is continuous

Figure 1. Controls requirement flow down

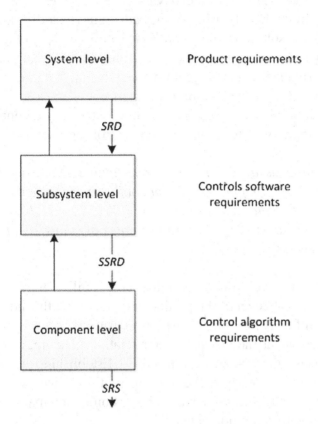

interaction between requirements, architecting and concept development along with plant model refinement, where plant model is used to assist these tasks. The objective is to leave any given level with requirements that are:

- Consistent with and allocated from the level above;
- Are flowed down to the next lower level of the product structure through a defined architectural allocation; and
- Are supported by a preferred concept selection that establishes they can be accomplished within the project's cost, schedule and technology risk constraints.

Further iterations occur between levels, which are time sequenced in a staggered manner. It is recommended that system-level requirements are captured unambiguously to make decomposition to the controls software-level more precise and traceable. This includes specifying acceptable tolerance ranges about the mean or nominal value (using lower (LSL) and upper specification limits (USL)), using significant digits (including trailing zeros) to specify value resolution to be controlled to, defining operating ranges, and the necessary linearity across the operating range. Given their importance to product performance, it is also recommended that all dynamic behaviors are flowed down and traced to the control design.

An illustrative system-level requirement that would communicate this important quantitative information to the controls engineer is:

When configured as a 17.5 ton air conditioning unit with the variable frequency drive indoor fan, the system shall provide an energy efficiency rating number of greater than or equal to 18.00 (LSL = 17.10, USL = 19.00) over the inclusive operating temperature range of minus 20.0 to plus 135.0 degrees Fahrenheit.

Model-based development provides the ability to predict design performance at each level of the product structure with the aid of analytical models. This information helps to explore sensitivity in terms of what needs to be specified, what the key parameter relationships are, and establishes requirement feasibility prior to design and test. Establishing design alignment with the requirements early in the development cycle increases confidence that the solution will be responsive to the customer and market's needs and at the same time that solution is feasible.

Often, the controls analysis using models such as the controllability analysis is ongoing in parallel with the controls requirements development and can be used to identify missing or infeasible controls requirements. The system or component modeling may help understand a critical parameter relationships, or identification of an unexpected transient response. This leads to more iteration with the requirements at the controls subsystem and control algorithm levels. The "correct" requirements and behavior of the controls software and control algorithm often are evaluated on the resultant component and product behaviors, and the challenge is to define and correlate what the control algorithm needs to do to achieve that component and product behaviors. It is often difficult to fully and accurately define the control software and control algorithm's behavior without having done some conceptual or exploratory design and analysis based on a plant model. This iteration is a top-down process. It also shows that the control algorithm requirements flow down from the agreed-to controls software (subsystem) behaviors and drive the control algorithm design, which then influences the performance of the end product.

The top down requirement flow down is combined with the bottom up requirement refinement and iteration may be required to obtain the final set of requirements. In some cases, such as when the desired component or product performance cannot be achieved, the requirement iteration takes place to reconcile product and controls characteristics. The intent is to ensure that when controlled by the proposed control software design the end product behavior (what the customers see) is acceptable. If undesirable, unintended or missed behaviors show up at the product behavior level, then the control software and control algorithm requirements are refined. This will drive another algorithm design and modeling iteration. Once the control algorithms and hence the control software provides the desired product behavior, then the control algorithm and control software requirements are considered complete. At the control algorithm level this iteration is on the control performance indexes using modeling and analysis. At the control software level, the iteration is on the controls architecture design and decomposition, for example centralized control versus decentralized control, constraint handling, and control mode and logic. The criteria for whether or not the control algorithm design is good are twofold, 1) whether or not it meets the control algorithm requirements levied on it; and 2) whether or not the component performs as desired (i.e. were the control algorithm requirements specifying the correct component behaviors). Likewise, the criteria for whether or not the control software design is good are twofold, 1) whether or not it meets the control software requirements levied on it; and 2) whether or not the product performs as desired (i.e. were the control software requirements specifying the correct system behaviors).

Control Software Requirements Development

Control subsystem behaviors are derived from system behaviors in response to the environment and the user. Controls requirements are derived through an analysis of the system-level requirements. This analysis utilizes dynamic modeling to support the requirement decomposition and the requirement quantification. The product architecture design and component (here means a piece of equipment or device of the product) design are the product internal design artifacts that help determine the control subsystem requirements. Developing the controls software requirements includes two major steps: the first step being to define the control subsystem: control related components, their behaviors and relationships; the second step being to analyze these to break out the controls related behaviors and translate these into requirements.

Define Control Subsystem Behavior

Inputs to this step are system requirements, system architecture, component concept and inputs/outputs, and key components under selection. The system architecture and component selection identifies the component to be controlled and its characteristics that influence control design (single speed, variable speed, multiple fans, etc.). The output of this first step is a documented understanding of the control subsystem component functions, key dependencies between the components, how the components are to be controlled (inputs and outputs) and the operating range of the components. The sub-steps involved with extracting control subsystem behavior are the following and described next.

1. Define control components
2. Define control component performance
3. Define control component relationships
4. Define control component constraints

1. Define Control Components

First, existing information about the system concept, selected component and necessary performance is consolidated. The system requirement document (SRD) includes information that defines the system boundaries and the functional layout of the system. This also identified the key system components. The system requirements or architecture design will also include interface definition and partitioning. This information is used to define the components to be controlled, the actuators, valves or switches that can be used to control them, as well as the sensors or switches that will provide system feedback.

At this point the plant model must be consistent with the baseline product concept (preferred concept selection). On some projects, the performance of multiple concepts may need to be modeled. Component dependencies (such as relationships between compressors and fans for an air conditioning system) are important to capture, as well as configurations or options which may drive system operation modes (such as multiple compressor or multiple heat exchanger concepts that require switching, lead/lag arrangements, hybrid power sources or part load/full load configuration differences). System operation modes influence the controls strategy and implementation.

2. Define Control Component Performance

In addition to identification of the components to be controlled and the control and feedback interfaces, the dynamic component performance is also captured. The product system engineer will define from domain specific analytical modeling the operating condition ranges, performance maps or profiles, and the accuracy necessary for the components to meet product requirements. Considerations for component performance that drive controls software requirements include:

- System operation modes (user observable at the overall product level, i.e. Heating, cooling, ventilation, automatic fan control)
- Individual component operation modes (i.e. On/off, normal/protected modes, etc.)
- Operation range and safety limits for component protection
- Operation at extreme conditions (i.e. Prevent freezing at low temperatures)
- Parallel operation modes (i.e. Perform heating and cooling to different zones simultaneously)
- Response time (i.e. Pull down time, time to achieve setpoint, startup time)
- Efficiency/energy usage (how is this being monitored and controlled in the system, repeatability/consistency to meet regulatory constraints)
- Accuracy over time (i.e. Keep within 0.5 degree of the set point)
- Transitions (i.e. When is the second compressor or additional fans engaged, when is circuit 2 turned off)
- Transition exceptions (i.e. Tolerances are relaxed during transition periods such as when first starting a compressor, or it takes some time for a fan to reach the commanded rpm)
- Existing component diagnostics capabilities (i.e. Does the compressor provide an alert, how does the controls tell if a sensor is bad, etc.).

Capturing the component performance will clarify the design problem for the controls engineer, and will ensure that the correct dynamic behaviors are modeled in the plant model and specified in controls software requirements.

Note that dynamic behaviors will exist at the system or subsystem level (i.e. maintain cooling output capacity) as well as the individual component level (i.e. manage compressor speed). This will likely result in a hierarchy of control algorithms that will need to be structured further during the controls architecture definition activity.

3. Define Component Relationships

In this step, the relationships amongst the control subsystem components are identified and understood. The overall control subsystem behavior is at the system level, which is different from behavior of individual components. Components are interconnected and organized in a way to provide the functions required at the system level. Thus it is important to identify the connections and dependencies among various components. For example, in a vapor compression air conditioning system, if there are multiple refrigerant circuits, multiple heat exchangers, and multiple compressors, the way in which they are connected together affects the controls design and the system level performance.

4. Define Component Constraints

In order to ensure proper and comprehensive controls design it is important to capture constraints resulting from the component, layout or network choices made during design. Due to physical limitations, performance constraints are imposed on devices. Actuation devices have magnitude and rate limitations. Transducers have range limits, response speed limits and resolution limits. Constraints of all components relevant to the control design should be accounted for.

For example, for a heating ventilation air conditioning (HVAC) system consider:

- Equipment minimum/maximum on and off times (i.e. Once compressor is started it must run for at least 3 minutes, this significantly impacts how the controls cycles the compressor and the ability to provide continuous setpoint accuracy)
- Equipment minimum/maximum operating pressures or temperatures (i.e. Protection limits, and the desired behavior when they are exceeded)
- Valve or actuator minimum/maximum ranges
- Valve or actuator resolution (i.e. Continuously variable in 1.00 degree increments, three fixed steps, on/off, etc.)

- Minimum settings (i.e. Damper manually set by installer to minimum ventilation position based upon building size)
- Response times (i.e. How long does compressor inlet guide vane motor take to adjust position after being commanded to a new position).

Develop Controls Software Requirements

Inputs to this step are system requirements, component performance, relationships and constraints from the first step. The output of this step is the controls software requirements. Controls software requirements should be written consistent with the guidance of a template approved by the engineering organization. Use cases, state diagrams, simulations and legacy information are useful sources to get ideas on what should be specified. This step is led by the system engineer, but as decisions are being made to allocate functionality between hardware and software components, engineers responsible for different engineering disciplines such as controls, software and hardware are involved in supporting roles. They will guide the system engineer in terms of technology feasibility and requirement allocation to a specific technical domain. They will review proposed requirements as they emerge to ensure clarity as well as understanding what needs to be implemented at the next layer of decomposition (i.e. control algorithm level). The steps to develop the controls software requirements are

1. Split system requirements
2. Decompose control subsystem functions
3. Group functions into modes
4. Analyze behaviors using modeling
5. Capture controls software requirements.

This is an iterative, evolutionary process as additional requirements may be identified well downstream of the first pass of the initial "Split system requirements" step, requiring that the process updates the requirements and reiterates the prior activities using the new requirements information.

1. Split System Requirements

The system requirements cover the entire product including the control subsystem along with other subsystems. In the previous step, the components under control are identified along with their dynamic behavior and interactions.

This step begins to allocate the system requirements to the control subsystem: what the controls software needs to do to meet system requirements. The controls engineer and the software engineer begin to establish the boundaries for the transactional or application software versus the controls software and how it integrates into the overall product software structure. The completion of this step builds upon the component definition step, and results in a list of behaviors and constraints specific to what the controls must do.

This is a key step in which all control related system requirements are collected. These control related requirements dictate how the components under control should be dynamically managed such that collectively the product dynamic behaviors meet the system level requirements. This happens by defining the requirements that directly or indirectly determine the component dynamic behavior and the control objectives they should be controlled to achieve.

2. Decompose Control Subsystem Functions

Within all requirements, functional requirements are structured around the functional hierarchy. Functions define what the product needs to do without getting into the how it is accomplished. The functional requirements also define how well the functions they are specifying have to be performed. Controls functionality should be grouped at the system-level if possible in order to provide a clear flow down to the controls software level. Having a well-organized functional hierarchy allows ease of translation and mapping into the controls architecture.

One of two approaches can be used for organizing the functions:

- By life cycle stages (start up, run/operate, manage faults, shut down, etc.), or
- By grouping like behaviors (cohesiveness).

Each approach tends to work better for different products, dependent upon what the most important behaviors are or where the project's most significant risk is located.

Figure 2 shows an example of controls functions that are grouped by functional cohesiveness. The functions are organized by functional topics, with the thick-outlined boxes representing those that would be allocated to the control subsystem.

Figure 2. Example functional hierarchy: cohesive grouping

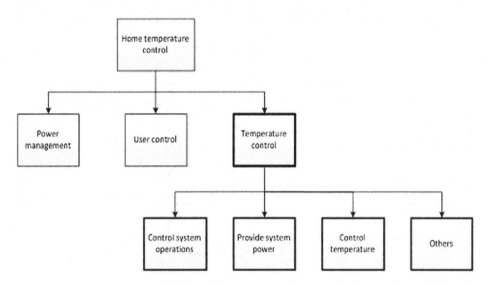

An example functional hierarchy following the life cycle stage approach is shown in Figure 3. The overall function of "Manage equipment" was the lowest-level function in the system functional hierarchy and was allocated to the software system which includes controls software, and thus is the starting point for decomposition at the subsystem level. Again, the thick-outlined third level boxes represent those functions that the software engineer and controls engineers decided would be implemented by the controls software, and as can be seen represent those dealing with dynamic feedback loops.

The functional hierarchy provides an initial perspective as to what the controls needs to do and what its structure might be. It is necessary (through the use of functional flow down or use cases) to derive lower-level functions for the controls in order to verify the subsystem level functions and provide more inputs for identifying which behaviors are necessary in which operation modes. It is recommended that product lines establish a functional hierarchy pattern that supports a clean flowdown as well as architectural modularization and reuse.

3. Group Functions Into Modes

Top level control logic includes operation modes and each mode provides a set of functions. Mode is a control architecture element for organizing functions. It is important to understand from a controls perspective which

Figure 3. Example functional hierarchy: life-cycle flow

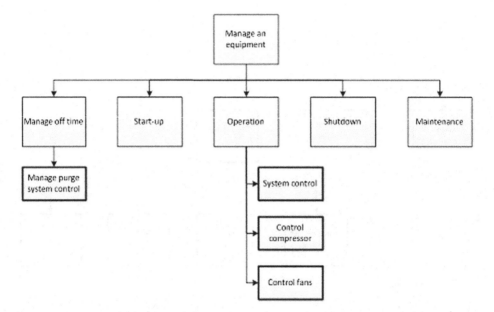

functions or behaviors occur in which operation modes as this will require logic to detect and implement. Certain capabilities may have to be prevented or locked out if the system is in a specific mode. This is often represented as a simple function (row) and mode (column) matrix or in more detailed state flow diagrams which align well with how the controls are modeled. It is often the case that a function is available in multiple modes, such that this is an important criterion for establishing the controls architecture. A function used in multiple modes may require different control strategies with respect to component control and reuse. For example, different indoor fan control is required for heating and cooling mode. Other considerations may include what types of diagnostics can be run while operating the system (run time diagnostics) versus which are interruptive and require going into a special off-line test mode, or a manual override mode in case of a failure.

4. Analyze Behaviors Using Modeling

The desired component behaviors are interpreted in terms of parameters that are managed by the controls. These parameters are often not fully characterized through the use of legacy lab test data or supplier data, so dynamic modeling can be used to further analyze the product behaviors and quantify relationships among the parameters. First, the underlying physics and what needs to be controlled or managed is identified and this activity helps also to identify the modeling requirements.

Once the basic relationships between the desired component behavior and the relevant parameters are defined, the relationship between them must be quantitatively determined. This can be done by modeling the plant and then performing sensitivity analysis on each parameter. Some parameters will also have dependencies with other parameters, and in this case the use of design of experiments and analytical techniques should be applied. The analysis in this step extends the steady state sensitivity analysis that was done by the product design team to the dynamic behavior domain. The significant parameters influencing product behavior will need to have their characteristics defined in requirements. This is where the controls performance begins to become quantifiable. Examples of what need to be documented as requirements for parameters are maintaining a given parameter above a certain limit or within a certain range, or achieve a target value within a specific amount of time.

Translating the problem from the component behavior to the parameters to be managed by the controls is a critical step, as it begins to isolate the controls software behaviors represented by physical parameters from the component being controlled itself. This step will likely require combinations of dedicated physical test data as well as modeling and simulation analysis.

5. Develop Controls Software Requirements

The previous step identified the critical parameters that the controls will use to manage the product to achieve the desired dynamic behavior. This subsequently allows the overall product to achieve the system level requirements. The dynamic modeling of the components under control provided the analytical results as to the ranges and values that the parameters need to be managed to and helped understand which parameters were critical and the dependencies amongst the parameters. The final step is to write the actual controls software requirements. Specific wording and format guidance for writing controls requirements within an engineering organization should be established for the benefits of reuse and ease of communication. As mentioned, the requirements are organized around the functions in the controls functional hierarchy. The intent is to describe each function individually, and specify how one could determine if it is implemented properly or not (that is it is testable). Questions to ask include:

- What behaviors would you look for?
- What you would measure?
- What are the criteria used to judge if it is working properly or not?

When writing the requirements, there is a balance that has to be achieved between properly specifying the black box performance (what) versus getting into implementation details (how) that unnecessarily restricts the design space.

Some requirements may be captured as constraints or non-functional requirements, which are organized around constraint categories, but most controls software requirements will be in the functional requirements category. Also note that additional requirement attributes can be used for requirement management, for example filtering of requirements, as well as capturing rationale and implementation guidance that should not be official part of the requirement text. At the controls software level it is not necessary to define explicit software data point or parameter names within the requirements.

Example controls software (control subsystem) requirements for a HVAC system:

1. **Fire Shutdown:** Upon the Fire input becoming active and Factory Test is inactive, the controls subsystem shall deactivate all indoor fans in less than or equal to 2.0 seconds.
2. **Thermostat Interface:** When the unit is configured for thermostat control, the controls subsystem shall use the Y1, Y2, Y3, W1, W2 and G inputs to determine cooling, heating and ventilation demands.
3. **Setpoint Accuracy:** When configured, the controls subsystem shall manage capacity to maintain the conditioned space temperature such that it is within the inclusive range of less than 1.50 degree Fahrenheit plus the active cooling set point.
4. **Optimal Start Time:** When in the unoccupied mode and connected to space temperature sensors, the controls subsystem shall select a start time to achieve the next scheduled occupied setpoint temperature within an inclusive range of 1.0 minutes prior to the scheduled occupied time.
5. **Optimize Energy Savings:** When in the unoccupied mode and connected to space temperature sensors, the controls subsystem should select the compressor speed, fan speeds and damper position to achieve the next scheduled setpoint temperature using the least amount of energy.
6. **Compressor Off Time:** When providing mechanical cooling and the compressor is turned off, the controls subsystem shall maintain the compressor off for greater than 3.00 minutes.

The controls software level requirements specify what the control software needs to do to manage the component behaviors to collectively meet the system level dynamic behavior requirements. Modeling of the physical system is used to understanding the parameters of the components and how they should be managed under various conditions, making the controls software requirements testable and measurable. Controllability analysis can be performed to assist in selecting the manipulated variables, the controlled variables, the measured variables and discover any product physical limitations to achieving the specified control requirements. If these limitations are indeed discovered during this analysis, the product design either needs to be modified, for example, selecting different components and vary the system architecture, or the system requirements and correspondingly the controls requirements need to be refined or relaxed.

Control Algorithm Requirements Development

With the completion of the controls subsystem (control software) requirements at the subsystem level, the next step is to further decompose these requirements into specific requirements for each control algorithm following the controls architecture design. The control algorithm requirements are written at a more detailed level such that they allow development of and testing the correctness of standalone and independent control algorithms. Additional requirements may also be added to ensure compatibility with the overall application software, which may drive additional needs beyond just component control. The steps to develop the control algorithm requirements are the follows, with descriptions of each step following.

1. Allocate subsystem requirements to algorithms;
2. Define control parameter characteristics;
3. Define software interfaces; and
4. Develop algorithm requirements.

1. Allocate Subsystem Requirements to Algorithms

Inputs to this step are controls software requirements and controls architecture or structure. The outputs of this step are behaviors allocated to specific control algorithms. This step is performed by the controls engineer.

The controls architecture defines the individual control algorithms and how they are organized into a whole control system. The hierarchical structure of subordinate levels in controls represents the hierarchy in controls decision making, as there are system type decisions made at higher levels (does the building need ventilation, should the unit switch to cooling) versus derived decisions made at the specific component level (what speeds should the fans be set to, should both compressors be turned on, etc.). Controls functional decomposition assists the allocation of control subsystem requirements to algorithms requirements. Based on the allocated functional requirements for each control function, the requirements for each algorithm are defined. Traceability is established in this process between system and component level requirements.

Controls software requirements are then aligned to control algorithms which they apply to. Some controls software requirements, especially constraint or interface requirements, may apply to multiple control algorithms. The allocations can be captured as a simple matrix or by using attributes in a requirements management tool.

To ensure consistent software development and testing, the parameter names used in the control algorithm requirements need to reflect the actual application software parameter names, as they now define a specific instance of an interface to a sensor, valve or actuator. Parameters or variables that are used to manage the component should be defined in the control algorithm requirement. In this step, the parameter list from the controls software requirements is made consistent with the formal data dictionary or variable list supporting the software architecture. If the lower level (algorithm level) controls modeling has been performed at this time, this can be used as another input source to identify missing or additional parameter instances that may not be included in the controls software level requirements initially.

2. Define Control Parameter Characteristics

Inputs to this step are allocated algorithm requirements and control algorithm level models. The control algorithm performance and constraint values are the outputs of this step.

An allocated algorithm requirement may include dependent behavior that gets distributed across multiple control algorithms. For example, a setpoint accuracy requirement may be influenced by concurrently running individual control algorithms. In this step, the algorithm level requirements are reframed to align with the controls hierarchy and controls modes represented in the controls architecture. Allocated algorithm requirements are translated to requirements on control design parameters using specific controls terms such as controlled variable, manipulated variable, measured variable, bandwidth, overshoot, settling time, etc. The control design parameters need to be specified are also related to the selected control design method, for example for the classical frequency domain design, bandwidth, gain margin and phase margin are usually specified along with controlled variable step response characteristics such as the settling time and the steady state error; for state-space design using the pole placement technique, the pole locations (natural frequency and damping ratio) are specified.

Additional modeling is often used to help understand how the control algorithms influence each other and what parameter tolerance levels are acceptable within a single control algorithm, continuing the flow down of the overall error or accuracy budget. This targeted modeling specifies control algorithm characteristics in both the time domain and the frequency domain that are necessary to achieve the controls software level requirements.

3. Define Software Interfaces

Inputs to this step include the allocated controls requirements to specific control algorithms, software architecture, controls architecture, software data points list or data dictionary. The outputs are detailed control algorithm interfaces: behaviors or constraints necessary to interact among control algorithms, to interface with the application software or input/output drivers. This step involves both the controls and the software engineers.

For deployment to an embedded controller, control algorithms will be compiled within the overall application software. As such, they may be required to perform behaviors not directly associated with component control, such as setting a flag when in a certain mode or using a specific protocol or pattern to command an actuator. These can be thought of as additional requirements to the control algorithm required by the application software for administration purposes beyond those derived to manage the component dynamic behavior. These additional requirements are necessary for the control algorithms to work with and integrate to the non-controls software. This step reviews the software architecture, communications protocols, and established software patterns to generate additional control algorithm requirements. This is most effectively done with the controls engineer working directly with the software engineer, and reviewing the software architecture. New requirements generated should be consistent with those defined for the feature or transactional software modules. The outcome of this step will be additional structural requirements allocated to specific control algorithms.

4. Develop Control Algorithm Requirements

Inputs to this step include allocated behaviors to specific control algorithms, data dictionary point names aligned with control algorithm parameters, control algorithm performance and constraints values, and detailed control algorithm interfaces. The outputs are control algorithm requirements. This step is mainly performed by the controls engineer.

The previous steps gather the information in preparation for writing the control algorithm requirements. Some of the previous steps will apply more or less to an individual product dependent upon its maturity and complexity and may also occur more iteratively than what is shown. However, after properly completing the above steps the necessary set of information will have been gathered to generate the control algorithm requirements. As they are more detailed and reflect many higher-level design decisions, the control algorithm requirements will reflect more controls technology terminology. With the above captured information, the controls engineer writes the control algorithm requirements following the outline of the Software Requirements Specification (SRS) established within the engineering organization.

A SRS may be generated for a single major control algorithm, or may combine several related control algorithms. The SRS documents will follow the structure of the controls architecture, but it is not necessary to have an individual document for each architectural element. In cases where the control algorithms are so tightly coupled that they cannot be broken apart for development or for a very simple, small project, the project may combine the requirements in one SRS. Note that a separate SRS should still be done even though the scope is then the same as the subsystem requirements for above cases, as the control algorithm requirements provide more specific testable behaviors at the algorithm level. Specific behaviors unique to the control algorithm are specified in the SRS, along with specific software parameter or data point names being used for interfaces.

Example control algorithm requirements for a HVAC system:

1. **Low Speed Cool:** When free cooling is inactive, mechanical cooling is active (MECHCOOL), and only compressor A1 is on, the Cooling algorithm shall command indoor fan speed to the low cool fan speed.
2. **Compressor Protection Range:** When in the cooling mode and the ambient temperature is in the inclusive range of 40.0 to 55.0 degrees Fahrenheit for greater than 3.0 minutes, the Low ambient algorithm shall

stop all compressors in less than 5.0 seconds if the saturated suction temperature:

- ○ Is less than 20.0 degrees Fahrenheit for greater than 5.0 minutes; or
- ○ Is less than or equal to 15.00 degrees Fahrenheit for greater than 4.0 minutes.

3. **Space Temperature Overshoot:** When transitioning from unoccupied to occupied set points, the Heating algorithm shall manage heating capacity such that the occupied setpoint is not exceeded by greater than 0.5 degrees Fahrenheit.

4. **Pressure Settling Time:** Following the start of a compressor, the System Control algorithm shall manage EXV position in order to achieve steady state discharge pressure in less than 5.0 seconds.

The control algorithm level requirements characterize individual variable behaviors. This enables evaluating the control algorithm performance and behavior prior to integration into the overall controls software. Modeling is used to quantify the required control algorithm characteristics in the time and frequency domains and understand allowable tolerance, variation, and performance. At this stage, the plant model needs to be accurate with detailed component models.

DOCUMENTING CONTROLS REQUIREMENTS

Requirements are recorded into documents called "specifications". A specification is written against a certain product or component, and aligned to different levels of the product structure. The outline of a specification should have been standardized in an engineering organization to provide common specification structure and contents, and to act as a checklist to ensure that nothing was left out. Requirements could be organized by type, for example

- Interfaces;
- Functional requirements; and
- Non-functional or constraint requirements.

The controls software requirements are captured in the subsystem requirements document (SSRD), and the control algorithm requirements are captured in the software requirements specification (SRS).

Specifications can be captured in Microsoft Word documents using pre-defined standard templates. Templates can be tailored to unique engineering organization needs. Specifications are also captured in requirements management tools such IBM Doors Next Generation (DNG). Using a requirements management tool is the preferred approach as it enhances reusability, allows the use of additional attributes, and enables making traceability links within the tool and externally to design artifacts such as Simulink models. Requirements management tools also allow for simultaneous multi-user access, which is helpful for globally distributed design teams. Requirement management tools ensure there is only one current version of requirements that all of the project team members are referring to. History, changes and baselines are automatically captured within the tool.

The specifications involved in documenting control requirements are summarized in the following table (Table 1).

Consistent with the notion of flowing down requirements from the customer to the component and part that implements the customer needs, these specifications form a hierarchy that resembles a pyramid as the system is decomposed (one system being broken down into multiple subsystems and pieces of components). Traceability is maintained as the requirements are decomposed, such that it is understood how the component-level requirements supports achievement of a customer need, and it is ensured that all customer needs have been allocated to a specific component or part for implementation. This hierarchy is referred to as a specification tree, and is illustrated in Figure 4 below.

Figure 4 also illustrates the allocation of system requirements to subsystems and components through requirement flow down, and the traceability between design and requirements provides evidence that all product requirements are satisfied in the design solution. These two characteristics, allocation and

Table 1. Specifications used to document control requirements

Specification	Acronym	Level	Written For
System Requirements Document	SRD	System	Overall product or end item delivered to customer
Subsystem Requirements Document	SSRD	Controls software (subsystem)	Controls or software subsystem; may also include computing platform hardware
Software Requirements Specification	SRS	Control algorithm (component)	Individual or group of related control algorithms (requirements – black box)
Algorithm Description Document	ADD	Control algorithm (component)	Individual or group of related control algorithms (design – white box)

Figure 4. Specification tree structure showing requirements flow down

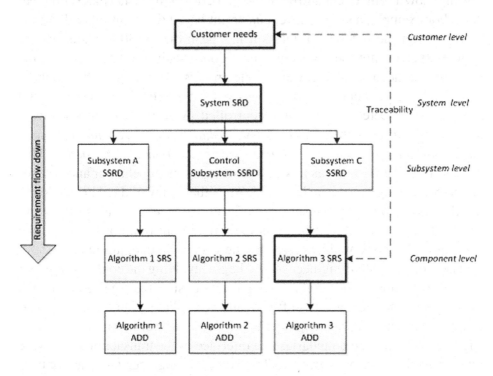

traceability, are inherent in the requirements analysis process when done using a structured approach. Besides tracing between different levels of requirements, design decisions can be substantiated by tracing back to the requirements which they implement. This is beneficial in case either the requirement or the design changes as it makes an impact assessment becoming easier.

Controls Software Requirement Format and Content

This section provides additional guidance on the content and format to consider when developing controls software level requirements. The topics of tolerance, accuracy, resolution and range (increased specificity) mentioned for the system-level requirements apply equally to the controls software (subsystem) level requirements.

As the control actions often extend across subsystem boundaries, the interface requirements take on more importance, ensuring that the components involved have the same expectation and corresponding requirements. Within the software or controls SSRD, the requirement wording reflects commanding and sensing (how a component is to be controlled), rather than what the component does. For example, a system-level constraint based upon fan reliability may be to not run the indoor fan unless it has been off for 30 seconds. At the system-level it is not specified how this is done (i.e. it could be implemented in software, mechanical hardware or electronics). However, at the controls software level the concept and analysis work has been done to understand the fan type selected and how it is controlled. A derived controls software requirement would then be *"The subsystem shall not send a command to start the indoor fan until it has been stopped for greater than 30.0 seconds."* This is a controls requirement, as it is devoid of component behavior and focuses on the control logic that is to be tested. An actual fan would not be needed to test this requirement. At the subsystem-level the "controls" are still thought of as a single entity (black box), as individual control algorithms and the controls architecture will be driven by these subsystem requirements.

The product system engineer should begin involving the controls engineer to gain exposure to the product design, and ensure that the requirements flowing down to the controls software and control algorithm level are clear and concise. The software engineer is involved and works with the controls engineer to define the boundaries and interface of the transactional software relative to the controls software. The software engineer and the controls engineer collaborate to ensure a controls architecture that supports the overall software concept is developed, and that the controls engineer knows how the controls software integrates into the overall software architecture. Often, the controls may need to coordinate with higher level software call functions or schedulers, or may need to go through software-provided drivers to command actuators, as the controls do not act in isolation. The test engineer begins to get involved at this point to ensure requirements are verifiable, and begin development of controls software level test cases.

Controls Software Requirements Content

Although the controls subsystem requirements are written for the overall controls software, they start to identify specific controls characteristics to implement the defined system behaviors. This is done by decomposing system requirements around control functions or features. The grouping of the controls subsystem requirements will provide the basis for the follow-on controls architecture design and the identification of the explicit control algorithms that will implement them. Requirement specification is always done at multiple levels of abstraction. As was previously mentioned, the analysis that occurs between the system and subsystem-levels breaks out the controls behaviors. Within the software SSRD, the analysis process allocates subsystem functions between the user interface, computing platform, transactional software, infrastructure and controls software. Finally, within the controls software requirements the analysis provides insight to the controls architecture. By thinking ahead to the next step, requirements are developed that can be efficiently decomposed at the next level down. So at the controls software level the requirement content should be structured to provide the information that is needed by the controls engineer to perform the next step of analysis. A preferred requirement pattern (focused on and repeated for each function) would include requirements that describe the following:

- **Algorithm:** Identify dynamic control function and mode or applicability (i.e. When in the cooling mode the controls subsystem shall manage ventilation …)
- **Objective:** What is the control algorithm trying to achieve (optimize comfort, reduce energy usage, maintain humidity within a range, reduce compressor cycling to a minimum, etc.)
- **Component:** What component does the algorithm control when doing this *(list plus I/O reference to interface requirements)*
- **Component Constraints:** What constraints need to be considered in controlling the component (cycles, minimum run/off times, temperatures/pressures) to not degrade reliability and/or safety?
- **Managed By:** Parameters or variables involved in doing this *(list)*
- **Range:** Range for each parameter to be maintained within
- **Worst-Case Behaviors:** System and component behavior when outside of desired parameter range (shut down, go to high speed mode, set alarm, etc.)

Obviously, not all functions will contain all of the elements listed above, but all of the topics should be thought through for applicability. The content areas above are often captured as a set of requirements for a single system-level behavior or function, thus this list can form the basis of a checklist for individual patterns of requirements.

Examples using the above content list follow below. It should always be clearly stated in the requirement that "the subsystem shall" do something. It should also be noted that as the problem domain is dealing with dynamic behaviors, most of the example requirements use the conditional requirement format of "when some condition occurs take some action" (specifically: Upon <condition>, the <Subsystem_name> shall <behavior> when/where <quality factor>.). The requirement set (content listed in the above) works to fully capture a specific system behavior, and when further decomposed will be allocated to a single control algorithm for implementation.

The following example states that when a certain set of conditions exist for a certain period of time, the controls shall apply special low ambient criteria, giving insight that within the controls architecture there likely will be a normal and low ambient mode or setting. For context, the system-level parent requirement might have been that the system needs to provide mechanical cooling down to 0 degrees. Again, it can be seen how the controls engineer would begin to dissect the below example to determine the necessary control logic and elements that will make up the controls architecture.

- **Algorithm:** "When in the Cooling mode for greater than 4.0 minutes and in the ambient temperature range of -10.00 to 40.00 degrees Fahrenheit for greater than or equal to 10.0 minutes, the controls subsystem shall control mechanical cooling using the low ambient temperature control function."

Following is an example of a requirement that states an objective. As many control problems are about multi-variable optimization (as opposed to a singular variable regulation) it is often good practice to ensure the controls engineer understands the intent of what is being asked. In this case note that it is important to use consistent terminology between requirements, such as here it would be expected that there would be another requirement that defines the "low ambient temperature range".

- **Objective:** "When providing mechanical cooling in the low ambient temperature range, the controls subsystem shall manage cooling performance to prevent the coils from freezing."

The next requirement example alerts the controls engineer as to the component that is manipulated when controlling in the low ambient range. The interface points should be consistently named to those defined in the SRD or software architecture.

- **Component:** "When providing mechanical cooling in the low ambient temperature range, the controls subsystem shall apply low ambient temperature control parameters to the following equipment:
  ○ **Compressors:** Through the compressor starter relay connections
  ○ **Outdoor Fans:** Through the ODF PWM connections."

The following example imposes a component constraint on the implementation of the low ambient control logic. In this case, from a hardware perspective the compressor reliability is known to drop if it is cycled on and off too frequently, so reliability testing was done to determine the optimal value.

- **Component Constraints:** "When providing mechanical cooling in the low ambient temperature range, the controls subsystem shall not cycle the compressor greater than or equal to 10 times per hour."

The controls software requirements relate the component behaviors to its physical parameters, which then allow definition of the relevant parameters. Parameters are individual variables that are used for control purposes. Best practice is to have an explicit requirement that relates the component control to the parameters that need to be monitored or managed. These parameters (controlled variables) will then be related to a sensor (measured variables) or actuator (manipulated variables) (that has accuracy, range and responsiveness characteristics), and will eventually become points in the software.

- **Managed by:** "When providing mechanical cooling in the low ambient temperature range, the controls subsystem shall manage the following system parameters:
  ○ Saturated discharge pressure
  ○ Saturated suction pressure
  ○ Saturated discharge temperature
  ○ …."

Range requirements define the performance or the operational space that the control algorithm needs to manage relevant parameters over. Note that in this example the value is expected to not be achieved during transitions (turning equipment on and off until it settles out), thus a warning was added that it only applies during steady state conditions.

- **Range:** "When providing mechanical cooling in the low ambient temperature range and with steady state equipment conditions, the controls subsystem shall maintain superheat temperature (SST) greater than 5.00 degrees Fahrenheit."

Finally, an example worst case behavior requirement is shown. This requirement tells the controls engineer what action to take in case the range that the parameter is to be kept in is exceeded. Most range requirements should have a corresponding worst case requirement. In this case, if a critical parameter was not available (such as caused by sensor or cable failure) then through modeling it was shown that the system could not be properly controlled. The team then decided the best alternative action was to not go into the low ambient cooling.

- **Worst-Case Behavior:** "When the saturated suction pressure value is not available, the controls subsystem shall prevent mechanical cooling from operating below an ambient temperature of less than or equal to 40.0 degrees Fahrenheit."

Also note that while it may be easier to combine some of the requirement content stated above, as the projects move to using requirements management and automated testing tools it is desirable to define independent areas separately such that the project team knows exactly where problems are at when problems occur and which specific behaviors have been verified. A good test to determine if multiple requirements are embedded in a single requirement statement is to ask if the software could be implemented in such a way that part of the requirement could be passed while another part failed. If so, then it would be best to separate the requirement out into multiple requirement statements. Each requirement should result in a clearly discernable pass or fail condition during testing.

Control Algorithm Requirement Format and Content

This section provides additional guidance on the content and format to consider when developing control algorithm level requirements. The flow down of controls subsystem requirements to control algorithm requirements is structured around the controls architecture, which defines the individual control algorithms and how they interact with each other as well as with the overall application software. As with system or controls software level requirements, component or control algorithm level requirements have a specific focus that impacts their content and style. Similar to the controls software level, there will be multiple requirements used to define the behavior of a given control algorithm. Typical requirement content at this level addresses:

- The desired function (i.e. Manage to desired capacity or comfort level);
- Protecting the component (i.e. Component constraints and fault setting); and
- Optimizing the system operation for energy usage, noise or component life.

Many controls challenges are to effectively manage or optimize competing system attributes (for example want it to function but do not want to use a lot of energy). When developing the algorithm using model-based techniques, it is important to ensure that the control algorithm requirements reflect only the black box performance of the algorithm. The Algorithm Description Document (ADD) will capture the white box details which will be an outcome of the modeling exercise and reflects the algorithm design. Thus, the control algorithm requirements provide the basis of the control algorithm concept, and then provide the basis for judging the success and quality of the control algorithm design upon completion.

Control Algorithm Characteristics

Being the lowest level requirements, control algorithm requirements will be the most detailed and will reflect many higher-level design decisions made during the requirement flow down process. Even though the control algorithm is controlling the hardware components, the control algorithm requirements need to be able to be verified independent of the component or the application software, so they should reflect "control" specific behaviors. It is important to always use the same terminology throughout the requirement set. When stating behavior that is complex or difficult to express textually, it is often valuable to add a diagram (like SysML state diagram) to clarify the starting or ending point, or exactly what disturbance is being specified, etc.

Each characteristic will matter more or less dependent upon the application and what is being controlled. The controls engineer needs to carefully consider the specific problem in order to determine what needs to be specified. Caution must be exercised to ensure that the requirement is needed and driven by another system need or constraint, as it is not desirable to over specify the algorithm as that leads to artificially limiting the design space. The objective trying to be achieved at this level is to not be concerned with "how" the control algorithm implements a function, but to ensure that if the control algorithm meets the performance requirement then it is suitable for use and supports the system achieving its overall customer requirements. Additional considerations for control algorithm requirements besides set point regulation include:

- Relationships with other algorithms
- Robustness against model uncertainty and disturbances
- Transitions between operation modes
- Disturbance rejection (demand/load change, oat change, compressor on/off, fans on/off/speed change, etc.)
- Configurability
- Adaptability
- Diagnostic capability
- Energy efficiency

From a technical perspective the control algorithm characteristics fall into either the time or frequency domain. The controls engineer should ensure both of these have been adequately specified in the control algorithm requirements set. Example common time domain characteristics include:

- Rising time
- Setting time
- Overshoot
- Steady-state tracking error
- On/off times
- Saturation limits
- Rate limits
- Sample time

Example frequency domain characteristics include:

- Closed loop/open loop bandwidth
- Sensitivity function peak magnitude
- Complementary sensitivity function magnitude
- Cycle times limit per period
- Gain margin

- Phase margin
- Sample frequency

Again, not all of these characteristics will be defined for all algorithms. If not important to achievement of the desired behavior, it is acceptable to leave these decisions to design. The characteristics that are driven by higher-level design choices and are critical to achievement of system performance over the operating envelope should be specified as control algorithm requirements. In other words, independent of the design solution the control algorithm needs to exhibit a specific behavior under a specific set of conditions as defined by the control algorithm requirements.

Control Algorithm Integration Requirements

There are two distinct needs that a control algorithm must fulfill. Firstly, as it was previously discussed it needs to manage component operation in order to deliver the desired system behaviors to the customer. Secondly, it must integrate into the overall transactional or application software architecture. This leads to the interface requirements. Requirements for the second objective will require the control algorithm and controls software to do things beyond what is strictly required to manage the component behaviors. This may include setting flags, responding to higher-level mode requests, capturing run time durations or detecting faults. To determine which parameters to use, the controls may need to read unit configuration data such as size or options from a software-provided table. This means that the control subsystem needs to support the overall software architecture defined interface points. For projects using a common parameter approach (i.e. data point, data element convention, such as a data dictionary), the formal parameter name should be referenced from within the requirement. This makes it easier for the implementer and the tester to know exactly which point to read or write to, and also ensures that unique parameter names are not introduced in the model-generated code that do not exist within the overall software architecture. Recall that the control software is compiled with the overall software application for implementation. Failing to model the controls consistent to the software architecture or data dictionary conventions will lead to rework during integration. For consistency purposes, the underlying algorithm model should use the same naming conventions and data types in order to improve consistency when using auto-code generation by the modeling tools such as Mathworks Simulink and IBM Rapsody.

Providing Requirement Context

The context of a system: how the system functions overall, how it interfaces with its users and other systems, how its subsystems interacts, shifts from system to subsystem to component level following the decomposition process. The context of a system, subsystem, and component correspondingly drives the system, subsystem, and component level requirements. The context of a set of requirements at each level needs to be well defined and well understood among the entire design team. As organizations use more globally distributed design teams, considerations must be given to the level of domain knowledge the implementers and testers may have. To ensure clarity, additional information beyond the requirement statement itself may be provided. Graphs and diagrams that clarify the component parameter being used or performance curves can be referenced from the requirement text or the rationale field.

It is desired that the requirement text itself be concise and represents the testable behavior being specified. The requirement statement should not be used to provide explanations or references. However, the "Rationale" field, which is not part of the testable requirement statement, can be used to provide additional information or guidance.

Models used to flow down and derive requirements should also be referenced in the Rationale field to alert others to their existence and location (where it captures the configuration/version data), and to keep the traceability to design artifacts in case the changes are made to the requirements which drives corresponding design changes.

Within the SRS (which specifies control algorithms) the functional or behavioral requirements are organized around functions, and include the function name, a functional description and then the requirements that specify how well that function has to be performed. The function description field can also be used to provide context for interpreting the requirements.

Control algorithm requirements illustrate behaviors that can be tested within the control algorithm software. The control algorithm requirements allows relating the manipulation of individual paramters to the perfomance effect on a control function and hence the end product behavior that the customer sees. This maintains the desired tracability link from customer needs to design. Breaking out the controls behaviors had previously occurred in the analysis step that led to the controls software level requirements. At the control algorithm level the analysis becomes more detailed and defines parameter characteristics. At this level behaviors specific to a single control algorithm are derived following the controls architecture and controls functional hierarchy. They no longer represent the overall controls software behavior (black box view) as was done at the subsystem level.

Finally, to illustrate the differences in requirement content and style at the different levels, a flow down example follows. Note that between each level of requirements is an analysis step (*<analysis step>*), that derives the next lower level requirements. For instance, while the customer simply stated "low temperatures", the analysis at the system level analyzed typical operating scenarios for data centers to understand what locations and tempreature ranges they might want to use this in, and then did a competitive benchmarking exercise to understand what the unit needed to do to effectively compete in the marketplace. When going from the subsystem to the component level, modeling was used to understand which specific parameters (not really known at the subsystem level) may cause the TXV (thermal expansion valve) to loose superheat control (this is a mechanical control, and changing other parameters too quickly can upset its balance), and then further analysis on the sensitivity of those parameters occurred to define the tolerable rate of change.

<voice of customer (VOC) analysis>

- **Customer Requirement:** "The unit should providing cooling at low temperatures."

<system requirements analysis>

- **System Requirement:** "The system shall provide continuous mechanical cooling at a capacity greater than or equal to the unit's lower specification limit at low ambient temperatures within the inclusive range of 0.0 to 50.0 degrees Farenheit."

<controls software requirements analysis>

- **Subsystem (Controls) Requirement:** "When operating in the low ambient temperature range at a constant cooling demand rate, the controls subsystem shall maintain software controllable parameters within ranges such that the TXV is able to maintain superheat control."

<control algorithm requirements analysis>

- **Component (Algorithm) Requirement:** "The low ambient algorithm shall make parameter changes affecting superheat temperature <SSTA> at a rate of less than 5.60 degrees Fahrenheit per minute."

<algorithm design>

MODEL REQUIREMENT DEFINITION

Plant model is at the core of the model-based design approach. The plant model is involved in requirement definition, control design and testing, developed in parallel with these activities, and refined or modified at different stages of the control development process. This section describes in some detail the process and steps of defining modeling requirements of physics-based dynamic plant system model for control design and verification. The intent is to outline the workflow and general guidelines of model requirement definition, also to provide step-by-step instructions, with the help of examples, on how to derive model requirements for developing a physical plant model.

Note that not only the modelling engineers should be concerned with and be responsible for model requirements. Since many system level decisions affect the scope and the level of accuracy of the plant model, system engineers, controls engineers and equipment engineers should all be involved in the process of defining model requirements. Model requirement definition is also iterative, a primitive set of model requirements are subsequently modified, augmented, and further refined based on the use cases, simulation and test results from the requirement analysis, controls design and verification and validation phases. This section provides guidelines for creating the first set of model requirements to start this iterative process. By the nature of engineering, many things can only be proved and finalized at the late stage of the development process; sound engineering judgments are relied on for making decisions in the beginning of defining the model requirements.

In model-based control development process, a physics-based dynamic plant system model is developed after the system requirements and the controls subsystem requirements are defined. The plant model can also help analyze the refine the system and subsystem level requirements. The model requirements are derived from the system requirements (functions and use cases) and the controls subsystem requirements described in the control subsystem requirement document (SSRD). Other design and implementation constraints may also impact modeling requirements, i.e. sensor accuracy. The dynamic plant model should capture the relevant physics of the product under control for its intended operation range and provide adequate level of precision for control design and verification. The first step in this model development process is the model requirement definition. This section describes how to derive model requirements from the controls requirements mainly by way of examples.

Developing Plant Model Requirements

In the workflow for physical plant model development, the first step is to define the plant model requirements. The two inputs to this step are the product and component description and the controls subsystem requirements (it is assumed here that the plant model is used for control development). The product description defines the physical system, namely the plant, to be modelled with its internal structure and components, physical limits, operation conditions and the interface to its user and environment. The controls subsystem requirement document defines the behaviors and the performance level of the behaviors or responses of the system under control for intended use scenarios. Other non-functional aspects of the control system such as safety and efficiency are usually described in the controls requirement document as well. The output of this step is the model requirements, which drives the subsequent model development and validation steps.

Guidelines for Defining Model Requirements

The physics-based plant system dynamic model represents the time-varying behavior of the product and is used for requirement flow down, control system design and verification. In order to ensure the designed control system meets the control system requirements, the physical plant model needs to be accurate enough to establish that the designed control design passes or fails the control requirements. Thus, the physical plant model should be built based on suitable model requirements which specify the intended use of the model, the operation conditions and the accuracy, for example what physics should be captured, what accuracy of the model response is expected at steady state and transient conditions.

In general, model requirements have three categories:

1. Use scenarios and operating envelope,
2. Accuracy,
3. Simulation requirements such as simulation speed, robustness to noise and random inputs.

The following paragraphs list the general guidelines in establishing model requirements with demonstrative examples.

1.   Use Cases and Operating Envelope Requirements

This type of requirements defines the physics to be modeled and the bounds within which the developed component and system model are expected to meet the accuracy and speed requirements. Use cases of a model represent the use cases of the product related to the control subsystem. Use cases for a model determine the purposes and functions of the model, thus deciding relevant physics that shall be captured by the model. Model operating envelope should be derived from product operation conditions and component operating envelope pertaining to the to-be-developed control algorithms. Based on the system model operating envelope, component model operating envelope can be estimated in terms of the component's input and output boundary conditions within the product structure. For instance, compressor component model's operating envelope could be the ranges of compressor speed, suction and discharge pressures.

The following steps should be followed to define a set of operation requirements:

1. **System Function:** Define the physics to be modeled based on the intended use of the product and its operation conditions
2. **System Boundary:** Identify product inputs, outputs, and their respective range; inputs and outputs may be further divided into measured/controlled outputs, unmeasured/uncontrolled outputs, manipulated inputs, and uncontrolled inputs.
3. **Subsystem/Component Characteristics:** Identify each component and its inputs, outputs, and parameters; determine component operating envelope and variable ranges.

The above steps follow the top-down identify-and-define approach, from system to subsystem to component. At each level, the relevant physics is identified and bounds and accuracy are defined on associated variables. Note that modeling accuracy requirements are more stringent at the subsystem and component levels.

Following examples illustrate the steps alluded to earlier.

Example 1: Capture the relevant physics

A rooftop unit provides mechanical cooling with outside air temperature as low as zero degree Fahrenheit (intended use). The condenser has two fans and there are two condenser fan staging scenarios (operation conditions): both fans on; one fan on and the other fan off, where air flows through the off-fan channel. To properly model this multistage fan sequencing, the bypass and convective flow through the off-fan channel (relevant physics) needs to be captured by the plant model for the one fan on and one fan off operating condition.

Example 2: Identify plant variables and their ranges

A vapor compression system diagram, Figure 5, shows its structure and components, respective inputs and outputs to each component. There are four components: compressor, evaporator, condenser, and expansion valve. Variables are classified as inputs and outputs with inputs further divided into controlled (manipulated) inputs and uncontrolled (disturbance) inputs.

Figure 5. Example 2: identify inputs and outputs

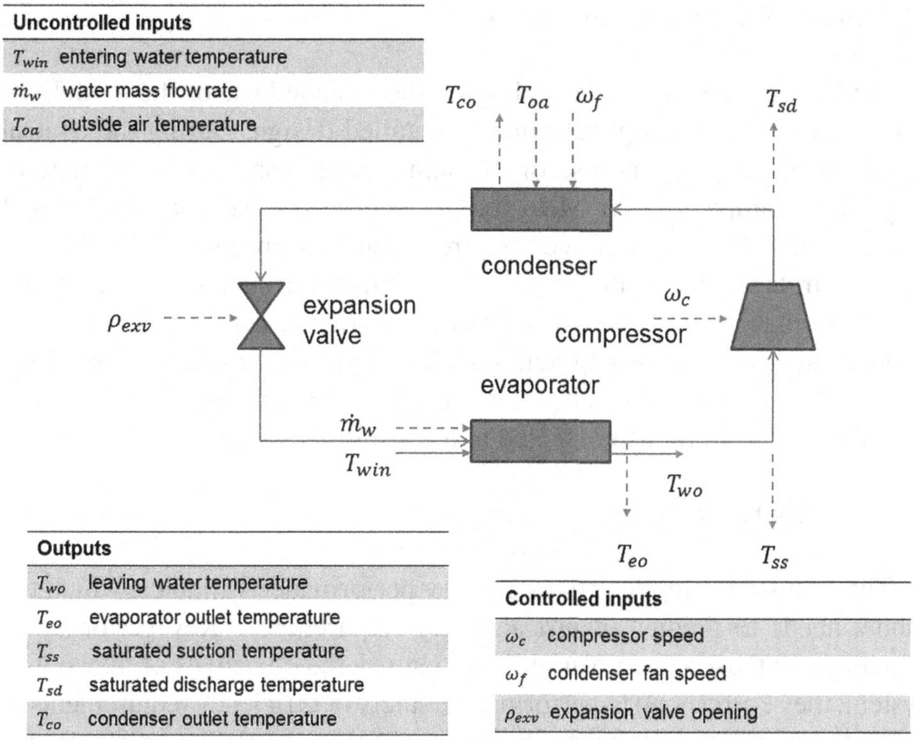
Uncontrolled inputs
T_{win} entering water temperature
$\dot{m}_w$ water mass flow rate
T_{oa} outside air temperature
T_{co}
T_{oa}
ω_f
T_{sd}
condenser
ρ_{exv}
expansion valve
ω_c
compressor
evaporator
$\dot{m}_w$
T_{win}
T_{wo}
T_{eo}
T_{ss}
Outputs
T_{wo} leaving water temperature
T_{eo} evaporator outlet temperature
T_{ss} saturated suction temperature
T_{sd} saturated discharge temperature
T_{co} condenser outlet temperature
Controlled inputs
ω_c compressor speed
ω_f condenser fan speed
ρ_{exv} expansion valve opening

Each plant variable should have a defined range based on the product design, for example, the expansion valve opening positioin is between 0 and 1; condensor fan speed is fixed, two stage or variable speed based on the design; the compressor speed is controlled by a variable frequency drive. Outside temperature range is determined based on the climates of targeted markets of the product, for instance North America or West Europe, which is a design factor.

Typical examples of component and system operating envelope include the maximum and minimum actuator commands, highest and lowest ambient temperatures, highest and lowest supply and return water or air temperatures. For some components, the operating envelope exists as design constraints for equipment protection: for example the compressor operating envelope is defined by the suction pressure and the discharge pressure. Model shall work for all compressor conditions within the given compressor design region.

Other requirements for internal variables, not part of inputs and outputs, include the suction supper heat limit, the condenser subcooling limit, and compressor minimum off/on time limit for example.

2.   Model Accuracy Requirements

Model accuracy varies depending on the intended use of the model, for example used for concept selection or detailed design. During the control development process, the use of the same model can vary from stage to stage, for example use for MIL or HIL, and so do the associated model requirements. Plant model accuracy requirements are essentially derived from controls requirements. This is to ensure that the plant model is accurate enough to enable control design and testing, and at the same time not to spend unnecessary time and costs modeling irrelevant physics or achieving accuracy levels which could negatively impact the model's numerical performance (simulation speed, robustness, etc.) and consume resources.

1.   Identify Key Performance Variables

The first step is to identify model key performance variables, which the model needs to predict against accuracy requirements. Key performance variables are these system variables serving as the objectives of the control system: they correspond to performance, safety or efficiency requirements in control subsystem requirement document (SSRD). Model key performance variables are typically measured variables used in the product's controller, for instance, compressor suction superheat is a key variable for compressor protection, if the expansion valve control algorithm is to be designed and verified. Another key performance variable example would be system capacity and power consumption if the control algorithm is to optimize system efficiency.

2. Identify Critical Components

This step determines which component models and parameters have the most effect on key performance variables. A natural step after identifying the critical components is to decide the modeling technique for each component. Questions such as should the component be a steady state model or a dynamic model, should the dynamic part be physics-based or data-driven, is information provided by the manufacturer of the component sufficient or we will need to obtain more data due to the effect on key performance variables, can be answered.

3. Determine Steady State and Dynamic Accuracy

Model accuracy requirements are specified in terms of maximum error allowed between model predicted key performance variables and experimentally measured ones. There are steady state accuracy requirement and transient state accuracy requirement respectively. Steady state accuracy is obtained by comparing model prediction at steady state against experimentally measured data at the same steady state. Transient state accuracy is obtained by comparing model predicted transient data against experimentally measured one. Experimentally measured data is usually lab data; in some case data of a higher fidelity model can be substituted.

Dynamic accuracy requirement can be given in both the time domain and the frequency domain. In the time domain, usually step responses at some selected operating conditions are compared in terms of quality indicators. For a first order system, a step response is characterized by the delay, the rise time, the overshoot, the settling time, and the steady state error. For a second order system, a step response is described using the peak time, the natural frequency, the damping ratio, and the settling time. Frequency responses can also be compared in terms of magnitude and phase error for a frequency range of interest. Control design is usually done using a linearized plant model around an operating point, where the classic frequency domain techniques are usually used for control design and analysis, thus imposing frequency domain dynamic accuracy requirements on the plant model.

Example 3: Derive Steady-State Model Requirements

For a specific model key performance variable (e.g. SST – Saturated Suction Temperature) the control requirement on SST is that it must be above freezing temperature, which comes directly from the operational requirement:

When operating in the low ambient temperature range, the low ambient algorithm shall maintain saturated suction temperature <SSTA> greater than or equal to 28 degrees Fahrenheit.

The model is required to be reasonably accurate in predicting SST. Therefore, it is defined through consulting the equipment team that the model must be capturing the steady state behavior of SST within a required accuracy of 5 degrees Fahrenheit.

Example 4: Derive Dynamic Model Requirements

Here, the key performance variable is a rooftop unit's Saturated Discharge Temperature (SDT). The relevant control algorithm is the rooftop's fan control algorithm for regulating SDT when operating in cooling mode at low ambient temperature conditions. It is required that the compressor on/off cycling frequency (due to minimum ON and OFF time) cannot be faster than the frequency ω_h.

Control requirements are often expressed in terms of bandwidth requirements in frequency domain for classical control design, e.g. how fast the controller needs to respond to changes of controlled variables. Based on controllability analysis for disturbance rejection(compressor on-off cycling is a disturbance to SDT), the SDT closed-loop control bandwidth ω_B should be greater than the compressor on/off frequency ω_h in order to reject the disturbance on SDT introduced by the compressor's on/off operation (refer to chapter four on controllability for details). In order for the plant model to be useful for control design, model dynamic precision requirements are also expressed in the frequency domain as the magnitude and phase accuracy requirements on model's frequency responses. As a rule of thumb, the plant model has to be accurate up to 3~5 times of the closed-loop control bandwidth (i.e. ω_B for SDT in the above rooftop example), because of the crossover frequency range is the most critical for the closed-loop stability and performance.

To verify that the plant model satisfies the frequency domain magnitude and phase requirements up to the desired frequency, frequency responses of the plant model within the desired frequency range are needed. The frequency response of the model at a frequency can be computed based on the steady state sinusoidal model response and a sinusoidal input to the model at the frequency. Frequency responses of the real plant system can be obtained in the same way using input and output data by exciting the plant using a sinusoidal input or by using an instrument such as the spectrum analyzer. The experimental data from the real system is then used against the frequency response data from the model to determine the model accuracy in the frequency domain.

In example 4, steady state error requirements are posed either in terms of absolute error or relative error (they are interchangeable). Transient error requirements are posed either in the time domain, i.e. the maximum error in the transient phase and in the frequency domain for a linearized model in terms of the magnitude and phase error for a frequency range. As mentioned earlier, control design usually is conducted using a linear model obtained by linearizing the nonlinear plant around an operating point.

3. Model Simulation Speed Requirements

Model simulation speed requirement should be derived based on how the model is to be used. If the model is to be used for Hardware-in-the-loop (HIL) control verification, the system model simulation speed has to be faster than real time, for example, model simulation CPU time shorter than real time at all time (not averagely). It makes sure that the model computation is completed within the sample time at each step of the simulation. The requirement applies to different HIL simulation hardware like NI PXI, and dSPACE.

If the plant system model will not be used for HIL application, then engineering effectiveness dominates the requirements. Typically, for control analysis using a dynamic model, the time to finish a transient simulation should at least be faster than real time. Note that along the model based control design tool chain, it is possible that the same model will be solved by different simulation platforms. It is important to keep in mind that the speed requirement should be applied to all simulation environments used in the control development process.

Simulation speeds of dynamic model are usually different in open loop fashion without controller and closed loop fashion with controller. Typically, simulation speed in open loop fashion is much faster than speed in closed loop fashion. Model can be tested in open loop fashion considering that controller model may not be available or it is complicated to test model in closed loop even if controller is already ready. However, input data of model should have similar form with the data fed by controller when running in closed loop fashion. For open loop test, the inputs of model include boundary conditions and actuator commands. Typically, average simulation time ratio (total CPU time/total Real time) should be less than about 0.1:1 for system normal conditions.

CONCLUSION

Model requirements definition guidelines are given along with steps and demonstrative examples. Requirements are driven by the intended use of the model. Different models have different sets of requirements. Also, at different phase of the design cycle, the requirements of the model may vary. Accuracy, speed, robustness are aspects, besides physics captured by a model and its operating conditions, of which model requirements are needed. Modelers together with the equipment engineer and the controls engineer define the detailed modeling requirements after control system requirement document is completed by the system engineer. Model requirement definition is iterative in its nature; control design outputs may require multiple rounds of model requirement refinements until the control design solution meets the controls requirements.

Chapter 3
Control Architecture and Controllability

CONTROL SYSTEM STRUCTURE DESIGN

Structure Design Problem

Control systems make the plant function in the specified ways, and are the critical components of many products. Controls systems vary in scale and complexity. With increasing functionalities and complexities in modern control systems, the control system structure design is an important step and often does not receive enough consideration from the engineers, in contrast to control algorithm design which is often focused in controls textbooks. Control system structure is the overall structural decisions made on the whole control system: these structural decisions include the selection of manipulated variables, controlled variables, measured variables as well as decomposition of the overall control system into smaller subsystems which are easier to deal with in design. The term control configuration is distinguished from the term control structure in this book. Control configuration is the structure of an individual controller and a control system may include many controllers like autopilot. We will discuss control system structure in this chapter; various control configurations used by individual controllers are introduced in Chapter Four on the controller design.

DOI: 10.4018/978-1-5225-2303-1.ch003

Control system structure design has been actively looked at in the process industry because of the needs to design a complex chemical plant which may have thousands of measurements and controls loops. Chapter 10 of Skogestad (1997) discusses the control structure design. Larsson and Skogestad (2000) published a paper on the plantwide control, where a review (references to other earlier works on this topic can be found there) and a new design procedure were given. Skogestad (2004) presented an expanded version of the plantwide control design procedure of Larsson and Skogestad (2000).

In practice, such as in a chemical plant, the control system is usually divided into several layers, (see Figure 1). For the chemical plant example, typically layers include scheduling (timescale of weeks), optimization layer (which is further divided into site-wide optimization (day) and local optimization (hour)), supervisory (advanced) control (minutes) and regulatory (base) control (seconds). These faster and slower layers are separated by different time scales and their relative positons in the hierarchy. The top layer is the planning and scheduling layer, where the overall operational decisions are made. For airplane avionics systems, a flight management system (FMS) is the top planning and scheduling layer. Given the flight plan and the aircraft's position, the FMS calculates the course to follow. The required course can be followed manually by the pilot or automatically by the autopilot (flight control system). The supervisory control layer and the regulatory control layer comprise the control layer, where the feedback control (and other control configurations such as feedforward) is implemented. In the supervisory control layer, the primary controlled variables are controlled to meet the overall system objectives and safety constraints and other constrains are handled. The regulatory control layer does not directly control the system level controlled variables; it regulates the secondary controlled variables. The objective of the regulatory control is to make it easier to achieve the primary control objectives in the supervisory layer. The regulatory control system stabilizes unstable modes, controls variables which otherwise drifts away due to large sensitivity to disturbances using local measurements and loops. The optimization layer determines the optimal operating point considering operational objectives and constraints. The optimization layer re-computes new set points at a longer time interval (i.e. an hour), while the control layer operates at a much short time interval (i.e. a minute and a second). These layers are linked by the controlled variables/measurements, whereby the set points are computed by the upper layer and implemented by the lower layer.

Why do we create layers in the control structure? One might image using a single optimizing controller which stabilizes the process, and at the same time coordinates all manipulated variables based on real time dynamic online optimization. There are fundamental reasons why such a solution may not be the best even with availability of the computing power needed. One fundamental reason is the cost of building and maintaining a dynamic plant model. Another factor is that feedback control when applied locally is very effective without the need for models. In fact, by cascading feedback loops, it is possible to control large plants with thousands of variables without using any models. The mode based control should be used only when the modeling efforts give enough benefits in terms of simplicity and /or improved performance. Other reasons could include maintainability, modularity and reuse.

According to Skogestad (2004), the control system structural design includes the following tasks:

1. Select manipulated variables (plant inputs);
2. Select controlled variables (variables with set points, plant outputs);
3. Select (extra) measurements (for control purposes including stabilization);
4. Select control configuration (the structure of the overall controller that links the controlled, manipulated and measured variables);
5. Select controller type (control law specification, e.g., PID, LQG, MPC, etc.).

In most applications, the controlled variables selection is straight forward; which variables should be controlled is naturally determined by the applications. For example, for a car cruise control system, the car speed is the controlled variable; for a home air-conditioning control system, the room temperature is the controlled variable; and for a printer, the print speed is the controlled variable for the paper feed control system. When the plants become very complex and they are a large number of variables available for control, i.e. a chemical plant, the selection of controlled variables becomes less obvious. In the latter case, Skogestad (2004) suggests that we first select the variables (primary controlled variables) directly related to ensuring optimal economic operation according to some cost function. In addition, we need to control additional variables (secondary control variables) in order to achieve satisfactory regulatory control. These variables are controlled in order to stabilize the plant with unstable and/or slow drifting modes such that the control objectives of the primary controlled variables can be better achieved. The secondary controlled variables are measured output variables, manipulated variables are used to control them. After the regulatory control

Figure 1. Typical control system hierarchy

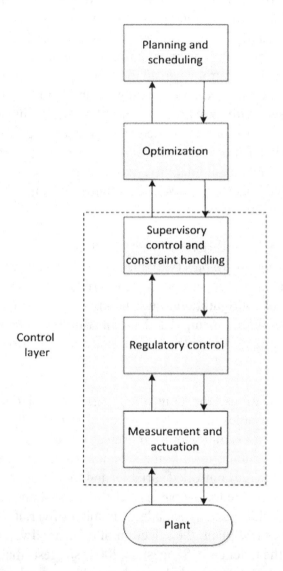

loops are implemented, their set points may be used as control degrees of freedom (manipulated variables) for the supervisory control layer.

Manipulated variables referred to here, are the physical degree of freedoms associated with actuators, i.e. valve positions or motor current or torque. Usually, what manipulated variables available for control design are given by the design of the plant itself: they are plant inputs. However, there may be some reasons to add more actuators or move their locations for improving the controllability of the plant after conducting a controllability analysis.

They are many variables in the control system that can be measured and usually the controlled variables are measured. Which variables to be measured, the number, location and accuracy of the measurement is a tradeoff between the cost of measurement and the benefits to control objectives. A controllability analysis is helpful to select which variables to measure. In most cases, the selection of measurements is considered simultaneously with the selection of the control configuration, i.e. for cascade control, extra measurements are needed besides the controlled variable measurements. In cascade control, the extra measurements are controlled locally and their set points are used as degree of freedom by the higher layer in the control hierarchy. For regulating the process, in some cases extra measurements are required to close the regulatory loop before controlling the controlled variables in the supervisory layer.

The control configuration is the structure of the controller that connects the measurements, set points to the manipulated variables. The controller itself can be structured (decomposed) into blocks both in the vertical (hierarchical) and horizontal (decentralized control) direction. Control configuration affects the controller design. Decomposing the controller can reduce the cost associated with defining the larger control problem and creating the detailed dynamic model required by a centralized control design. A decomposed control system is much less sensitive to model uncertainty since it uses a smaller model with less modeling uncertainty or use no explicit model.

General Structure Design Procedure

In principle, a top-down approach should be used to conduct the control structure design. We assume that control system requirements such as the product functional requirements and operating conditions have been developed and available. Based on these control system requirements, plus the knowledge of the potential measured, manipulated, and controlled variables, optimization methods could be employed to develop the control system structure design based on a comprehensive static or dynamic model of the plant. Such an approach may not be practical because of a large number of variables present in a complex control system and the costs of building and tuning a detailed physical model of the plant.

The traditional design procedure used for industrial control design has been a bottom-up, component by component approach. Even though it incorporates systematic methods to develop the control system structure, this approach relies on the heuristic design methods and rules of thumb developed from previous designs and experience of both the equipment and control engineers.

Control system structure design has been guided by logical, sequential, process-oriented methods proposed by many control researchers such as Skogestad (2004). However, it is unlikely that any proposed design procedure can generate a suitable structure design following a set of sequential steps in one pass. At every step of a given procedure, alternative options can arise, each leading to a different final design solution. The knowledge, skills, intuition of the controls team will always play a key role in making the final design decisions. There is no unique solution for a control structure design problem, different control engineers always come up with different designs due to their differences in the skill and knowledge levels and preferences.

Hierarchical design approach for control structure design is proposed to help making a large number of decisions in an organized and orderly manner. In this approach, detailed lower level design decisions are not made until important higher level questions on the system level have been addressed. Most industrial control system don not need a fully centralized control system, linking all of the controlled variables with all of the manipulated variables. Decentralized control system designs generally are more robust when operating conditions change and are more tolerant to individual component failures. An important analysis method for control system structure design is decomposition. Decomposition can be performed according to the various aspects of the plant. Decomposition can be based on the subsystems of the plant and subsequently the components of the plant. Decomposition of the overall design into smaller design problems at the subsystem and component levels can be efficient. The extent to which the overall control design can be broken down into smaller control design at the subsystem level, further broken down to the component level, determines how easily the control system can be designed, tuned, and maintained. Other ways of hierarchical decomposition are possible, for example based on the control objectives, and time scale. Control system structure shall support all system level functions. The system functional decomposition used earlier for control system requirements development also provides input information for control system structure design.

The intrinsically hierarchical characteristic of the control system structure design leads to design procedures that combine the best features of tip-down and bottom-up design methods. In general the following major steps are recommended for control structure design (appendix G; Seborg, Edgar, Mellichamp, & Doyce, 2011):

1. **Specify the Overall Control System Design Objectives:** State the overall control, economic objectives of a control system. Identify system and component constraints that must be satisfied, including safety, environmental, and quality constraints

2. **Perform a Top-Down Analysis:** Identify controlled variables, manipulated variables, measured variables, the source and nature of the major disturbances that must be rejected, perform control structure analysis, evaluate the possibility of decomposing the control problem. Establish the overall control structure in a conceptual form at the end of this stage.

3. **Develop a Bottom-Up Design:** Develop the strategies for regulatory control. Examine the potential of applying advanced control strategies (feedforward, cascade, MIMO control, etc.) for supervisory control and constraint handling. Evaluate the economic benefits of real time optimization.

4. **Validate Alternative Control Structure Designs and Down Select:** Check component and subsystem control designs. Check the effect of constraints and disturbances on the control system performance. Simulate the control system performance for a wide range of operating conditions. The final design solution shall meet all the objectives identified at step 1.

Skogestad (2004) and Larsson and Skogestad (2000) proposed similar combined top-down and bottom-up control structure design processes to complete the five tasks of control structure design. For the top-down analysis path, tasks 1 and 2 are performed and steps involved are:

1. **Definition of the Operational Objectives:** Use the information from control system requirement specification and functional decomposition.

2. **Manipulated Variables and Degrees of Freedom:** This step may show extra equipment is need for control for lack of control DOFs.

3. **Select Primary Control Variables:** Use the information from control system requirement specification and functional decomposition. And in the bottom-up analysis path, the following steps are performed for tasks 3, 4 and 5

4. **Regulatory Control Layer:** Select secondary controller variables and pair them with manipulated variables for stabilization and local disturbance rejection.

5. **Supervisory Control Layer:** Determine decentralized control or multivariable control. For decentralized control, choose input-output pairing. Decentralized control is preferred for non-interacting process and cases where active constrains remain constant. Controllability analysis tools can be applied for determining input-output pairing. Multivariable control is used for interacting processes and for easy handling of feedforward control. Use MPC with constraints handling for moving smoothly between varying active constraints to avoid using logic.

6. **Optimization Layer:** Identify active constraints and compute optimal set points for controlled variables.

7. **Validation:** Nonlinear dynamic simulation of critical components and operating conditions.

The procedure is generally iterative and may require several rounds going through the steps above, before converging at a feasible control structure solution.

In steps 4 and 5 for control layer analysis, a linear multivariable dynamic model is needed. Since, we are controlling variables at their set points using feedback, the steady-state part of the model is not important (except for controller using pure feedforward control). In Step 3 and 6, for the optimization layer analysis, a nonlinear steady-state mode is required; dynamic models are usually not needed. For control structure design, a generic model is considered sufficient versus a specific detailed model (for example, based on model identification) needed for controller design. Since a good control structure is generally insensitive to parameter changes, a generic model is generally sufficient for the control structure design purposes. This is the model where the structural part is correct, but where all the parameters may not match these in the true plant. A first principle theoretical model captures the salient physical properties of the plant is usually recommended for this.

Supervisory Control

In the control system hierarchy, the supervisory control layer is where the final control strategies are decided. The system control objectives are met by a satisfactory control design in this layer where controlled variables are regulated at their set points, the constraints for safe operation are enforced, and other optimization targets are achieved. Regulatory control design is completed before performing the supervisory control design. The plant under control for the supervisory controller is the original plant with the regulatory control implemented, which is a partially controlled system. The remaining manipulated variables except these used by the regulatory control, are utilized to control the primary controlled variables for achieving system level control requirements. An important decision at this level is if to use a centralized controller or to use a decentralized controller and it is a part of the control structure design. Other controls capabilities can be designed in this layer include estimation, adaptation, automatic controller tuning, and diagnostics, etc. To manage the complexity of the control functions and match up with the intended use cases and real operations of the final product, logic is needed to implement operation modes, decisions and to interface with the rest of the system (for example, user interface, remote monitor system). Constraints handling is another important design aspect considered at the supervisor control level. For a decentralized control system, how to handle the constraints with proportional-integral-derivative (PID) controllers are not easy. We will next talk about two ways of implementing control constraints: one involves using a finite state machine (FSM) and the other applies the override control.

Finite State Machine in Supervisory Control

In the supervisory control layer, after the regulatory control design is complete, the plant is to be controlled to meet all of the control objectives of the primary controlled variables. A controller, either decentralized or centralized depending on the level of interactions in the plant, is designed to achieve this. Logic usually is needed at this layer in addition to algorithmic computation for most industrial control applications. A control system can have different modes of operation, for example start up, shut down, normal operation, and diagnostics mode. In each mode, a different control algorithm is designed to meet the requirements of that mode. A finite state machine (FSM) is usually used to implement various modes of operation in industrial control applications: each mode corresponds to a state in the FSM. FSM is widely used for embedded control system modeling and programming in the industry. A FSM is a model of computation. It can be in one of a finite number of states and is only in one state at a time. It can change from one state to another when initiated by a triggering event or condition; this is called a state transition. A state represents the particular status of a system. A transition action is a set of actions to be executed when a condition is fulfilled or when an event takes place. Actions can also be associated with a state:

entry action which is performed when entering the state, exit action which is performed when exiting the state, during action which is performed when remains in the state. A particular FSM is defined by a list of its states and the transition condition for each transition. Hierarchy can be implemented in a FSM as well, that is a state contains lower level states within itself (which are called substates or child states) or be contained in another state (called a parent state or a superstate). The hierarchical structure of FSM makes implementing a complex process or task containing natural hierarchy easier such as the control system structure.

A control system is designed to operate over a range of operating conditions. Every subsystem and subsequently every component in the control system have an operating envelope. To keep the equipment safe, the subsystems and components need to stay within their individual operating envelop. Such operational requirements impose constraints for the control system such that the control design needs to satisfy. Consider a compressor control example, where for the compressor safety protection, the suction pressure and the discharge pressure shall stay within a specified region (see Figure 2). The suction pressure and the discharge pressure are treated as additional controlled variables for the compressor control besides the main control objective of controlling the speed of the compressor to meet the cooling capacity demand.

The control problem of controlling the cooling capacity and keeping the protected variables within safe operating region can be implemented using a finite state machine in Figure 3. There are three states in the finite state machine: one for the capacity, one for the discharge pressure (DP) and one for the suction pressure (SP). In each state, there is a distinct control loop running to meet the control target: in the capacity state, the control target is the cooling capacity; in the discharge pressure state, the control target is to keep the discharge pressure within the limits; in the suction pressure state, the control target is to keep the suction pressure within bounds. The control system starts in the capacity state and stays in that state until the suction pressure or the discharge pressure is out of bounds. The transition is taken when a pressure variable is outside the operating region, and the corresponding state for the pressure variable is entered and the control loop in the state is activated to take over the control of the pressure variable which is out of bounds. When the control action brings the out of bound pressure variable back into the safe operating range for a certain period of time and with a certain margin, then a transition takes place, and the capacity state is entered and the control loop in the capacity state is activated and the control target is switched back to the cooling capacity control again. When multiple

Figure 2. Safe operating region example for compressor

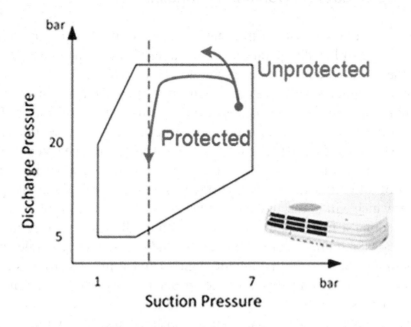

variables need to be kept with a safe region, there are situations that two or more variable are out of bounds, priority can be set on which variable will be controlled first, and which variable will be controlled next after the first controlled variable is brought within bounds. Using a finite state machine, a hierarchical protection mechanism with different priority levels assigned to the protected variables can be easily implemented.

Figure 3. Finite state machine example for supervisory control of the compressor

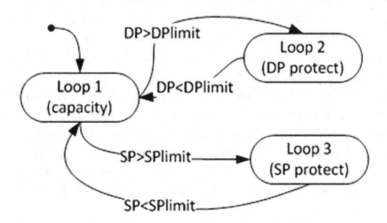

Override Control for Constraint Handling

We have seen how to use a finite state machine to implement supervisory control logic to handle operational constraints. Because at every point in time, the finite state machine can only be in one state, the operation of the controller within a state is not continuous, if switching out of that state and switching back to the state happen over time during the operation. Here different controllers in different states control the same actuator, the compressor speed in this case. Due to the switching, extra caution must be taken to make sure the same actuator command input is always smooth when it is under control of different controllers in different states. It is called the bumpless transfer which will be discussed in the later chapter on the controller design. Implementing a finite state machine, including all states, transitions, and state actions, requires careful logic design and check, also consumes more computing resources. With complex logic included in a control system, it becomes more difficult to maintain, debug and test; also it is prone to human error. For these reasons, using less logic in a control system is preferred. Another popular way of implementing constraint handling without using logic is the override control.

In the override control, no finite state machine is needed, controllers are running continuously and each controller is designed to implement a constraint, for example upper or lower limit for a variable. Controller outputs from each controller are compared and selected using Min, Mix or Min and Max selectors based on physics. The selected controller output is sent to the actuator as command. In override control, one controller can take over the command of the manipulated variable from another controller when the process would otherwise exceed some equipment limit or constraint. According to Shinsky, Shunta, Jamison, and Hohr (2005), override can be defined as "controllers that remain inactive until a constraint is about to be reached or exceeded, at which point they take over control of the manipulated variable from the normal controller through a selector and thereby prevent the exceeding of that constraint."

As an example, consider using override control to implement the high limit for the suction pressure of the compressor. The manipulated variable for controlling the suction pressure is the opening position of an electronic extension valve (EXV). The same EXV opening position is also used for superheat control during the normal compressor operation. There are two controllers for the compressor control: one controller for superheat control during normal operation and the other override control for keeping the suction pressure under the high limit. The set point for the override controller is the suction pressure limit. The two controller outputs are fed to a low-signal selector, which selects the lower of the two, in this example.

As long as the suction pressure set point is not exceed, the output of the override controller is blocked by the low signal selector and the EXV position is controlled by the normal superheat controller. When the suction pressure in the inlet of the compressor exceeds the set point of the override controller, the override controller output decreases, and when it drops below the superheat controller's output, it is selected for controlling the EXV opening position. In this way, the suction pressure override prevents the suction pressure from exceeding the high pressure limit. When override control takes over control of the EXV opening position, the superheat is not under control and controlling the suction pressure below the high limit becomes a higher priority over superheat for the control system.

Integral action in a PID controller will cause controller output to saturate if the controller has enduring control error because it has no access to the manipulated variable. Saturation of the controller output due to the continuous integration of the sustained error experienced by a PID controller is called reset windup. It can occur in override control, where a selector connects one controller output to the manipulated variable from among the outputs of two or more PID controllers while blocking the others. The controllers being blocked have no command of the actuator and their controlled variables are not regulated, so their outputs will wind up and the antiwindup needs to be implemented to stop integrating their errors when their outputs are not selected for commanding the actuators. External reset feedback is used for anti-windup for a PI or PID controller, and it can be used for a cascade loop and a feedforward loop (Shinsky, Shunta, Jamison, & Hohr, 2005).

Another type of external reset algorithm is created by adding to the standard PI algorithm a term that integrates the difference between the controller output and the feedback signal:

$$m(t) = k_p e(t) + k_p / T_i \int e(t) \, dt + 1 / T_i \int F(t) - m(t) \, dt \qquad (1)$$

where k_p is the proportional gain, T_i is the integral time constant, $F(t)$ is the external reset feedback signal which is the output of the selector, m(t) is the output of the controller. When the control is selected for controlling the manipulated variable, the feedback signal is its own output and the extra term is equal to zero. When it is not selected, the feedback signal which is the output of the selected control is different from the controller output and the integration occurs. This new term cancels out the normal integral action so the integral action is stopped until that the controller is selected. Equation 1 in effect leads to:

$$m(t) = k_p e(t) + F(t) \tag{2}$$

which shows that the unselected controller tracks the selected controller with an offset of $k_p e(t)$. This offset term causes the unselected controller output to rise above or fall below the selected controller output based on its own error, which can thus override the selected controller when being selected by a selector.

When designing an override control, one shall consider the following steps:

1. The process variables that are to be controlled by the manipulated variable (including the normal controlled variables and constraints);
2. The failure position of the final control element(actuator);
3. The safe set points for the controllers;
4. The required controller actions (control error increases or decreases the manipulated variable);
5. The type of selector required (high, low, other);
6. Selector series reflecting the constraint priority.

When there are more than two controller outputs, min and max selectors can be placed in serial one after the other. The first selector accepts two controller outputs and its output (selected controller output) is fed to the second selector together with the third controller output. The second selection takes place and it then continues in the same fashion. In this chain of selection, the selectors placed to the end of the chain have higher priority than these placed at the beginning of the chain, because they can override the outputs of selector in front of them. This feature can be used to design override control where there exist multiple constraints with different levels of priority, for example the constraint with the highest priority is implemented by the last selector.

CONTROLLABILITY ANALYSIS

Introduction

Input-output controllability of a plant is the ability to achieve acceptable control performance requirements. This section provides guidelines or rules for performing the input-output controllability analysis, including simple analysis tools which can be used to get a rough idea of how easy or difficult it is to control a plant given a defined control strategy or suggest better control strategies, without performing detailed controller designs and analysis.

The intended users of the controllability analysis include controls engineers, software, hardware, or system engineers with some control engineering background. It is assumed that the user has taken at least one undergraduate level controls course and understands frequency domain control analysis such as Bode plot, gain and phase. The users should also be familiar with linear algebra and matrix theory to apply the analysis tools.

Controllability analysis rules and tools presented in this section cover both single-input-single-output (SISO) systems and multi-input-multi-output (MIMO) systems. After a plant model is obtained in the modeling step and before the actual control design starts, the controllability analysis step should be performed to find out what control performance can be expected against the control requirements. This is an important step in the sense that it can catch fundamental limitations in the plant for achieving desired control objectives before conducting detailed controller design. Thus, it has the potential of saving development costs and time. Any limitations in the plant on control performance found at this step should be fed back to equipment engineers to improve the plant (equipment) design. The outcomes of this analysis help determine what the measured variables should be, what should be manipulated variables, and their pairings. It can also help sizing the actuators. After this analysis, it may be determined that a SISO controller can be designed for each control loop without considering interactions in a MIMO plant, i.e. decentralized control design, or a multivariable controller needs to be designed to accounting for strong interactions in the plant, i.e. centralized controller design.

Controllability Measures

Control system performance is limited by RHP zeros, RHP poles, time delays, input constraints, model uncertainties, and disturbances. Controllability measures are developed based on these limiting factors of the plant. These measures are simple and can be applied to give a rough idea of how easy the plant is to control, independent of the controller (Skogestad & Postlethwaite, 1997; Van de Wal & De Jager, 2001; Farsangi, Song & Lee, 2004; Ca & Yang, 2004). The following measures of controllability are introduced at a high level and in practice they can be combined in a controllability analysis.

Minimum Singular Value

In general, a large minimum singular value of the plant is preferred. The minimum singular value is the smallest gain for any input direction. If it is small, the ratio between the maximum and the minimum singular values is big. It shows that the plant is ill-conditioned, which means that the plant is sensitive to model uncertainty. To maintain independent control of all outputs, the rank of the plant needs to be equal to the number of the outputs. If the minimum singular value is close to zero, it implies the plant is close to losing rank and it is difficult to achieve independent control of all the outputs. Because there are input constraints, the minimum singular value should be large to have good tracking and disturbance rejection performance without using large inputs.

The Condition Number

The condition number, the ratio between the maximum and minimum singular value, is another common controllability indicator. A small condition number is preferred. It has been shown that plant with a small condition number is robust to both diagonal and unstructured multiplicative uncertainty at the plant input.

The Relative Gain Array

RGA was introduced by Bristol (1966) as a measure of interactions in decentralized control. The RGA is a matrix of the relative gains, which is the ratio of two gains in two extreme cases. The first case is the open loop case, and the gains are open loop gains. The second case is the all other inputs and outputs (except the output and input pair under consideration) are under perfect control. Each RGA element is independent of how other loops are paired. If a RGA element is close to 1, it means that the gain of that input output pair is not affected by closing other loops. Negative RGA elements are undesirable because it means that the gain for a given loop changes sign when closing other loops.

The RGA can be used to pair inputs and outputs for a MIMO plant. It is desirable to pair inputs and outputs such that diagonal elements of the RGA are as close as possible to one, which means there is less interactions among the different loops.

Plants giving rise to large RGA elements should be avoided, since they are difficult to control. It has been shown that plants with large absolute RGA elements are very sensitive (especially around the bandwidth) to diagonal multiplicative input uncertainty (realistic in practice) and are very sensitive to element-by element uncertainty (less realistic) in the plant. In practice, it is common to encounter the first type of uncertainty, i.e. neglected actuator dynamics.

Right Half Plane Zeros

The RHP zeros are undesirable because they limit the performance of the closed-loop. From the root locus analysis, we know that when the feedback gain increases, the closed-loop poles move from the open loop poles to the open loop zeros, which leads to high gain instability. However, high performance usually requires a high gain. RHP zeros limit the closed-loop bandwidth, it is bad when the RHP zeros are located close to the origin. A plant which has RHP zeros is called non-minimum phase plant, and it has inverse response behavior for a step change in the input. The output goes initially towards the opposite direction before it reverses the direction and moves towards the final steady state value.

Controllability Rules for SISO Plants

In controls courses offered through engineering programs at universities, controller design and stability analysis are usually emphasized. However, in practice the following three issues are often more important (Skogestad & Postlethwaite, 1997):

1. How well can the plant be controlled?
    Before starting any controller design and analysis one should first determine how easy the plant actually is to control. Is it a difficult control problem? Indeed, does there even exist a controller which meets the required performance objectives?
2. What control structure should be used?
    What variables should we measure, what variables should we manipulate, and how are these variables paired together?
3. How might the plant be changed to improve control?
    Should any components in the plant be changed to improve the control performance? For example, one may increase the size of a buffer tank to reduce the effects of disturbance in process control, or one may find the speed of response of a measurement device is important for achieving acceptable control.

The above three questions are each related to the inherent control characteristics of the plant itself. The term input-output controllability is introduced to capture these characteristics. In summary, a plant is controllable if there exists a controller that yields acceptable performance for all expected plant variations and disturbances, under all expected operating conditions. Controllability is independent of the controller, and is a property of the plant (or process) alone. It can only be affected by changing the plant itself, that is, by design changes. So, it is recommended that the equipment design and controllability analysis are performed concurrently and iteratively together, ensuring the product is feasible for meeting the specified control requirements.

Figure 4. Feedback control system

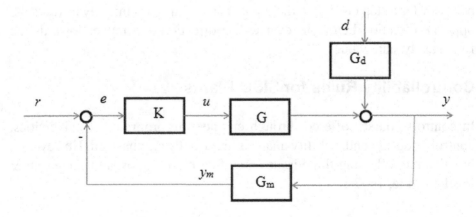

Consider the control system in Figure 4. The linear model in terms of transfer functions (one can extract transfer functions from data or physics-based models) is:

$$y = G(s)u + G_d(s)d.$$

$G_m(s)$ is the measurement transfer function representing the dynamics of the transducer. The disturbance d, the control input u, the controlled output y and the reference r are assumed to have been scaled using largest allowed (as defined in the controls requirements) or expected changes as outlined in Section 1.4. of Skogestad and Postlethwaite (1997), and therefore $G(s)$ and $G_d(s)$ are scaled transfer functions between the scaled controlled output y and the scaled control variable u, the scaled output y and the scaled disturbance d respectively. The scaling of variables is done such that, the allowed input $|u(t)|<1$, the expected disturbance $|d(t)|<1$, the allowed control error $|e(t)|<1$, and the expected reference signal $|r(t)|<R$, where R is the largest expected change in reference relative to the largest allowed control error.

Consider the control problem of adjusting the heat input Q to maintain constant room temperature T with the outdoor temperature T_0. The acceptable room temperature variation is 1K, so the room temperature T (output), the temperature reference and the temperature error are scaled by dividing them by 1K respectively. The heat Q is the control input, if the largest input change is 2000W, the heat Q is scaled by dividing it by 2000W. The disturbance is the outdoor temperature, if the expected change in the outdoor temperature is 10K, the outdoor temperature is scaled by dividing it by 10K.

Let ω_c be the gain crossover frequency; defined as the frequency where the open loop transfer function magnitude $|L(j\omega)| = |G(j\omega)K(j\omega)|$ crosses 1 from above. Let ω_d denote the frequency at which $|G_d(j\omega)|$ first crosses 1 from above.

If $|e(t)|<1$ is achieved, then the closed-loop is said to have tight control at this frequency.

The following set of controllability rules proposed by Skogestad (1994) apply:

Rule 1: Speed of response to reject disturbances.

Must require $\omega_c > \omega_d$. More specifically, we must require with feedback control $|L(j\omega)| > |G_d(j\omega)|$, $\forall \omega < \omega_d$.

Rule 2: Speed of response to follow set point changes.

Must require $\omega_c > \omega_r$, where ω_r is the frequency up to which tracking is required.

Rule 3: Input constraints for disturbances.

Must require $\left| G(j\omega) \right| > \left| G_d(j\omega) \right|$, $\forall \omega < \omega_d$.

Rule 4: Input constraints from set points.

Must require $|G(j\omega)| > R$, $\forall \omega < \omega_r$.

Rule 5: Time delay θ in $G(s)G_m(s)$.

Must require $\omega_c < 1/\theta$.

Rule 6: A RHP-zero in $G(s)$ at $s=z$.

For a real RHP-zero, must require $\omega_c < z/2$ and for a complex RHP-zero, must require $\omega_c < |z|$ for tight control at low frequencies.

Rule 7: Phase lag constraints.

In most practical cases (e.g., with PID control) require $\omega_c < \omega_u$. Here the ultimate frequency ω_u is where $\angle G(j\omega_u) G_m(j\omega_u) = -\pi$ or $-180°$.

Rule 8: Real open-loop unstable pole in $G(s)$ at $s=p$.

We need high feedback gains to stabilize the system and we approximately require $\omega_c > 2p$.

These rules are necessary conditions, minimum requirements, in order to obtain acceptable control performance. The reason they are not sufficient is that they are derived by considering one effect at the time.

In summary, Rules 1, 2 and 8 tell us that we need high feedback gains, or fast control, in order to reject disturbances, to track set points and to stabilize the plant. On the other hand, Rules 5, 6 and 7 tell us that we must use low feedback gains in the frequency range where there are RHP-zeros, delays or where the plant has a lot of phase lag.

These requirements for high and low gain have been formulated as bandwidth requirements (at frequencies lower than the bandwidth, feedback gain is high and at frequencies higher than the bandwidth, feedback gain is low). If they somehow are in conflict then the plant is not controllable and the only remedy is to introduce design changes to the plant itself which may include:

- Changing the apparatus itself, e.g. type, size, etc.;
- Relocating sensors and actuators;
- Adding new equipment to dampen disturbances;
- Adding extra sensors;
- Adding extra actuators;
- Changing the control objectives;
- Changing the control configuration already in place.

Example 1: Room Heating (Skogestad & Postlethwaite, 1997)

Consider the problem of maintaining a room at constant temperature. Let
y be the room temperature, u the heat input and d the outdoor temperature.
Feedback control should be used. Let the measurement delay for temperature
be $\theta_m=100s$. Consider the following two questions:

1. Is the plant controllable with respect to disturbances?
2. Is the plant controllable with respect to set point changes of magnitude
   $R=3$ ($\pm3K$) when the desired response time for setpoint changes is
   $\tau_r=1000sec$ (17min)?

Let us perform the controllability Analysis. A critical part of controllability
analysis is scaling. A model in terms of scaled variables was derived following
the process shown earlier as follows

$$G(s)=\frac{20}{1000s+1}; \quad G_d(s)=\frac{10}{1000s+1}$$

The frequency responses of $|G|$ and $|G_d|$ are shown in Figure 5.

Question 1: Disturbance Rejection

From Rule 1 $\omega_c>\omega_d$. Feedback control is necessary up to the frequency
$\omega_d=0.01$rad/sec, where $|G_d|$ crosses 1(0dB). From Rule 3 no problems with
input constraints are expected since $|G|>|G_d|$ at all frequencies. From Rule 5
$\omega_c<1/\theta$. The upper bound given by the measurement delay is $1/\theta=0.01$rad/
sec. The requirements of Rule 1 and Rule 5 conflict with each other, we
therefore conclude that the system is barely controllable for this disturbance,
which means the requirement $|e(t)|<1$ could be violated.

Figure 5. Frequency responses for room heating example

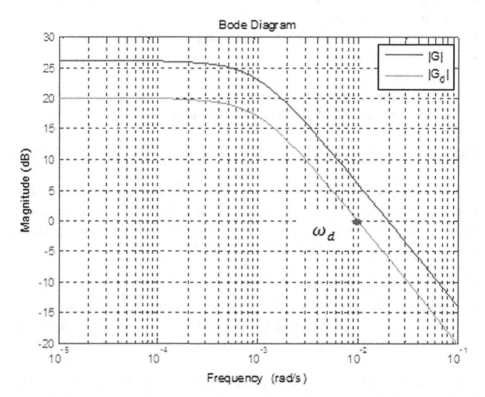

These conclusions are supported by the closed-loop simulation in Figure 6 for a unit step disturbance (corresponding to a sudden 10K increase in the outside temperature) using a PID controller. The output exceeds its allowed value of 1 for a very short time after about 100seconds, but then returns quickly to zero. The input goes down to about -0.8 and thus remains within its allowed bounds of +/-1. Note there is a measurement delay of 100seconds, the plant output is already at 1 after 100seconds, so no PID could ever meet the requirement.

Question 2: Set Point Tracking

Rule 5 is satisfied. The delay of 100 seconds is much smaller than the desired response time of 1000 seconds. Rule 4 is satisfied. $|G(jw)| \geq R=3$ up to about $\omega_1 = 0.007$rad/s which is seven times higher than the required $\omega_r = \dfrac{1}{\tau_r} = 0.001 rad / s$. In fact, we should be able to achieve response times

Figure 6. Disturbance step responses

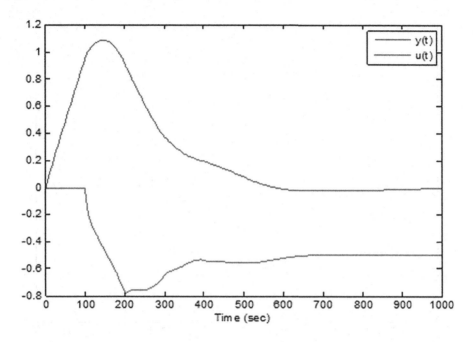

of about $\dfrac{1}{\omega_1} = 160s$ without violating the input constraints. This is confirmed in Figure 7 for a desired set point change of 3/(200s+1) using the same PID controller as before. For this set point change, $\omega_r = \dfrac{1}{\tau_r} = 0.005 rad/s$, Rule 2 requires that $\omega_c > \omega_r$ which is satisfied adequately with $\omega_c = 0.011 rad/s$ as shown in Figure 8, which plots the frequency response of the open loop transfer function, $L(s) = G(s)K(s)$.

MIMO Plant Controllability

When there are multiple manipulated variables and multiple controlled variables for a plant, we are dealing with a MIMO plant. MIMO plants are often encountered in industrial control problems. Compared to SISO plants, controllability analysis of MIMO plants are in general more difficult and more advanced mathematical tools are needed. Besides mathematical analysis, good physical understanding of the plant under control is beneficial. In some cases, selection of inputs and outputs and pairing of inputs and outputs can

Figure 7. Set point step response

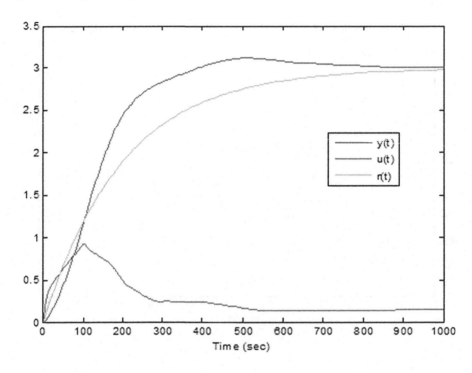

Figure 8. Open loop Bode plot

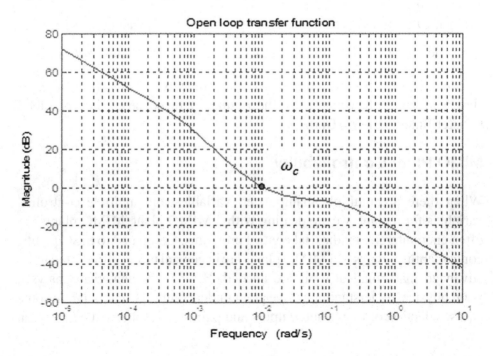

be made based on knowledge of physics of the plant, which, subsequently, will be confirmed by the mathematical analysis.

There is interaction between inputs and outputs for true MIMO plants: an input generally affects all outputs. The main difference between a SISO system and a MIMO system is the presence of directions in the latter. For example, in a MIMO system, disturbances, the plant, RHP poles and RHP zeros each have directions associated with them. This makes it more difficult to consider their effects separately as for SISO case. For example, a MIMO plant may have a RHP zero and a RHP pole at the same location, but their effects may not interact if they are in completely different parts of the system (remark 5, Skogestad & Postlethwaite, 1997, p. 135).

For a MIMO plant, the controllability analysis usually considers the issues of functional controllability, RHP zeros, RHP poles, disturbances, input constraints and uncertainty. A typical MIMO controllability analysis may proceed as follows, following Skogestad and Postlethwaite (1997):

1. Scale all variables to obtain a scaled model $y = G(s)u + G_d(s)d$.
2. Obtain a minimal realization
3. Check functional controllability. To be able to control the outputs independently, we need at least as many inputs as outputs. Second, we need the rank of $G(s)$ to be equal to the number of outputs.
4. Compute the poles and directions of RHP poles.
5. Compute the zeros and directions of RHP zeros.
6. Obtain the frequency response $G(j\omega)$ and compute the RGA matrix $\Lambda = G \times (G^{-1})^T$. Plants with large RGA-elements at crossover frequency range are difficult to control and should be redesigned.
7. Compute the singular values of $G(j\omega)$ and plot them as a function of frequency. Also consider the associated input and output singular vectors. The minimum singular value is a useful controllability measure and it should be as large as possible for frequencies where control is needed.
8. Consider disturbances effects on the outputs and control inputs.

In step 8, the elements of the disturbance matrix $G_d(s)$ are considered. At frequencies where elements are greater than 1, control is needed. If we consider one disturbance at a time (the column g_d of G_d), we must at least require $\underline{\sigma}(S) \leq 1/\|g_d\|_2$.

9. Uncertainty. If the condition number $\gamma(G)$ is small then we expect no particular problems with uncertainty. If the RGA elements are larger, we expect strong sensitivity to uncertainty.
10. Ask if the control requirements are compatible based on results from the previous steps. For example, look at disturbances, RHP poles and RHP zeros and their associated directions.

To complete the steps in the above controllability analysis process, certain mathematical tools are needed, such as singular values and singular vectors, condition number, relative gain array (RGA). They are introduced next.

Analysis Tools

In this section, useful analysis tools are introduced and their applications to MIMO control system analysis are also discussed.

Definition 1: Unitary matrix. A complex matrix U is unitary if:

$$U^H = U^{-1}$$

U^H is the complex conjugate transpose of U.

Definition 2: Singular Value Decomposition (SVD). Any complex $l \times m$ matrix A may be factorized into a singular value decomposition

$$A = U \Sigma V^H$$

where the $l \times l$ matrix U and the $m \times m$ matrix V are unitary, and the $l \times m$ matrix Σ contains a diagonal matrix Σ_1 of real, non-negative singular values, σ_i arranged in a descending order as:

$$\Sigma_1 = diag\{\sigma_1, \sigma_2, ..., \sigma_k\}; \quad k = \min(l, m)$$

and

$$\bar{\sigma} \equiv \sigma_1 \geq \sigma_2 \geq ... \geq \sigma_k \equiv \underline{\sigma}.$$

The unitary matrices U and V form orthonormal bases for the column (output) space and row (input) space of A. The column vectors of V, denoted v_i, are called right or input singular vectors and the column vectors of U, denoted u_i, are called left or output singular vectors.

Output and input singular vectors are output directions and input directions of a plant in control. These input and output directions are related through the singular values. SVD is used for analyzing the gains and directionality of multivariable plants. Singular values of a MIMO plant represent the gains of the plant and are usually plotted as a function of frequency in a Bode magnitude plot with a log-scale for frequency and magnitude. The maximum singular value, $\bar{\sigma}$, and minimum singular value, $\underline{\sigma}$, are particularly useful for MIMO system control design and analysis.

SVD is easily performed in MathWorks MATLAB, a computing environment widely used by control engineers. For example, consider a matrix:

$$G = \begin{bmatrix} 5 & 4 \\ 3 & 2 \end{bmatrix}$$

The following MATLAB commands accomplish SVD of this matrix

```
>> G=[5, 4; 3 2]
G =
         5        4
         3        2
>> [U, S, V]=svd(G);
>> U
U =
    -0.8718    -0.4899
    -0.4899     0.8718
>> S
S =
     7.3434            0
          0       0.2724
>> V
V =
    -0.7937     0.6083
    -0.6083    -0.7937
```

Definition 3: Rank. The rank of a matrix is equal to the number of non-zero singular values of the matrix.

Definition 4: Functional Controllability. An m-input l-output system $G(s)$ is functionally controllable if the normal rank of $G(s)$ is equal to the number of outputs. The normal rank of $G(s)$ is the rank of $G(s)$ at all values of s except at the zeros of $G(s)$.

An example of functional uncontrollability is when none of the inputs affect a particular output which would be the case when one of the rows in $G(s)$ is identically zero. Another example is when there are more outputs than inputs.

Definition 5: Condition Number. The condition number of a matrix A is defined as the ratio:

$$\gamma(A) = \bar{\sigma}(A) / \underline{\sigma}(A).$$

A matrix with a large condition number is said to be *ill-conditioned*. The condition number has been used as an input-output controllability measure and if the condition number is small, then the multivariable effects of model uncertainty are not likely to be serious.

Definition 6: Relative Gain Array. The relative gain array of a complex non-singular $m \times m$ matrix A, denoted $RGA(A)$ or $\Lambda(A)$, is a complex $m \times m$ matrix defined by:

$$\Lambda(A) \triangleq A \times \left(A^{-1}\right)^{T}$$

where the operation $\times$ denotes element by element multiplication.

RGA is a useful measure of interactions and is the matrix of relative gains: ratios between gains of open loop and gains when other loops are closed under perfect control. RGA has a number of useful control properties:

1. It is independent of input and output scaling.
2. Its rows and columns sum to one
3. The RGA is a good indicator of sensitivity to uncertainty, esp. uncertainty in the input channels (diagonal input uncertainty) caused by uncertain or neglected actuator dynamics. This is the uncertainty usually occurring in practice.

4. RGA and RHP zeros. If the sign of an RGA element changes from $s=0$ to $s=\infty$, then there is a RHP zero in G.
5. Diagonal dominance. The RGA can be used to measure diagonal dominance, by the simple quantity:

$$RGA\_number =\| \Lambda(G) - I \|_{sum}.$$

For decentralized control, we prefer pairings for which the RGA number at crossover frequencies is close to 0. Also, rearranging the inputs and outputs to make the plant diagonally dominant with small RGA number makes multivariable design easier.

6. RGA and decentralized control
    a. For stable plants avoid input-output pairing on negative steady-state RGA elements.
    b. Prefer pairings corresponding to an RGA number close to 1 at crossover frequencies.

Applications of Analysis Tools

In this section, we use two examples to show how the mathematical analysis tools may be applied towards the controllability analysis of MIMO plants.

Example 2: An Academic Case

This example is taken from Astrom (2013) to demonstrate the usage of RGA and SVD for inputs-outputs selection and pairing.

Consider a system with a zero frequency gain matrix of the scaled linear model:

$$\begin{pmatrix} y_1 \\ y_2 \\ y_3 \end{pmatrix} = G(0) \begin{pmatrix} u_1 \\ u_2 \\ u_3 \end{pmatrix} = \begin{bmatrix} 0.48 & 0.9 & -0.006 \\ 0.52 & 0.95 & 0.008 \\ 0.9 & -0.95 & 0.002 \end{bmatrix} \begin{pmatrix} u_1 \\ u_2 \\ u_3 \end{pmatrix}.$$

Compute RGA:

$$\Lambda\big(G(0)\big) \triangleq G(0) \times \big(G(0)^{-1}\big)^{T} = \begin{bmatrix} 0.7100 & -0.16 & 0.4501 \\ -0.3557 & 0.7925 & 0.5632 \\ 0.6456 & 0.3677 & -0.0133 \end{bmatrix}$$

Recall that RGA is a measure of loop interactions which tells us how the open loop gain in one loop is affected when other loops are closed under perfect control. For example λ_{11}=0.710 indicates that the static open loop gain between output one and input one is decreased about 30% when the other two loops are closed under perfect control; λ_{12}=-0.16 indicates that input two affects output one in a opposite way when the other two loops are closed; λ_{13}=0.4501, compared to λ_{11}=0.710, indicates that the gain from the third input to the first output is more impacted by the loop closure in the other two loops.

Compute the singular values:

$$\bar{\sigma} = 1.6183, \ \sigma_2 = 1.1434, \ \underline{\sigma} = 0.0097$$

Compute the condition number:

$$\gamma = \bar{\sigma} / \underline{\sigma} = 166$$

Very small minimum singular value and a large condition number indicate the plant is difficult to control.

Very small minimum singular value implies the plant is almost singular. In other words, the first two rows of $G(0)$ are almost parallel, which indicates that the first and second output cannot be controller independently, which is consistent with the functional controllability definition, So, we need to reduce the 3 by 3 plant to a 2 by 2 plant. We need to pick two inputs. Compare the three columns in $G(0)$, the elements in the third column is very small compared to elements of the other two columns, obviously the first and second input should be chosen.

If choose (y_1, y_3) as outputs, then γ=1.51 and RGA:

$$\Lambda\big(G(0)\big) = \begin{bmatrix} 0.3602 & 0.6398 \\ 0.6398 & 0.3602 \end{bmatrix},$$

so, y_1 is paired with u_2, y_3 paired with u_1.

If choose (y_2, y_3) as outputs, then $\gamma=1.45$ and RGA:

$$\Lambda(G(0)) = \begin{bmatrix} 0.3662 & 0.6338 \\ 0.6338 & 0.3662 \end{bmatrix},$$

thus, y_2 is paired with u_2, and y_3 paired with u_1.

Example 3: Commercial HVAC Plant Model

This example demonstrates the application of SVD, RGA, RGA number in the controllability analysis of a HVAC plant model during control design.

The HVAC plant has 70kW cooling capacity, there are three control inputs and three controlled outputs. The identified linear model at an operating condition is as follows:

$$G(s) = \begin{bmatrix} \dfrac{-0.0006(1+32.6s)}{(1+10.7s)(1+6.3s)}e^{-0.6s} & \dfrac{0.014}{1+12.7s}e^{-15s} & \dfrac{-0.077}{1+14.5s}e^{-7.4s} \\[3mm] \dfrac{0.0024}{1+1.4s}e^{-0.3s} & \dfrac{-0.57}{1+9.7s}e^{-s} & \dfrac{0.14}{1+13.2s}e^{-12.7s} \\[3mm] \dfrac{0.009}{1+10.8s} & \dfrac{0.23}{1+13s}e^{-8.9s} & \dfrac{-0.75}{1+14.8s}e^{-1.1s} \end{bmatrix}$$

This model is unscaled. Note that scaling is an important step before any attempt of controllability analysis. Scaling is applied and the scaled model is given by:

$$G_s(s) = (S_y)^{-1} \cdot G(s) \cdot S_u$$

where

$$S_y = I, \ S_u = diag(2900, 12, 100).$$

Compute the steady state RGA:

$$\Lambda\big(G(0)\big) \triangleq G(0) \times \big(G(0)^{-1}\big)^{T} = \begin{bmatrix} 0.3539 & -0.0688 & 0.7150 \\ 0.0298 & 1.0271 & -0.0570 \\ 0.6163 & 0.0417 & 0.3420 \end{bmatrix}$$

Now consider the main diagonal RGA number for diagonal pairings:

$$RGA\_number = \| \Lambda\big(G(j\omega)\big) - I \|_{sum}$$

and the off-diagonal RGA number for off-diagonal pairings:

$$RGA\_number = \Lambda\big(G(j\omega)\big) - \begin{bmatrix} 0 & 0 & 1 \\ 0 & 1 & 0 \\ 1 & 0 & 0 \end{bmatrix}_{sum}.$$

The two RGA numbers are plotted as a function of frequency for evaluation. Recall that RGA number measures diagonal dominance, smaller RGA number is better. Based on the RGA numbers plot, in the feedback effective frequency range, the main diagonal RGA number is smaller than the off-diagonal RGA number. Thus the original inputs outputs pairings (diagonal) are kept, instead of choosing the off-diagonal pairings. This contradicts the steady state RGA, but pairings giving RGA number close to 0 in the crossover frequency range is preferred for decentralized control.

Singular values and the condition number are also plotted versus frequency for examination respectively. No major control difficulties are found based on the plots if the closed-loop bandwidth is not too high, i.e. beyond about 0.2 rad/sec because when the control bandwidth is higher than this frequency, the minimum singular value drops below 1 which should be avoided.

REFERENCES

Astrom, K. J. (2013). *Foundation of Controls* [PDF document]. Lecture Notes.

Bristol, E. H. (1966). On a new measure of interactions for multivariable process control. *IEEE Transactions on Automatic Control, 11*(1), 133–134. doi:10.1109/TAC.1966.1098266

Farsangi, M. M., Song, Y. H., & Lee, K. Y. (2004). Choice of FACTS Device Control Inputs for Damping Interarea Oscillations. *IEEE Transactions on Power Systems*, *19*(2), 1135–1143. doi:10.1109/TPWRS.2003.820705

Larsson, T., & Skogestad, S. (2000). Plantwide control-A review and a new design procedure. *Modeling, Identification and Control*, *21*(4), 209–240. doi:10.4173/mic.2000.4.2

Seborg, D. E., Edgar, T. F., Mellichamp, D. A., & Doyce, F. J. (2011). Process Dynamics and Control (3rd, ed.), Wiley.

Shinskey, F. G., Shunta, J. P., Jamison, J. E., & Rohr, A. (2006). Selective, Override, and Limit Controls. In B. G. Liptak (Ed.), Instrument Engineers' Handbook: Process control and Optimization (4th ed.; vol. 2, pp. 336-344). Boca Raton, FL: CRC Press, Taylor & Francis Group.

Skogestad, S. (1994). *Input-Output Controllability Analysis*. Invited Lecture, Reglermote, Vasteras, Sweden.

Skogestad, S. (2004). Control structure design for complete chemical plants. *Computers & Chemical Engineering*, *28*(1-2), 219–234. doi:10.1016/j.compchemeng.2003.08.002

Skogestad, S., & Postlethwaite, I. (1997). *Multivariable Feedback Control: Analysis and Design*. John Wiley & Sons Ltd.

Van de Wal, M., & De Jager, B. (2000). A Review of Methods for Input/Output Selection. *Automatica*, *37*(4), 487–510. doi:10.1016/S0005-1098(00)00181-3

KEY TERMS AND DEFINITIONS

Decentralized Control: A simple approach to MIMO control design using a diagonal or block-diagonal controller.

Gain Crossover Frequency: The frequency where the open loop transfer function magnitude crosses 1(0dB) from above.

(Input-Output) Controllability: The ability to achieve acceptable control performance; that is, to keep the outputs (y) within specified bounds or displacements from their references (r), in spite of unknown but bounded variations, such as disturbances (d) and plant changes using available inputs(u) and available measurements (y_m or d_m).

MIMO: Multiple-input multiple-output.

Model Uncertainty or Uncertainty: The differences between the actual system and the model of the system.

Poles: The complex roots of the denominator polynomial of a transfer function for SISO system, or the characteristic equation of a plant (SISO or MIMO).

RGA: Relative gain array.

RHP: Right half plane of the complex number plane.

Scaling: The first step in controllability analysis. Scale (normalize) all variables (inputs, outputs, disturbances) to be less than 1 in magnitude (i.e. within the range -1 to 1).

SISO: Single-input single-output.

SVD: Singular value decomposition.

Transfer Function: A mathematical representation of a dynamic system in Laplace or *s*-domain (as opposed to time-domain). The ratio of the Laplace transform of the output and the Laplace transform of the input.

Zeros: The complex roots of the numerator polynomial of a transfer function for SISO system (excluding zeros at infinity) or values at which the transfer function matrix loses rank.

Chapter 4
Control System Development

INTRODUCTION

The control system development process includes the selection of a control configuration and control algorithm development. Besides analytical analysis and numerical simulation, aspects relating to implementation of the control algorithms are important practical issues. This chapter discusses various types of control loops commonly used for industrial control systems. It provides guidelines for controller design, analysis and implementation. Practical examples are used to demonstrate the applications in real control systems.

The intended readers of this chapter include controls engineers, software engineers, hardware engineers, and system engineers with some control engineering background. It is assumed that the reader has taken at least one undergraduate level controls course offered through an engineering program and understands frequency domain control analysis and design techniques such as Bode plot, Nyquist stability criterion, gain margin, and phase margin. The users should also be familiar with linear algebra and matrix calculations.

Controls systems could have multiple actuators (control/manipulated variables) and multiple properties to be regulated and controlled (controlled variables). In other words, they are multi-input, multi-output (MIMO) systems. However, we can apply either single-input-single-output (SISO) design approaches or MIMO design approaches for a MIMO control system.

DOI: 10.4018/978-1-5225-2303-1.ch004

- SISO control design techniques are used most commonly in industry. SISO tools and methods consider the effect of one control variable (e.g. a DC motor terminal voltage) on a controlled variable (e.g. rotational speed of a DC motor) as if other control variables have little effect on that controlled variable (in controls terminology they are considered as decoupled). Proper decoupling techniques could be used to enable a SISO control design.
- MIMO control system design is less commonly used in industry and usually introduced when there are strong interactions among control variables and controlled variables and independently designing a SISO control loop for each controlled variable becomes insufficient. Also, MIMO techniques are used when control requirements for several controlled variables have to be met simultaneously, where a centralized controller is preferred to multiple independent SISO control loops. MIMO techniques are more difficult to use as they involve advanced system concepts, such as the controllability and observability structural properties, and system/signal norms. The design of MIMO control systems will be briefly discussed in this chapter at a high level.

As discussed above, when the control requirements for a control system are less stringent (which occurs in majority cases in industry), a decentralized controller may be used, that is a single controller is designed for each individual control/controlled variable pair ignoring the interactions with other variables in the plant. This approach results in designing a number of SISO controllers. This chapter focuses on the control design based on decoupling techniques and SISO control methodologies.

When a specific design method is adopted, the reader should reference controls textbooks or literature for details of the method. This chapter only presents what steps should be taken to design an industrial control system and discusses a number of techniques, but does not substitute for formal training in control system design.

Control design in the scope of this chapter includes two steps:

1. Control configuration selection, and
2. Control algorithm development.

General control configurations found in industrial control systems such as cascade control, feedforward control and feedback control, are discussed. Implementation aspects such as bumpless transfer, noise filtering, magnitude and rate saturations are also discussed in this chapter.

Overview of Control Design

Starting from some fundamental principles, control system development is an iterative process that consists of a number of phases:

1. Controls requirements definition
2. Controllability analysis
3. Control system architecture definition
4. Control algorithm design and tuning

Details of developing controls requirements are presented in chapter two. Control architecture design and controllability analysis are discussed in chapter three. Control loop structure and control algorithms design are topics of the current chapter. The following is a brief discussion of each of the four phases.

Control systems generally are designed to meet the following requirements:

*   **Safety and Reliability:** Protect product, in particular ensuring critical components operate within prescribed "safety" boundaries.
*   **Performance:** Provide control functions as needed.
*   **Efficiency:** Minimize energy consumption and harmful emissions.

The definition of more detailed dynamic functional requirements and their translation into controls requirements are first carried out to define HOW the control system is supposed to perform. Examples of controls requirements include:

*   **Set Point Regulation:** How close to a desired set point a controlled variable should be
*   **Limits:** Admissible values for key state variables (e.g. the discharge pressure of a compressor shall be always less than a prescribed value).
*   **Operation Range:** The range of ambient conditions where the system should be operating.

- Required dynamic behavior, e.g. a temperature must reach a set point in a prescribed time, and it should not exceed a prescribed value during the transient.

Requirements should be achievable, and compatible with the capability of the plant. The capability of a plant may be limited by its own design, the selection of sensors and actuators. For example, it would be impossible for a controlled variable to reach the set point in seconds if the corresponding actuator can change position within minutes.

For this reason, an input-output controllability analysis should be conducted after a physical model of the plant is obtained to identify the plant limitations and determine if controls requirements can indeed be achieved. An equipment or system under control has a pre-determined operation range or envelope, i.e. in terms of pressure and temperature ranges it operates within. It always subjects to external disturbances, i.e. outside air temperature, and measurement noises. A controller designed should automatically control the system within the entire operation envelope, subject to disturbances and noises under specified levels, while meeting all performance requirements. It is usually a difficult task and requires rigorous analysis and design. Plant models are built and used for analysis and design. Obtaining a high-quality model itself is a difficult task. Since certain dynamic effects are too difficult to model using physical principles in the first place or too costly to model, a model at best captures salient features of the plant dynamics. In addition, the plant dynamics may vary with time and with the operating conditions. After a physical model is developed, a plant model for control design (usually transfer functions) relating the controlled variables to the control variables, can be identified based on the responses generated by the detailed physical model under prescribed input signals. The plant model thus obtained (referred to as "plant model" in this book) is used for controllability analysis and subsequent controller design and analysis. The resulting difference between the actual plant dynamics and the dynamics captured by the model is called model uncertainty. The amount of model uncertainty allowed, in other words, the level of model accuracy is determined by the requirements and other constraints such as time and cost, and should be clearly defined and accounted for when using a nominal plant model for control design.

Models used for control design are usually linear, time invariant (LTI), although the true dynamics is most likely to be nonlinear and time varying. The reasons of using LTI models are two-fold: first, plant dynamics around an equilibrium point is approximately linear; second, it is much easier to deal with LTI models, there are a lot more analysis and design methods available for LTI systems. Since, a LTI model is used for design, despite of a nonlinear plant, all conclusions drawn using linear theory are valid under small signal conditions around the equilibrium point the linear time invariant model is obtained. Extensive simulations using a higher fidelity physical plant model (i.e. Dymola model) is usually needed to verify that the designed controller meets all control requirements within the entire operation envelope. At this level, system constraints if there are any, are also checked to assure that they are not violated in operation. In control algorithm implementation (usually digital implementation), additional issues arise which effect the eventual control performance such as aliasing, sampling, switching.

Given the system requirements and the operation envelope, linear models at multiple points in the operation envelope (may include corner points and central points, or points on a defined grid) are developed. These LTI models are compared to determine how much the plant dynamics vary over the operation envelope. If the variation is small, an average model (i.e. model at the center of the envelope) is used to design a single controller. If the variation is large, gain scheduling can be used with one set of gains for each operating point. A controller of a specified structure (i.e. a PI controller) is designed for every LTI model. Then, the controller gains are scheduled using gain tables based on measurable scheduling variables.

In most industrial applications, the control design boils down to designing a controller for a single or group of LTI model(s) subject to disturbances, noises, and model uncertainty. A loop structure is first selected based on available manipulated inputs and measurements, such as feedback, cascade loop, and feedforward. A single degree-of-freedom feedback control loop is commonly used in industry. Given a control loop structure and a control plant model, a control algorithm, determining control variables based on measurements, is then developed to render the desired closed-loop properties. For most industrial applications, a PI control law is used. When the plant dynamics is of the second or higher order, a PID controller is required for phase compensation. In most cases, control loops are designed one at a time. This is always the case for SISO control system design. For a MIMO plant, it is the case if a decentralized controller is designed. When interactions in a MIMO plant cannot be ignored, a centralized controller is designed, where all loops are closed at the same time.

When PI or PID controllers are used, some tuning rules exist. For tuning a PI or PID controller, a first order plus time delay (FOPTD/FOTD) plant model or second order plus time delay (SOPTD/SOTD) plant model is needed.

A FOPTD or SOPTD model can be identified using step response data. A step response is easily obtained either from simulation using a physical plant model or from laboratory test.

In the chapter, fundamentals of feedback controls are reviewed. Various control loop structure are discussed, and guidelines for designing corresponding controllers are presented. Implementation issues are also discussed. For detailed information on certain control topics and methods, users should consult standard controls textbooks such as Brogan (1990), Skogestad & Postlethwaite (1997), Franklin, Powell, & Emami-Naeini (1986), and Franklin, Powell, & Workman (1990), Horowitz (1993) and numerous controls literature.

INTRODUCTION TO FEEDBACK CONTROL SYSTEM

Feedback Fundamentals

Feedback control system design needs to consider the following four aspects: load disturbance, measurement noise, process/plant variations and uncertainty, and command/reference following/tracking. Consider the general two degree-of-freedom (2DOF) feedback control system (Figure 1), showing the plant/process P (G is also used in controls engineering), the feedback controller C (also denoted by K), and the pre-filter F. The disturbance d (shown entered at the plant input, it can also enter at other point, i.e. plant output) drives the system away from the desired set point, the measurement noise introduced by sensors n corrupts the feedback signal x.

For this feedback control system, the response variable x should follow the reference r amid the disturbance, noise and plant variation or plant/model mismatch (model uncertainty). The functionalities of a control system are:

Figure 1. 2DOF feedback control system

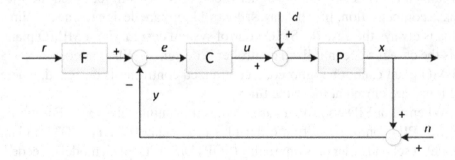

to reduce the effects of disturbances on the controlled response variables, to reduce the effects of the measurement noises, to make the closed-loop robust against plant variations and model uncertainty, and to make the controlled variables to follow the commands. The performance of a closed-loop system is expressed by its response to command signals, rejection of load disturbances, and attenuation of measurement noises. Robustness of the closed-loop system is expressed by its sensitivity to disturbances and model uncertainty. The system in Figure 1 has 2DOF according to Horowitz because the signal transmissions from reference r to control u and from measurement y to u are different. The feedback controller C is designed to achieve disturbance rejection, noise reduction, and robustness to plant variation and model uncertainty. The pre-filter F is designed to achieve command following. In the case of a one degree-of-freedom control loop, F=1, design goals cannot be separated, that is C is also designed to make the response to track the command.

Consider the responses of the control system in Figure 1:

$$X = \frac{P}{1+PC}D - \frac{PC}{1+PC}N + \frac{PCF}{1+PC}R,$$

$$Y = \frac{P}{1+PC}D + \frac{1}{1+PC}N + \frac{PCF}{1+PC}R, \tag{1}$$

$$U = -\frac{PC}{1+PC}D - \frac{C}{1+PC}N + \frac{CF}{1+PC}R.$$

The feedback properties of the closed-loop are characterized by four transfer functions, called *the gang of four (GOF):* $\dfrac{P}{1+PC}, \dfrac{PC}{1+PC}, \dfrac{1}{1+PC},$ $\dfrac{C}{1+PC}$. Note that it is important to consider all four transfer functions simultaneously to make sure that the closed-loop is really stable. The *gang of six (GOS)* for a 2DOF closed-loop includes two additional transfer functions $\dfrac{PCF}{1+PC}$ and $\dfrac{CF}{1+PC}$. Robustness to process variations is expressed by the sensitivity function S and the complementary sensitivity function T:

$$S = \frac{1}{1+PC}, \quad T = \frac{PC}{1+PC}, \text{ and } T+S=1. \tag{2}$$

115

Response of x to load disturbance d is expressed by:

$$G_{xd} = \frac{P}{1+PC} = PS \tag{3}$$

Response of control u to measurement noise n is expressed by:

$$G_{un} = -\frac{C}{1+PC} = -CS \tag{4}$$

Response to the command r is expressed by:

$$G_{yr} = \frac{PCF}{1+PC} = TF, \quad G_{ur} = \frac{CF}{1+PC} = CFS \tag{5}$$

Now, consider the open loop plant response to disturbance and noise:

$$y_{ol} = n(s) + Pd(s) \tag{6}$$

and the corresponding closed-loop system response is:

$$y_{cl} = \frac{1}{1+PC}\left(n(s) + Pd(s)\right) = Sy_{ol} \tag{7}$$

The sensitivity function S shows the effect of feedback. At frequencies such that $|S(j\omega)| < 1$, disturbance and noise responses are reduced by feedback, at frequencies such that $|S(j\omega)| > 1$, feedback amplifies the noise and disturbance responses. This is an example the tradeoff has to be made in control design. A typical sensitivity function is shown in Figure 2, where the magnitude is small within the control bandwidth, becomes greater than 1 in the crossover region, and approaches 1 at high frequencies.

Look at another relationship connecting open loop and closed-loop process variation effect:

$$\frac{dT}{T} = S\frac{dP}{P} \tag{8}$$

Figure 2. Sensitivity function plots: Bode magnitude plot

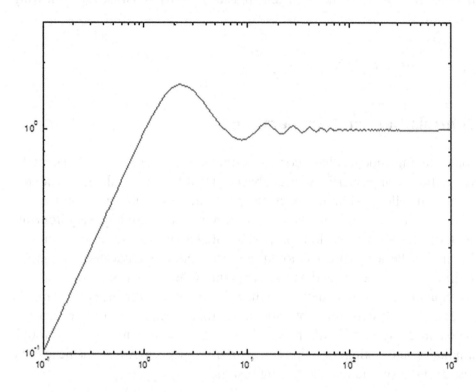

Thus plant variation effect is reduced by feedback at frequencies where $|S(j\omega)|<1$, in other words, the closed-loop system is less sensitive to plant variation at these frequencies.

For a finite plant variation, the stability condition is:

$$|C\Delta P| < |1 + PC| \quad \text{or} \quad \left|\frac{\Delta P}{P}\right| < \frac{1}{|T|} \tag{9}$$

where $\dfrac{\Delta P}{P}$ is the multiplicative model uncertainty whose magnitude $\left|\dfrac{\Delta P}{P}\right|$ poses a constraint on the magnitude of the closed-loop transfer function T.

Various stability margins are defined for checking the closed-loop stability. Most familiar to controls engineers are the gain margin g_m and the phase margin φ_m. Other important stability measures are the maximum sensitivity peak $M_s=\max|S(j\omega)|$, and the maximum complementary sensitivity peak

$M_T = \max|T(j\omega)|$. And the gain and phase margins satisfies the following inequalities:

$$g_m \geq \frac{M_s}{M_s - 1}, \quad \varphi_m \geq 2 arcsin \frac{1}{2M_s} \tag{10}$$

Controls Design Considerations

For achieving good feedback control system performance, as alluded to in the last section, four properties of a feedback control system should be considered in the controller design: disturbance rejection, noise attenuation, command following, and sensitivity to plant variation or model uncertainty. Requirements rendering the four closed-loop properties satisfactory should be determined at the onset of the design process. Requirements should be achievable, accounting for intrinsic limitations in the physical plant. Refer to controllability analysis in chapter three for more details on the achievable performance of a plant. At the end of the design, after obtaining a control algorithm, the performance of the feedback system should be verified against these requirements through simulation and testing. Iterations on the requirements may become necessary based on the simulation and testing results.

Disturbance Rejection

Feedback control is used widely for disturbance rejection in real applications. If there is no disturbance on a system to be controlled, it may not be necessary to use feedback and open loop control could be sufficient. There are always some disturbances in control systems, either representing the influences from the external environment or some internal effects. When using the cruise control to drive a car, the slopes on the road the car is travelling on are external disturbances to the cruise control system. For a home air conditioning control system, cooking, opening a window, and visitors etc. are disturbances to the control system. For servo control systems, the cogging and the detaining torque in the motor, the stiction and frictions in the drive mechanism are internal disturbances the servo control systems need to deal with. Disturbance rejection is a major design consideration for a control system. In the next chapter, we will show real examples of disturbance effects in motion control applications and techniques to reject disturbance.

Consider disturbance rejection of a feedback loop (Figure 3), where the transfer function from the disturbance to the control variable and the transfer function from the disturbance to the controlled variable are:

$$G_{xd} = \frac{P}{1+PC} = PS, \quad G_{ud} = \frac{C}{1+PC} = CS \tag{11}$$

The open loop disturbance response and the closed-loop disturbance response is related by the equation:

$$y_{cl} = \frac{1}{1+PC}\left(n(s)+Pd(s)\right) = Sy_{ol}. \tag{12}$$

According to Equation 12, feedback attenuates the disturbance at frequencies where $|S(j\omega)|<1$, and this frequency range is defined by the closed-loop bandwidth ω_B. The disturbance rejection requirement is usually expressed in the frequency domain as a lower bound on the loop transfer function $L(s)=P(s)C(s)$ magnitude over the low frequency range. Consider a controller with integral action, at low frequencies $C(s)\approx k_i/s$, k_i is the integral gain, thus:

$$G_{xd} = \frac{P}{1+PC} \approx \frac{1}{C} \approx \frac{s}{k_i}. \tag{13}$$

Figure 3. Disturbance rejection

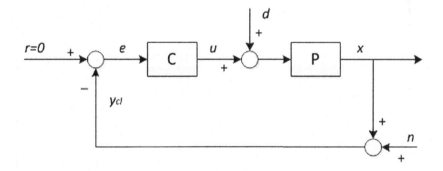

At high frequencies:

$$G_{xd} = \frac{P}{1+PC} \approx P,$$ (14)

and the magnitude upper bound:

$$|G_{xd}| = |P||S| < |P|M_s, \quad |G_{ud}| = |CS| < |C|M_s.$$ (15)

A typical disturbance transfer is shown in Figure 4 with its low and high frequency approximates.

In the time domain, disturbance rejection performance is measured using the integrals of the error:

$$IE = \int_0^\infty e(t)\,dt, \quad IAE = \int_0^\infty |e(t)|\,dt$$ (16)

Figure 4. Disturbance transfer function: magnitude (solid); low frequency approximate, s/k_i (dash dot); high frequency approximate, P (dash dot)

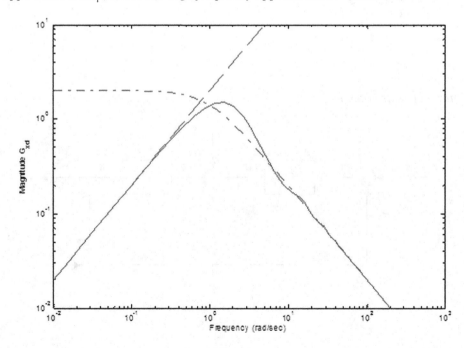

And for a PID controller, we have:

$$IE = \int_0^\infty e(t)\,dt = \frac{1}{k_i} \tag{17}$$

The integral error is inversely proportional to the integral gain to a unit step disturbance applied at the plant input.

Measurement Noise

Next, consider the effect of the measurement noise on the feedback system. Noise enters the feedback path when the controlled variable is measured and is then amplified by the controller at frequencies below the bandwidth. Measurement noise usually has high frequency contents, if noise has frequency components within the closed loop bandwidth it can cause the actuator to react to noise instead of the error. Also, derivative action in the controller, i.e. a PID controller, can amplify noise. In these cases, the measurement should be filtered, and the loop transfer function $L(s)=P(s)C(s)$ should roll off quickly at high frequencies and this is usually expressed by an upper bound on the loop transfer function magnitude at high frequencies. In Figure 3:

$$G_{un} = \frac{C}{1+PC} = CS \approx C \quad \text{at high frequency} \tag{18}$$

For a PI controller, at high frequency:

$$C = \frac{k_p s + k_i}{s} \approx k_p \tag{19}$$

For a PID controller with a low pass filter, at high frequency:

$$C = \frac{k_d s^2 + k_p s + k_i}{s\left(1 + T_f s\right)} \approx \frac{k_d}{T_f} \tag{20}$$

The combined magnitude bounds on open loop transfer function for disturbance rejection at low frequency and noise attenuation at high frequency is shown in Figure 5.

Figure 5. Typical requirements on the open loop transfer function

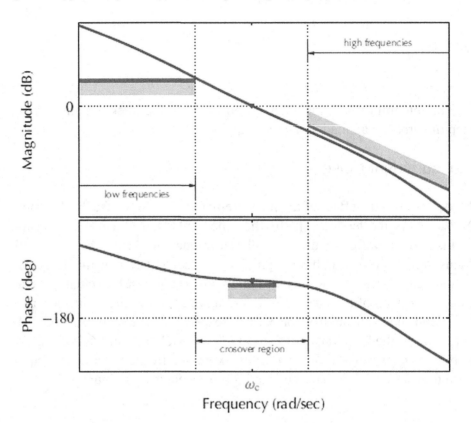

Robustness

Stability margins include the gain margin, the phase margin, the sensitivity peak and the complementary sensitivity peak. The gain margin and phase margin are computed from the open loop frequency response, and can be found from the Bode plot, shown in Figure 6a; the sensitivity peak is the maximum magnitude of the sensitivity function of the closed-loop, where the inverse of the sensitivity peak is the shortest distance from the loop transfer function to the critical point, -1 on the Nyquist plot, shown in Figure 6b; the complementary sensitivity peak is the maximum magnitude of the closed-loop transfer function. Usually, requirements on gain and phase margins are given for control design.

Figure 6. Stability margins: a) Bode plot; b) Nyquist plot

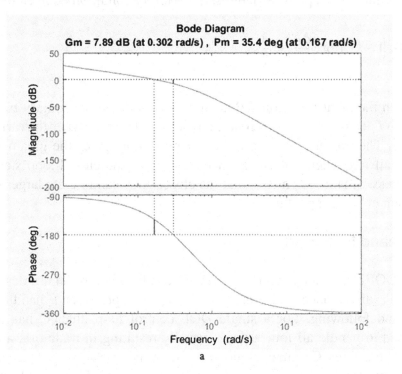

a

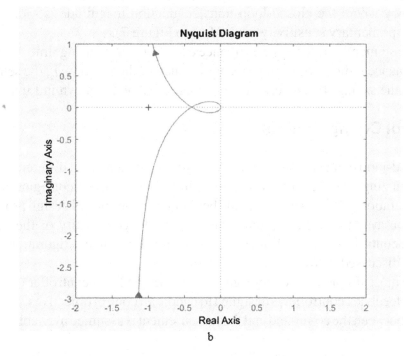

b

For finite (large) plant variations, the stability condition is given by:

$$|C\Delta P| < |1 + PC| \quad \text{or} \quad \left|\frac{\Delta P}{P}\right| < \frac{1}{|T|} \tag{21}$$

When the plant variation ΔP is quantified, the complementary transfer function T needs to satisfy this condition such that T is small when the variation is large. The transfer function peak $M_T = \max|T(j\omega)|$ gives the greatness of T over all frequencies and it is an indication of the closed-loop stability robustness. Smaller M_T means that the closed-loop can tolerate larger plant variation or more model uncertainty.

Command Following

For a 2DOF closed-loop control system, the feedback controller C is designed to handle disturbance, noise and robustness. The pre-filter F handles the command following. For a single DOF control loop, then C has to be designed to handle all four aspects, usually resulting in trade-offs among control objectives. Command following requirements can be specified in the frequency domain on the closed-loop transfer in terms of bandwidth ω_B, the frequency where the closed-loop transfer function magnitude is -3db, and the complimentary sensitivity peak M_T (see Figure 7).

Or, command following performance can be specified using time domain performance indices for the step response, such as the rise time t_s, the setting time t_r, the steady state error, the percentage overshoot, shown in Figure 8.

Control Configurations

A closed-loop control system can have multiple elements and different ways of organizing these elements, resulting in various control configurations. Configuration selection is done at the beginning of the control design process based on available measurements and actuations, complexity of the plant and the control objectives. Some common control system configurations are briefly discussed below.

The most simple control configuration is the one DOF controller (Figure 9). The feedback controller is designed to handle all control objectives, and the error e between the command and the measurement is assumed available here.

Figure 7. Frequency domain command following requirements

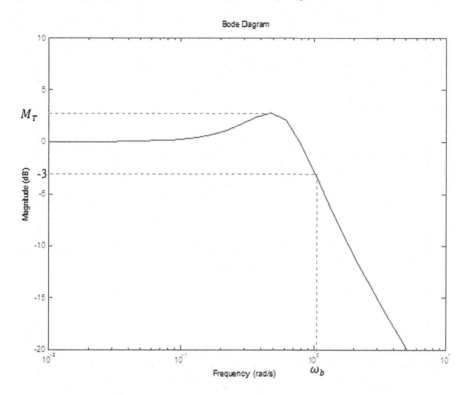

A two DOF controller is shown in Figure 1. As already discussed, the introduction of the pre-filter F, leads to a separation in the controller design: the feedback controller handles the disturbance, noise, and plant variations, while the pre-filter handles the command following.

Besides feedback, feedforward is also often applied to reject disturbances and improve commanding following. Figure 10 shows the application of feedforward for disturbance rejection. In next chapter, real examples of using feedforward for disturbance compensation are given. Figure 11 shows using feedforward for command following, where the forward controller is an inverse of the plant.

Cascade control configuration (Figure 12), is applied when there are extra sensor measurements in addition to the controlled variables, i.e. internal state variables, and needs for tight feedback regulation for dealing with disturbance and model uncertainty. It is an example of regulatory control in the control layer when control system architecture is discussed in chapter three.

Figure 8. Time domain step response indices

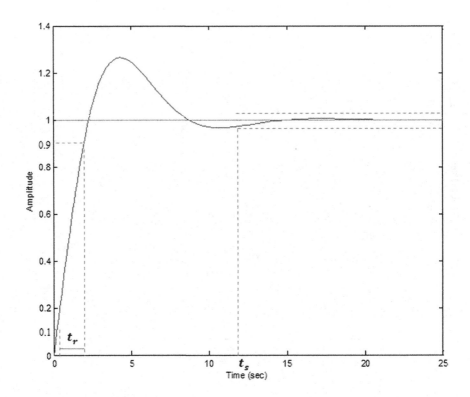

Figure 9. One DOF control loop

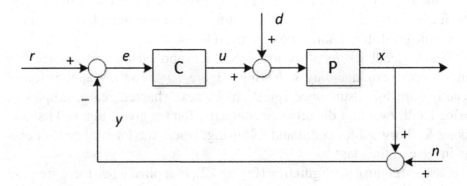

Figure 10. Feedforward for disturbance rejection

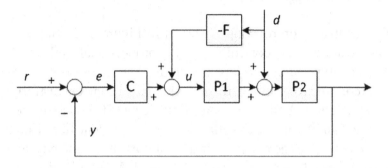

Figure 11. Feedforward for command following

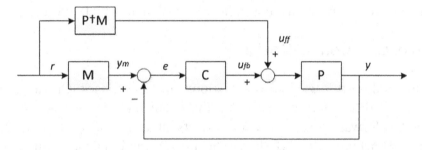

Figure 12. Cascade control loop

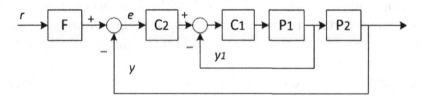

Control Algorithm Design

A complete control system may be hierarchical, i.e. with a higher level supervisory layer and a lower level control layer. The lower level control layer consists of one or multiple controllers. The basic control loop is single-input-single-output (SISO): one control signal controlling one controlled variable. After the control design requirements have been defined and the loop configuration has been selected, control algorithms are developed to determine the control variable based on measurements and control system performance analyzed. This section describes the design of controllers in more detail.

One DOF Controller Design

One DOF feedback control loop is shown in Figure 9. In most industrial control applications, the controller C is a proportional and integral (PI) controller. This type of controllers are simple, yet effective, providing zero steady state command tracking error and rejection of constant disturbance due to the integral action. A first order plus time delay (FOTD) plant model P is needed for design of the PI controller, which can be identified from the step response data of either the real plant in a laboratory test or the physical model of the plant in simulation, i.e. a Dymola model. Many identification tools and approaches are ready to be applied, i.e. MathWorks MATLAB System Identification toolbox. After obtaining the model, the PI tuning procedures are applied to determine the controller proportional and integral gains.

Feedforward Control Design

Feedforward is often used in combination with the feedback. One feature of feedforward different from feedback is that it can never destabilize a system. Using feedforward can reduce the effects of disturbances and improve command tracking. Figure 10 shows a feedforward and feedback combination where feedforward is used for better disturbance rejection. In this control system, the disturbance is an internal variable to the plant or process, and the control signal u cannot directly cancel off the disturbance because of the plant dynamics part P_1. The disturbance compensation control F is designed to generate additional control signal for u such that the disturbance effect is eliminated.

Consider the transfer function from disturbance to plant output in Figure 15:

$$G_{yd} = \frac{Y}{D} = \frac{P_2\left(1 - P_1 F\right)}{1 + P_1 P_2 C} = P_2\left(1 - P_1 F\right) S \tag{22}$$

The disturbance is eliminated if:

$$F = P_1^{-1} \approx P_1 \tag{23}$$

where P_1 is the pseudo inverse of P_1. When the disturbance is not measured or cannot be measured, estimation techniques can be applied to obtain an estimation of the disturbance. Wu (2009) gives an example of estimating the DC motor cogging torque using a disturbance estimator. Wu (2015) used both offline and online disturbance estimation and compensation. These approached are discussed in Chapter 5. Figure 11 shows using the feedforward for improving command following with desired command response model M.

Transfer function from the reference to the plant output is:

$$G_{yr} = M + \left(PP -1 \right) MS \approx M$$

The desired command response is specified by M and the feedforward control is given by P M. Some care must be taken for the feedforward control to be realizable. Unstable plant zeros must be zeros of M, the time delay of M must be larger than the plant time delay, and the pole excess over zero of M must be greater than or equal to the pole excess of the plant. Approximate plant models can be used for the feedfoward control design. Using feedforward for improving the command response is common in motion control application. Using feedforward, the command tracking can be faster. Younkin (2003) showed the benefit of using feedforward to a position servo with a velocity inner loop. The closed-loop position servo is type 1 and it is not possible for the position to track a constant velocity position command without error. When the velocity feedforward approach is applied, the position output can track constant velocity position command with zero steady state error. In this example, the closed loop position servo with feedforward becomes type 2, since it can track a ramp command with zero steady state error. For eliminating position errors for constant acceleration and deceleration moves, commercial servo drive manufacturers use the additional technique of acceleration feedforward (Younkin, 2003).

Cascade Control Design

Cascade control configuration, shown in Figure 12, is common when additional measurements of the plant are available. Under the situation of large plant variation, significant sensor noise and nonlinearity, cascaded-loop control can be applied. By introducing the inner loop, the nonlinearity or plant variation is reduced and resulting compensated plant would be easier to control by the controller in the outer loop. Cascade control is commonly used in servo control systems, where the position servo is closed around a velocity servo, and the velocity servo is closed around a current closed loop of the motor for torque regulation (Younkin, 2003).

Design of cascade-loop control is sequential. Usually, the inner (faster) loop is closed first, obtaining the secondary controller Cs/C_1, then the slower outer loop is closed to obtain the primary controller Cp/C_2. This is the inner-outer design procedure. The inner-loop is usually closed arbitrarily and its effect on the outer-loop cannot be predicted. Thus iterations may be required. A method exists that explicitly bounds the closed-loop uncertainty of the inner-loop through the design of the inner controller, removing design iteration (Wu, 2001). Outer-inner design is also frequently used.

In the inner-outer procedure, the secondary controller is designed for plant P1, then the primary controller is designed for the effective plant:

$$T_{inner} = \frac{P_2 P_1 C_s}{1 + P_1 C_s} \tag{24}$$

It is a good practice to keep the outer-loop bandwidth three to five times slower than the inner-loop bandwidth. Bandwidth separation between the inner-loop and the outer-loop is also discussed in detail in YounKin (2003) for position servos when there are resonances in the drive mechanism, where a velocity servo inner loop is used inside the position loop. To make the cascaded-loop stable, the bandwidth of the position loop is an half or a third of the bandwidth of the velocity loop (Younkin, 2003).

Gain Scheduling

When a control system has a large operation envelope, and the system dynamics varies significantly over the operating envelop, the gains of the controller can be adjusted based on scheduling variables. For example, aircrafts usually have a large operation envelope in terms of airspeed and altitude, and gains of the autopilot controllers, i.e. pitch controller, are scheduled using the airspeed and the altitude. For gain scheduling control design, operating points inside or on the operation envelope are selected and at each operating point a controller is designed. During operation, the controller gains are interpreted using the gains obtained at these design points, saved in a gain table, based on the scheduling variables.

Issues should be considered when designing a gain scheduled controller include: choice of scheduling variables, granularity of the scheduled gains, interpretation methods, bumpless transfer between gain changes, and gain table generation and tuning.

Multi-Input-Multi-Output Control Design

Multi-input-multi-output (MIMO) plants possess unique properties compared to SISO plants, e.g. interactions and directions. It is intrinsically more difficult to design a MIMO controller, although some of the ideas and techniques for SISO systems analysis and design may be extended to MIMO systems. State space approaches are suited for MIMO control systems analysis and design (Brogan, 1990), where concepts such as controllability, observability, linear quadratic regulator (LQR), state observer, separation principle, Lyapunov stability are utilized. Design methods are based on minimizing some objective function (or norm). Optimization in controller design became prominent in the 1960's with "optimal control theory". Later, other approaches and norms were introduced, such as $\mathcal{H}_2$ and $\mathcal{H}_\infty$ optimal control. Chapter 7 in Skogestad & Postlethwaite (1996) discusses practical methods such as Linear Quadratic Gaussian method (LQG), loop transfer recovery (LTR), $\mathcal{H}_2 / \mathcal{H}_\infty$ control, $\mathcal{H}_\infty$ loop-shaping design. Horowitz introduced a robust frequency domain approach called Quantitative Feedback Control (QFT) (Horowitz, 1993).

Consider the feedback system in Figure 13. In Figure 13, note that we use different notations: G for the plant, and K for the controller. The disturbance affects the controller output through the dynamics G_d. A conceptually simple approach to multivariable control is given by a two-step procedure in which you first design a compensator to deal with the interactions in G, and then design a diagonal controller using methods similar to those for SISO systems. The most common approach is to use a pre-compensator, $W_1(s)$, which counteracts the interactions in the plant and results in a new shaped plant:

$$G_s(s) = G(s)W_1(s) \tag{25}$$

which is more diagonal and easier to control than the original plant G(s). After finding a suitable $W_1(s)$ we can design a diagonal controller $K_s(s)$ for the shaped plant $G_s(s)$. The overall controller is then:

$$K(s) = W_1(s)K_s(s) \tag{26}$$

Figure 13. One DOF feedback configuration

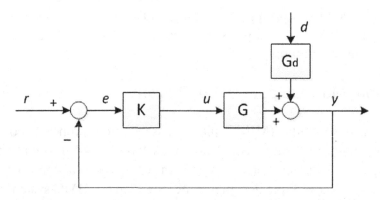

Decoupling control results when the compensator is chosen such that $G_s(s)$ is diagonal at a selected frequency. There exist several cases: dynamic decoupling where $G_s(s)$ is diagonal at all frequencies; steady-state decoupling, $G_s(0)$ is diagonal; approximate decoupling at ω_0, $G_s(j\omega_0)$ is as diagonal as possible and the bandwidth frequency is a good selection for ω_0.

Another simple approach to multivariable controller design is to use a diagonal controller:

$$K(s) = diag\{k_i(s)\} = \begin{bmatrix} k_1(s) & 0 & 0 \\ 0 & \ddots & 0 \\ 0 & 0 & k_m(s) \end{bmatrix} \qquad (27)$$

This is often referred as decentralized control. If off-diagonal elements in $G(s)$ are large, the performance with decentralized control may be poor because no attempt is made to counteract the interactions. Before decentralized controller design, an input-output pairing selection is conducted to achieve diagonal dominance using tools such as relative gain arrays (RGAs) and RGA-number. The design of decentralized controller involves two steps:

1.   The choice of pairings;
2.   The design of each controller, $k_i(s)$.

There are two useful rules for pairing inputs and outputs:

1. To avoid instability caused by interactions in the crossover region one should prefer pairings for which the RGA matrix in this frequency range is close to identity.
2. To avoid instability caused by interactions at low frequencies one should avoid pairings with negative steady state RGA elements.

The controllers are commonly designed sequentially in practice when the bandwidths of the loops are quite different. In this case, the outer (slow) loops are tuned with the inner (fast) loops in place, fast loops are closed first, and each step may be considered as a SISO control problem. The sequential design may involve many iterations because the closing of a later loop may cause "disturbances" (interactions) into previously designed loops.

An example of decentralized control is given below. Inputs-outputs pairings were determined by RGA and RGA number to give the following plant model:

$$G(s) = \begin{bmatrix} \dfrac{-0.000555(1+32.6s)}{(1+10.7s)(1+6.3s)}e^{-0.6s} & \dfrac{0.01382}{1+12.7s}e^{-15s} & \dfrac{-0.07724}{1+14.5s}e^{-7.4s} \\[3mm] \dfrac{0.002438}{1+1.4s}e^{-0.3s} & \dfrac{-0.5654}{1+9.7s}e^{-s} & \dfrac{0.138}{1+13.2s}e^{-12.7s} \\[3mm] \dfrac{0.008988}{1+10.8s} & \dfrac{0.2308}{1+13s}e^{-8.9s} & \dfrac{-0.7458}{1+14.8s}e^{-1.1s} \end{bmatrix}$$

A PI controller for each single loop was designed using the diagonal element from the MIMO plant model, $\dfrac{-0.000555(1+32.6s)}{(1+10.7s)(1+6.3s)}e^{-0.6s}$, $\dfrac{-0.5654}{1+9.7s}e^{-s}$, and $\dfrac{-0.7458}{1+14.8s}e^{-1.1s}$ respectively, as for a SISO plant.

PI CONTROLLER DEVELOPMENT PROCESS

PI Controller Design Process

Most industrial control systems are designed by using a one Degree-Of-Freedom (DOF) loop structure and a PI controller (Figure 9), where d is the disturbance and it may enter at the plant input, as shown, or at the plant output, x the controlled variable, u is the control variable, e is the control error, and r is the reference command. The controller design process for this type of control system is illustrated in Figure 14.

In Figure 14, the process starts with given controls requirements and the system operation envelope. Linear plant models at selected operating points within the operation envelop are derived; operating points selection shall cover the entire operation range, i.e. normal operating conditions, worse case conditions. A controller is designed for each model, corresponding to the controller design iteration around models, shown as the outer loop in Figure 14. For a given control system, the plant can be either SISO or MIMO. For a MIMO plant, decentralized control is assumed applicable in the design process. If decentralized control is not feasible due to strong interaction in the plant, then help from a controls expert is needed to perform a centralized control design. When applying decentralized control, multiple SISO control loops are designed for a MIMO plant, corresponding to the design iteration around each plant input-output pair, shown as the inner loop in Figure 14. For a SISO control design, a PI controller is usually used in a feedback configuration. In some cases, feedforward control can be utilized for better disturbance rejection and command following. Cascade control is also used sometimes, where PI controllers in both the inner and outer loops are designed. Usually, inner loop controller is designed first, followed by the outer loop controller design. Gain scheduling control is applied when plant dynamics varies significantly through the operation range. The same controller structure, i.e. PI, is used with control parameters adjusted according to some scheduling variables. Gain tables are created for looking up the control parameters when updating the control loop. The three cases, feedforward control, cascade control, and gain scheduling control, are also covered in the standard control design process, shown in Figure 14.

Non-Applicable Scenarios

The standard control design process applies to stable plants with monotonic step responses such as these modeled by FOPTD models, where basic frequency domain analysis and design tools such as Bode plot, gain margin and phase margin, work well. In cases of more complex plant dynamics, precautions must been taken when applying the standard process. In particular, the process doesn't apply to the following cases. The user should consult a controls expert for guidance in these cases.

Figure 14. PI controller development process

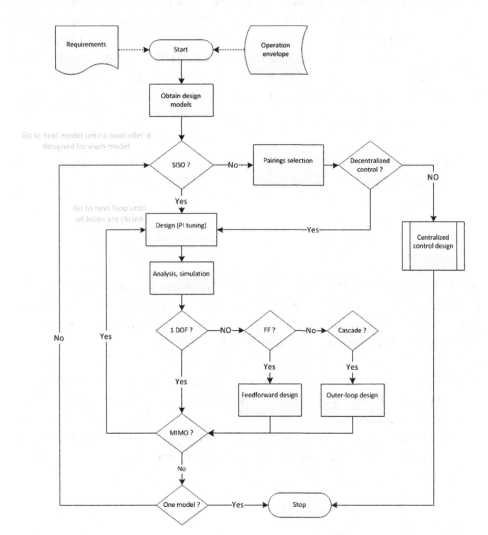

- **Unstable Plants:** Feedback is required for stabilizing an unstable plant. An unstable plant might be a rare case in some industrial applications. When dealing with the stability of an unstable plant, simple stability tools of gain margin and phase margin are not sufficient; Nyquist stability criterion should be applied for the stability test. A closed-loop system may seem to be stable in terms of gain margin and phase margin, but is actually unstable because of incorrect number of negative encirclement around the critical point in the Nyquist plot.

- **Non-Minimal Phase Plant:** A non-minimal phase plant, characterized by right-half-plane (RHP) zeros, has more phase lags compared to a minimal phase system. It limits the achievable closed-loop bandwidth. A characteristic of a non-minimal phase system is that its step response initially goes in the opposite direction, then turns around moving towards the right direction. Figure 15 shows the step response of the non-minimal phase plant $G(s) = \dfrac{-s + 0.2}{(s + 0.2)(s + 1)}$.

- **Long Time Delay:** When the time delay is much longer than the time constant, i.e.

$$G(s) = \frac{k_p}{s + 1} e^{-3s},$$

where the time constant is 1sec, but the time delay is 3sec, then PI control performance may be poor or oscillation may occur. In such cases, first action that is recommended is to investigate the reason for the long time delay and the location of the sensor is the usual suspect.

- **Higher Order Dynamics:** When the step response is monotonic, its dynamics is well captured by a FOPTD model, or a SOPTD model. However, if the step response is oscillatory, the dynamics is of another type and trying to fit the step response data using a FOPTD model is incorrect. Consider a typical mass-damper-spring type of system:

$$G(s) = \frac{\omega^2}{s^2 + 2\zeta\omega s + \omega^2} = \frac{1}{s^2 + 0.6s + 1} \tag{28}$$

whose natural frequency is 1rad/sec, and the damping ratio is 0.3. Its step response is oscillatory, shown in Figure 16 and its dynamics cannot be modeled by a FOPTD model.

- **Strong Plant Interactions:** Strong interactions in a MIMO plant indicate that a decentralized design may not work, instead a centralized should be designed. Consider an idealized model of a distillation column (Skogestad & Postlethwaite, 1996)

Figure 15. Non-minimal phase plant step response

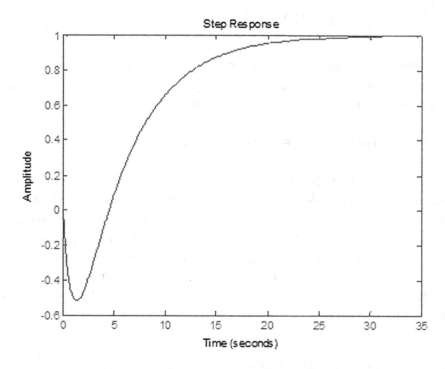

Figure 16. Plant with oscillatory behavior

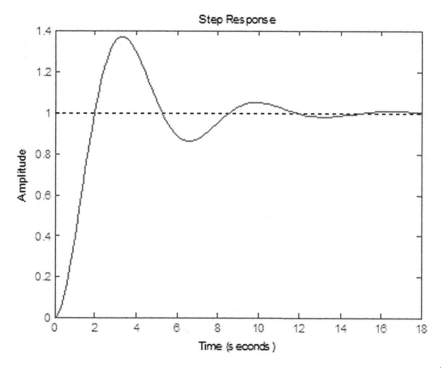

$$G(s) = \frac{1}{75s+1} \begin{bmatrix} 87.8 & -86.4 \\ 108.2 & -109.6 \end{bmatrix}$$

The step responses of the plant in Figure 17 show strong interactions among inputs and outputs, i.e. a step change in input one causes large step changes in both outputs, which suggests that the plant is difficult to control.

Define Control Requirements in Analytic Form

One of the inputs to the control design process is control requirements, either at the control subsystem level in the form of Control Subsystem Requirement Document (SSRD) or at the algorithm level in the form of Algorithm Requirement Document (ARD) or Software Requirement Specifications (SRS). At this stage, requirements are typically expressed in natural language for readability and ease of communication among team members. In order to enable the control design process, requirements need to be expressed in analytical form. Specifically:

Figure 17. Interactions in MIMO plant

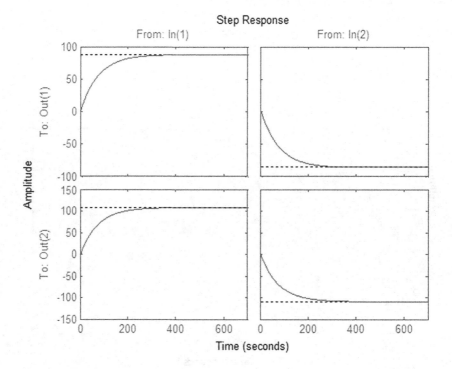

- Control requirements are assigned to four categories: disturbance rejection, noise attenuation, command following and robustness.
- Control requirements are translated from natural language textual form to analytical expressions that describe constrains/requirements on open loop and/or closed-loop control metrics in the time domain or in the frequency domain.

Metrics specifying control requirements are expressed either in the time or frequency domain. In the frequency domain, these include the open/closed-loop bandwidth, the sensitivity function peak magnitude, the gain margin, the phase margin, etc.; in the time domain, metrics are the rise time, the settling time, the steady state error, the percent overshoot for step response, etc.

IMPLEMENTATION ASPECTS

Actuator Saturation

Actuators have physical limitations on how large the outputs can become and how fast the outputs can change. When an actuator works at its magnitude limit and/or rate limit, the actuator is saturated and the closed-loop is no longer operating in the linear regime. This saturation nonlinearity in actuator usually degrades the feedback system performance, even destabilizes it.

Magnitude Saturation

A well-known case is the integrator windup. Integral windup refers to the phenomena where the discrepancy between the PI controller command and the actuator output which is saturated, causes the integrator output to grow larger and stay beyond the physical limits of the actuator while the actuator stays saturated. As a result, it needs large error in the opposite direction to bring the integral output down to the saturation limit of the actuator such that the actuator can respond to the error in the way that is designed. Windup can cause large overshoot, oscillations or even instability. Back-calculation (also known as external-reset feedback) technique is commonly used in industrial PI controller to avoid integral windup. Figure 18 shows the structure of a PI control with back-calculation anti-windup. In the reset-feedback (back-calculation) scheme for anti-windup, when the actuator reaches its limit, the integral part of the PI controller is recomputed so that its new PI output gives a value close to the limit. A time constant, T_t, is applied to the difference between the PI output and the actuator value and determines how quickly the integral is reset. T_t can be parameterized as $T_t = N_i * T_i$ (T_i is the integral time constant) and N_i is recommended as $N_i = 0.9$ (Astrom & Wittenmark, 1997). Note that in the figure, there is an actuator model block. This model is used when the actuator output is not actually measured. Placing the actuator model in front of the actuator keeps the actuator always operating in the linear range.

Rate Saturation

How fast an actuator signal can change is also limited by physics such as power limitation. This results in the rate saturation. Skew rate of operational amplifier is an example. It also has adversary effects on a feedback system and should be deliberately dealt with in the control design. A simple actuator model simulating the rate limiting may be used for control design purpose, such as that in Figure 19.

Figure 18. PI controller with anti-windup based on back-calculation

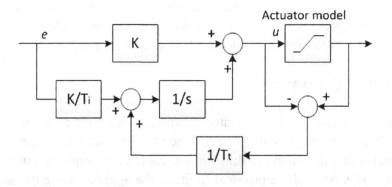

Figure 19. Rate saturation model

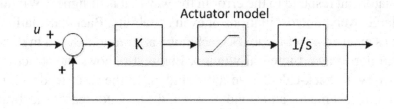

Rate saturation compensation is demonstrated below using an example.

Plant model is: $G_p(s) = \dfrac{2}{1s+1} e^{-0.5s}$.

PI controller is: $C(s) = 0.5\left(1 + \dfrac{1}{s}\right)$

The step responses are shown in Figure 20.

Consider the actuator having rate saturation with rate limited in [-0.5, 0.5]. A rate limiter model with a large gain K to give fast tracking of the control command in the linear operating mode of the actuator is used in the design of rate saturation compensation. The back-calculation scheme is applied on the saturation block within the rate limiter model, instead of the actuator input and output as in the magnitude saturation case.

The Simulink closed-loop model diagram with rate limiter and back-calculation rate saturation compensation, where the anti-windup time constant Tt=1, is shown in Figure 21. Figure 22 shows the step response and the control signal rate with and without the rate compensation. It is evident

Figure 20. Open loop and closed loop step response with the tuned PI

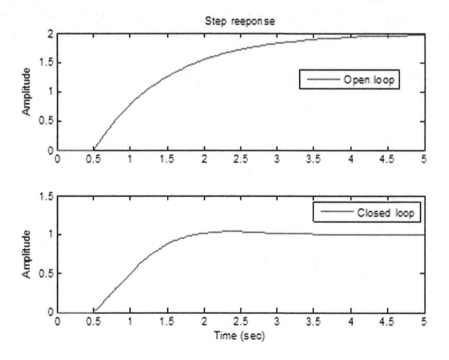

that applying back-calculation scheme for rate saturation compensation is effective, eliminating the large overshoot with the presence of rate limiting.

We demonstrated using an example that the integral reset anti-windup scheme can also be applied for rate saturation: in this case the control rate is modified instead of the magnitude by the scheme. Note that the controller is a simple PI controller. For more complex controllers not of the PID type, it is not clear how to apply this simple scheme. In this case, more systematic design process should be followed to design rate saturation compensator. A frequency domain design method was developed using a local feedback loop around the rate saturation element, where the rate saturation compensator was designed to guarantee the robust stability and the robust performance (Wu, 2001).

Magnitude and Rate Saturation

When an actuator has both magnitude and rate saturation, for a PI controller loop, the back-calculation scheme can be applied twice to deal with two saturation elements in the actuator.

For the closed-loop system shown in Figure 23 which is the system used for rate saturation design earlier, assume the actuator has magnitude limits +/-0.57 and rate limits +/-0.5. Figure 24 presents the closed-loop responses with and without the magnitude and rate saturation compensation, which shows the effectiveness of the integral reset for saturation compensation. For

Figure 21. Actuator rate saturation compensation using back-calculation

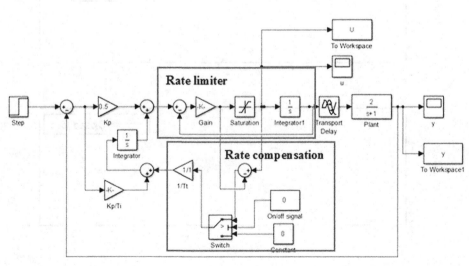

Figure 22. Step responses for actuator with rate saturation

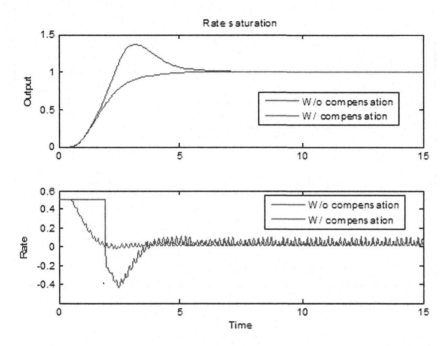

a general frequency domain robust design method, compensation for both magnitude and rate saturation is achieved by using two local feedback loops around the magnitude saturation element and the rate saturation element (Wu, 2001), where two additional local controllers are designed systematically accounting for both the closed-loop stability and performance.

Figure 23. Compensation for magnitude and rate saturation

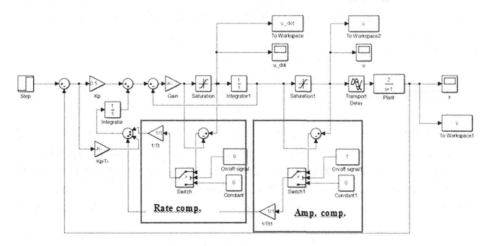

Figure 24. Closed-loop responses with magnitude and rate actuator saturation

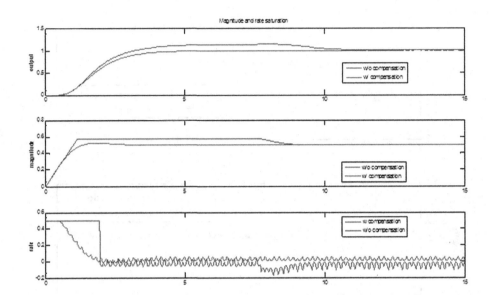

Extra Time Delays

The single most important impact of implementing a control system digitally is the delay associated with the D/A converter. Due to zero order hold, on the average, the continuous control signal generated by D/A has a delay of $Ts/2$, with Ts the sample time (Franklin, Powell, & Workman, 1990). One should incorporate this $Ts/2$ delay in the continuous design of a digital system. Delays in sensors and the delay in the computational unit, *latency*, should also be considered during the controller design if they are not negligible. Usually, adequate phase margin is required in the controller design to account for the extra time delays in the control system, and time delays are introduced during the simulation to analyze system stability and performance.

Controller Update Rate

In real time implementation, the controller algorithm is computed at a fixed time interval, the reciprocal of this time interval is the controller update rate or sample rate. Analog output signals of sensors measuring the controlled variables are sampled through ADCs (analog-to-digital convertor) at a fixed rate before computing the control outputs. The control update interval shall be selected between the sampling interval of the sensor reading (feedback signal for PI controller) and 1/15 -1/20 of the dominant time constant of the closed-loop control system. If the control update rate is fast enough, then the controller can be tuned using a continuous plant model and the controller performance achieved for the continuous plant model can be preserved in the discrete implementation. For example, for most HVAC/R systems, the sampling interval is set at 1 second for temperature and flow rate. The sampling interval for pressure can be as short as 0.2 second. A sampling interval of 1 second and a control update interval of 5 seconds are common practice in HVAC/R systems.

Filtering

Now, most control systems are implemented digitally with feedback signals sampled and control signals updated with a fixed sampling time Ts. $fs = 1/Ts$ is called the sample rate. When the controller is designed in continuous time and implemented in discrete time, to preserve the desired performance of the designed analog control system, the sample rate has to be fast enough, usually 15 to 20 times faster than the bandwidth of the control system. If the sample rate is limited, then the sampling effect has to be explicitly accounted for in the control design, the controller should be designed in discrete time. Sampling also introduces an unexpected phenomenon, called Aliasing. After sampling, higher frequency signal appears as a low frequency signal, for instance, the frequency of a signal S is 5/6HZ, when it is sampled at 1Hz sample rate, the sampled signal Sa has a frequency of 1/6Hz.

Pre-filtering is required to remove aliasing in sensor signals. An anti-aliasing filter effectively eliminates all signal components with frequencies above half the sample rate. A second-order Butterworth filter is commonly used. The dynamics of the filter is often significant. It should be accounted for in the control design by combining it with the plant dynamics.

Bumpless Transfer

A control system can have multiple operational modes, such as automatic mode and manual mode, cooling or heating mode. When a mode switch occurs, the actuator input switches from the current control output to a new control output. The two controllers may have different output values at the instant of switching, so switching can introduce a jump or discontinuity in the actuator input signal, which consequently cause undesired change in the controlled output. Bumpless transfer mechanism is applied to ensure the transition between the controller output signals being smooth. The bumpless transfer for a PI controller is demonstrated below. Assume that controller #1 is connected to an actuator and the controller output is:

$$u_1 = k_{p1}e_1 + k_{i1} \int e_1 dt \tag{29}$$

where e_1, k_{p1}, k_{i1} are error, proportional gain and integral gain for controller #1, respectively. At the instant when the controller #2 overrides the controller #1, the integral part of the controller #2 is reset such that the output of controller #2 is equal to the output of the controller #1, so there is no jump in the actuator input, avoiding destabilizing the controlled output.

$$u_2 = k_{p2}e_2 + k_{i2} \int e_2 dt, \text{ where } k_{i2} \int e_2 dt = u_1 - k_{p2}e_2. \tag{30}$$

When there is no mode switch, the controller parameters such as the proportional gain and the integral gain can still change, causing the controller output to be discontinuous. In these situations, proper bumpless transfer techniques should also be applied for parameter change during the operation. Consider that the integral gain is changed from k_{i_old} to k_{i_new}. At the instant of parameter change, the integration of the error is reset such that the integral part of the PI controller remains unchanged under the parameter change:

$$\int edt = \left(k_{i\_old} \int edt \right) / k_{i\_new} \tag{31}$$

Then, the controller output is updated using the new parameter as usual:

$$u = k_p e + k_{i\_new} \int edt. \tag{32}$$

If the proportional gain changes, similar to integral gain change, the process can be applied to adjust the integral part to keep the PI output smooth.

PID CONTROLLER TUNING

Introduction

A PID controller is the cornerstone feedback controller of industrial control systems. In the process control, more than 95% of the controllers are of the Proportional-Integral-Derivative (PID) type. The PID controller is the most popular among all controllers. The determination of proportional, integral and derivative gains are known as PID controller tuning. The PID controller is given in transfer function as:

$$c(s) = k_p \left(1 + \frac{1}{T_i s} + T_d s \right)$$

where k_p is the proportional gain, T_i is the integral time constant (k_p/T_i is the integral gain) and T_d is the derivative time constant ($k_p T_d$ is the derivative gain). Proper tuning of the PID parameters is critical for the PID controller to function as expectedly. This section describes the PID tuning procedures, i.e., how to obtain the tuning parameters from measurements and calculations made from the system under control.

The PID controller is usually applied to systems with a stable, low-order dynamic behavior. Furthermore, the proportional-integral (PI) controller, a special class of PID controller, is sufficient for the majority of industrial control applications. Therefore, the tuning procedures described here are applicable to components or equipment under control that exhibit such stable, low-order dynamic behaviors. The tuning procedures presented in this section only consider a single control loop. However, a real control system is usually made of multiple PI controllers regulating key controlled variables by means of several control loops. Single loop tuning procedures can be used for multi-PI controller systems as long as interactions in the plant dynamics are limited, i.e. if changing a control variable associated with an actuator generates a large change on the corresponding controlled variable and relatively small changes on other controlled variables under control of other PID loops.

Controller Tuning Within Overall Controller Design Workflow

A typical controller development process consists of the following steps:

Step 1: Define control loop performance requirements.

This set of control performance requirements are derived from the product requirements and generally cover four aspects of a closed loop control system: command following, disturbance rejection, noise attenuation and robustness to process variations. These requirements are usually expressed in control terminology such as the rise time, the settling time, the overshoot and the steady state error requirements for a closed loop step response in the time domain or the gain margin and the phase margin, and bandwidth requirements for certain loop transfer functions in the frequency domain.

Step 2: Create an open-loop test plan to be carried out on a real unit or plant model (e.g. a validated Dymola model).

Create a test plan for step response tests on the system under control. A step change can be introduced in a control input or disturbance input. One input variable is changed at a time. The step test can be conducted either in the open loop or the closed loop fashion. For the same input, a series of step responses can be designed for different operating conditions to test the variation of the system dynamics over the operating envelope.

Step 3: Carry out open-loop test plan to generate step response data.

Step 4: Identify system dynamics from step response test data. In most application cases, the dynamics can be represented as a FOPTD or SOPTD model.

Step 5: Tune PI parameters according to a selected tuning rule.

Step 6: Determine other parameters in the closed loop, such as the control update rate, the anti-windup parameter, the noise filter time constant, and the command pre-filter.

Step 7: Create a closed-loop test plan to be carried out on a real unit or simulation model.

Step 8: Carry out closed-loop test plan to verify controls performance against its requirements.

Step 9: PI tuning iterations and adjustment if needed.

There is no guarantee that the PI controller tuned according to selected tuning rules meets all control requirements, i.e. when a second order dynamics is approximated by a first order plant model or other elements in the closed loop are neglected during the tuning step. More fine tuning based on the test results may be needed.

Step 10: Create the control algorithm description documentation (ADD).

Document in detail the control loop structure, the control algorithm, assumptions, limitations, and implementation aspects.

PI controller tuning in Step 5 in the above controller design process is described in detail next. It is assumed that Steps 1 to 4 have been completed and a plant model, i.e. a FOPTD or SOPTD model, has been obtained before the controller tuning is performed.

PID Controller Tuning

The proportional-integral-derivative (PID) controller has three parameters, but it is not easy to determine their values. Many PID controllers are still manually tuned on site, and a large number of PID controllers operating in industrial factories are poorly tuned. Ziegler and Nichols (1942) first introduced a classical tuning method. Since then, a large amount of research has been done to modify and improve the original tuning rules such as analytical tuning approach, optimization methods, gain and phase margin optimization, etc. Rivera et al. (1986) introduced IMC PID tuning, Smith and Corripio (1985) presented direct synthesis tuning rules, Skogestad (2002) proposed the widely used SIMC PID controller tuning, Astrom and Hagglund (1995) discussed optimization based tuning methods with the goal of ensuring good stability and performance.

Ziegler-Nichols Method

This open loop tuning method was presented in the 1940s, it is still widely used in the process control and it motivated the broader research on better PID tuning rules since then till today. This method uses the reaction curve, which is the open loop step response curve. Dynamics of the plant in the form of the open loop step response is represented by two parameters, the time delay L (originally called "lag" by Ziegler and Nichols) and the unit reaction rate R_i. The unit step response of the process/plant is obtained by introducing the unit change in the plant input. This requires that the plant is stable. The reaction curve is usually S-shaped. The unit reaction rate is the maximum rate of the unit step response and occurs at the inflection point of the unit step response curve. Where the tangent line to the inflection point intersects the time axis gives the time delay.

For a proportional controller, the proportional gain is given by:

$$K_p = \frac{1}{R_1 L} \tag{33}$$

For a proportional-integral controller, the proportional gain and the integral time constant are given by:

$$K_p = \frac{0.9}{R_1 L}, \quad T_i = 3.3L \tag{34}$$

And, for a proportional-integral-derivative controller, the proportional gain, the integral time constant and the derivative time constant are given by:

$$K_p = \frac{0.9}{R_1 L}, \quad T_i = 2L, \quad T_d = \frac{L}{2} \tag{35}$$

If the plant dynamics is modeled by a first order plus time delay model, given below:

$$G_p(s) = \frac{k}{1 + Ts} e^{-Ls} \tag{36}$$

Then for a proportional controller, the gain is given by:

$$K_p = \frac{T}{kL} \tag{37}$$

For a proportional-integral controller, the gain and time constant are given by:

$$K_p = \frac{0.9T}{kL}, \quad T_i = 3.3L \tag{38}$$

And for a proportional-integral-derivative controller, the gain and time constants are given by:

$$K_p = \frac{1.2T}{kL}, \quad T_i = 2L, \quad T_d = \frac{L}{2} \tag{39}$$

For a PID controller tuned using this method, the transfer function is:

$$C(s) = 0.6\frac{T}{k}\frac{\left(s + \frac{1}{L}\right)^2}{s} \tag{40}$$

The PID controller has a pole at the origin and two zeros at $s = -\frac{1}{L}$. The open loop gain kK_p, according to the formulas for K_p, is proportional to the ratio of the plant time constant to the plant time delay $(\frac{T}{L})$.

Ziegler-Nichols method is simple, it requires the minimal amount of information of the process. It often gives good performance for load disturbances in terms of a small integrated absolute error (IAE), the drawback is the poor robustness of the closed-loop (Guzman, Hagglund, Astrom, Dormido, Berenguel, & Piguet, 2014). It gives good disturbance response for integrating process, but otherwise known to give aggressive settings, and also gives poor performance for delay dominated processes (Skogestad, 2002).

Hen-Coon Method

In this method, the process reaction curve is first obtained by an open loop step test, and then the process dynamics is approximated by a first order plus time delay model, as given by Equation 36.

After the determination of the three parameters of the process model, the controller parameters can be determined using Cohen-Coon rules (Seborg, Edgar, & Mellichamp, 1989). These rules were developed empirically to provide a closed-loop step response with a ¼ decay ratio. Note that Ziegler-Nichols tuning rules give a ¼ decay ratio in the closed-loop step response.

For a proportional controller:

$$K_p = \frac{1}{k}\frac{T}{L}\left(1 + \frac{L}{3T}\right);$$

(41)

For a proportional-integral controller:

$$K_p = \frac{T}{kL}\left(\frac{9}{10} + \frac{L}{12T}\right), \quad T_i = L\frac{30 + 3L/T}{9 + 20L/T};$$

(42)

And for a proportional-integral-derivative controller:

$$K_p = \frac{T}{kL}\left(\frac{4}{3} + \frac{L}{4T}\right), \quad T_i = L\frac{32 + 6L/T}{13 + 8L/T}, \quad T_d = L\frac{4}{11 + 2L/T};$$

(43)

AMIGO Tuning Method

Approximate M-constrained Integral Gain Optimization (AMIGO) was developed by Hagglund and Astrom (2002) in the spirit of Ziegler and Nichols tuning res. In this method, robust loop shaping techniques were applied to a large set of representative processes. The design objective is to optimize load disturbance rejection performance, which optimizes the integral gain, with robustness constraints on the sensitivity and the complimentary sensitivity peak $M_s = M_t = 1.4$. The controller parameters obtained through the design were then correlated with the three parameters of the process dynamics such as the process gain, the time constant, and the time delay. It gives tuning rules f PI controller. The tuning rules gave good results for all processes in a large test batch ranging from integral process to pure time delay process. The following formula are given for proportional and integral (PI) controllers:

$$K_p = \frac{0.15}{k} + \left(0.35 - \frac{LT}{(L+T)^2}\right)\frac{T}{kL}, \quad T_i = 0.35L + \frac{13LT^2}{T^2 + 12LT + 7L^2}.$$

(44)

And the tuning rules for PID controllers are:

$$K_p = \frac{1}{k}\left(0.2 + 0.45\frac{T}{L}\right), \quad T_i = \frac{0.4L + 0.8T}{L + 0.1T}L, \quad T_d = \frac{0.5LT}{0.3L + T}. \tag{45}$$

AMIGO tuning rules are conservative robust tunning rules with lower performance compared to MIGO tuning rules (Astrom & Hagglund, 2004). AMIGO PID tuning rules are similar in structure to Cohen-Coon tuning rules, compared Equation 45 to Equation 43, but parameters are very different.

SIMC Tuning Rules

The starting point of SIMC-PID tuning rules is the IMC-PID tuning rules, which has widespread application in the industry. The rule for the integral term has been modified to improve load disturbance rejection performance for integrating processes. There is just one set of tuning rules for both a first-order time delay model and a second –order time delay model (Skogestad, 2002).

Consider an approximate first-or second order time delay model:

$$G_p(s) = \frac{k}{(1 + T_1 s)(1 + T_2 s)} e^{-Ls} \tag{46}$$

where $T_1 > T_2$ is the dominant lag time constant. For a dominant second-order process where $T_2 > L$, the second-order lag time constant T_2 is included in the model. To get a PID controller, one starts from a second -order model, and to get a PI controller, one starts from a first-order model with $T_2 = 0$. PID control with derivative action is recommended for processes with dominant second order dynamics with $T_2 > L$ approximately. The same rules used for both PI and PID controller are given below.

$$K_p = \frac{1}{k}\frac{T_1}{T_c + L}, \quad T_i = \min\{T_1, 4(T_c + L)\}, \quad T_d = T_2. \tag{47}$$

The only tuning parameter is the first-order closed-loop response time constant T_c. This time constant is determined by a trade-off between setpoint change and disturbance rejection performance and robustness and input usage. SIMC rule for the tuning parameter leading to good performance and good robustness is:

$$T_c = L \tag{48}$$

SIMC PI tuning rules were recently improved for better performance for time delay processes (Grimholt & Skogestad, 2012) as follows:

$$K_p = \frac{1}{k} \frac{T_1 + L/3}{T_c + L}, \quad T_i = \min\{T_1 + L/3, \ 4(T_c + L)\}. \tag{49}$$

Example 1: The plant model (a simplified FOTD model approximating the real system behavior) is

$$G_p(s) = \frac{2}{1s + 1} e^{-0.5s}$$

Determine the closed loop time constant:

$$T_c = L = 0.5$$

Compute the proportional gain:

$$K_p = \frac{T}{K(T_c + L)} = 0.5$$

Compute the integral time constant:

$$T_i = \min(T, 4(T_c + L)) = 1$$

PI controller:

$$C(s) = 0.5 \left(1 + \frac{1}{s}\right)$$

Figure 25 shows the step responses of the plant with and without PI controller.

Next, let us consider actuator saturation. Usually, Saturation causes the oscillatory behavior with larger overshoot and longer settling time. This control system was used earlier to demonstrate rate saturation and compensation.

Figure 25. FOPTD plant model: open loop and closed loop step response (closed loop with the tuned PI)

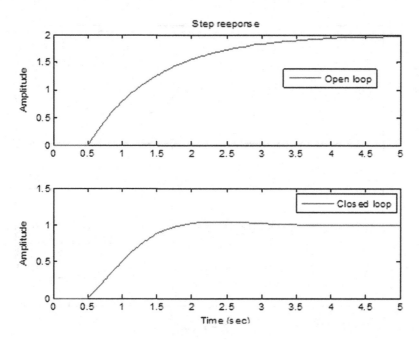

Assume the actuator output is in the range of [-0.57 0.57]. The nonlinear response under actuator saturation is presented in Figure 26, showing windup in the integrator and its effects on the output. We use back-calculation for anti-windup in this example. In the reset-feedback (back-calculation) scheme, which is introduced earlier in this chapter, for anti-windup, when the actuator reaches its limit, the integral part of the PI controller is recomputed so that its new PI output gives a value close to the limit. A time constant, T_t, is applied to the difference between the PI output and the actuator output and determines how quickly the integral is reset. T_t can be parameterized as $T_t=N_i*T_i$ and N_i is recommended as $N_i=0.9$. The effect of changing the anti-windup time constant is illustrated in Figure 27.

Fine Tuning of PID Parameters

Starting from one of the tuning rules, the values of the PID parameters can be calculated. However, implementing these PID settings may not lead to satisfactory closed-loop performance or robustness properties. These tuning rules assume an idea process dynamics, represented by a first-order or second-

Figure 26. Step response of the system in example 1 showing actuator saturation and integrator windup

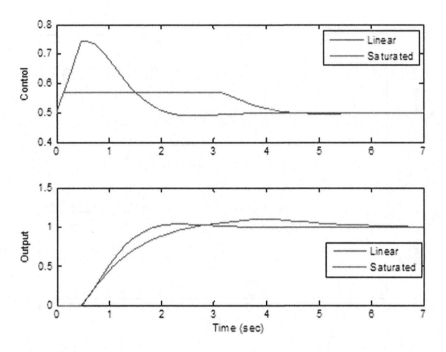

Figure 27. Closed-loop step responses for different anti-windup time constants

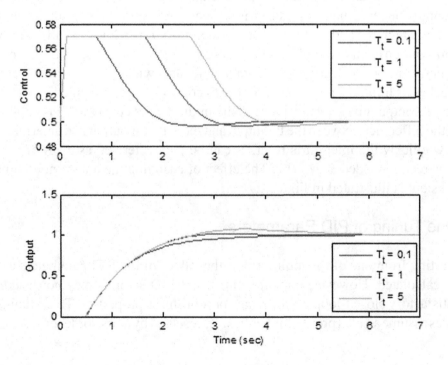

order plus time delay model. There may exist higher order process dynamics or the identified first-order or second-order model parameter values are not precise. In these cases, the PID parameter values need to be manually adjusted.

The adjustments are performed based on simple guidelines for changing parameters. Astrom and Hagglund (2005) gave a set of simple rules: performance is improved by increasing the proportional gain or decreasing the integral time constant; robustness is improved by decreasing the controller gain or increasing the integral time constant; control signal variation is reduced by decreasing the proportional gain. Increasing the proportional gain makes the closed-loop response faster, however, too much gain can make the closed loop system unstable. The integral action has the fundamental property to eliminate in most cases the steady state error between the controlled variable and its desired reference. However, too much integral action can also cause instability due to a decrease in the phase margin. Too much actuator movements can lead to actuator saturation, i.e. integrator wind-up, which leads to large overshoot, oscillation and sometimes instability.

Tuning for Second-Order Time Delay Model

For a SOPTD plant model approximation, the model needs to be further approximated using a FOPTD model. Once the FOTD approximation is obtained, the PI tuning follows the same rules as described for FOPTD system. Higher order dynamics model can be reduced by applying the half rule (Skogestad, 2002): "The largest neglected (denominator) time constant (lag) is distributed evenly to the effective delay and the smallest retained time constant." Rules for approximating the pole zero pair $\dfrac{Ts+1}{\tau s+1}$ were also given by Skogestad (2002). Applying these rules, the following table (Table 1) describes different cases for the approximation of a SOPTD system using a FOPTD model.

Example 2: SOPTD plant model approximation:

$$G_p(s) = \frac{K(T_0 s + 1)}{(T_1 s + 1)(T_2 s + 1)} e^{-Ls} = \frac{2(s+1)}{(1.1s + 1)(0.5s + 1)} e^{-0.5s}$$

FOPTD plant model is further approximated by applying the reduction rules described above:

Table 1. Cases for approximation of SOPTD system using FOPTD model

SOPTD Transfer Function	FOPTD Transfer Function Approximation
$G_p(s) = \dfrac{K}{(T_1 s+1)(T_2 s+1)} e^{-Ls}$ *(T1>T2)*	$G_p(s) \approx \dfrac{K}{(T_1 + T_2/2)s+1} e^{-(L+\frac{T_2}{2})s}$
$G_p(s) = \dfrac{K(T_0 s+1)}{(T_1 s+1)(T_2 s+1)} e^{-Ls}$ $(T_0 > 0,\ T_1 > T_2)$	$G_p(s) \approx \begin{cases} \dfrac{KT_0/T_2}{T_1 s+1} e^{-Ls}, & T_0 \geq T_2 \geq L \\[2mm] \dfrac{KT_0/L}{T_1 s+1} e^{-Ls}, & T_0 \geq L \geq T_2 \\[2mm] \dfrac{K}{T_1 s+1} e^{-Ls}, & L \geq T_0 \geq T_2 \\[2mm] \dfrac{KT_0/T_2}{T_1 s+1} e^{-Ls}, & T_2 \geq T_0 \geq 5L \end{cases}$
$G_p(s) = \dfrac{K(T_0 s+1)}{(T_1 s+1)(T_2 s+1)} e^{-Ls}$ *(T0 < 0, T₁>T₂)*	$G_p(s) \approx \dfrac{K}{(T_1 + T_2/2)s+1} e^{-(L+\frac{T_2}{2}-T_0)s}$

$$G_p(s) = \frac{KT_0/T_2}{T_1 s+1} e^{-Ls} = \frac{4}{1.1s+1} e^{-0.5s}$$

Next, we apply SIMC PI tuning rules. First, determine the closed loop time constant:

$$T_c = L = 0.5$$

Next, compute the proportional gain:

$$K_p = \frac{T_1}{KT_0/T_2 (T_c + L)} = 0.275$$

And compute the integral time constant:

$$T_i = \min(T_1, 4(T_c + D)) = 1.1$$

PI controller resulted is:

$$C(s) = 0.255\left(1 + \frac{1}{1.1s}\right)$$

Figure 28 compares FOTD and SOTD model frequency response in the Bode plot.

Figure 29 shows the step response of the plant without PI control (open loop), the plant with PI control, and the FOTD plant model approximation with PI control respectively. Since the PI controller is tuned using the FOTD model, which approximates the SOTD plant model, the response of the closed loop with FOTD plant model is better than that of the closed loop with the actual SOTD plant model. However, the controller actually regulates the plant represented by the SOTD model, the PI controller tuned based on the FOTD model may be further tuned to meet the requirements, e.g. the gains should be increased to have a faster response for this example.

Figure 28. Comparison of FOTD approximation and SOTD

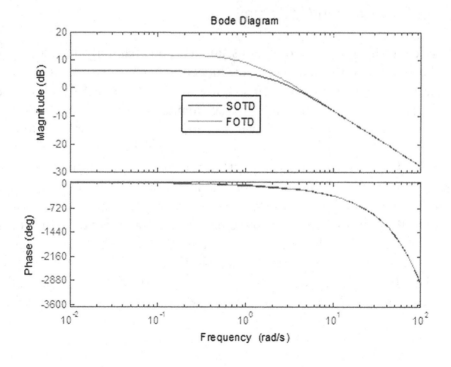

Figure 29. Step responses for example 2

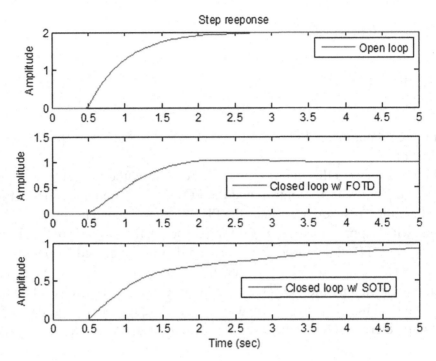

PI Controller for On/Off Actuator

The PI controller output is continuous, and it follows naturally that the signal will be sent to a continuous actuator. Indeed, for majority of the cases the actuator is continuous, such as direct current (DC) motor or VFD (Variable Frequency Drive) fan. In many product applications, however, there are actuators operating at discrete level. For multi-stage actuators, the tuning process introduced above is not affected, and the PI controller output is discretized to the nearby actuator output level. The second case is on/off actuator having only two stages or levels. For example, most of the compressors are digital (on/off) compressor. Many fans are fixed speed fans. In such cases, PI controller can still be used, and the on/off actuator will operate on a duty cycle. The actuator will have a cycle period, T_{cycle}, and a duty cycle signal, which is the PI controller output, u, ranging from 0% to 100%. A duty cycle signal of 30% means that during the current cycle period, 30% of the time the actuator will be ON, and the rest 70% of the time the actuator will be OFF.

The open loop step test for on/off actuator will be limited to step change from OFF to ON (or ON to OFF), this is equivalent to a step change of a continuous actuator from 0% to 100%, although for a continuous actuator, the step change size is usually set at 10% of the full range (i.e. from 50% to 60%).

T_{cycle} becomes an additional configurable parameter of the control algorithm when the PI controller determines the duty cycle of an ON/OFF actuator. T_{cycle} should be much longer than the control update interval, T_s, but smaller than the ultimate period of the FOPTD or SOPTD plant model, estimated to be 3 times of the time delay. Thus the guideline to determine T_{cycle} is to have a T_{cycle} between *10T$_s$* and *3L*: *10T$_s$ <= T$_{cycle}$ <= 3L.*

For duty cycle control, taking into account of the effective time delay introduced by the cycle period, the closed loop time constant should be determined by the following guideline:

$$T_c = max \ (L + 0.5T_{cycle}, \ 0.5T).$$

Corresponding SIMC tuning rules become:

$$Kp = \frac{T}{K(Tc + L + 0.5T_{cycle})},$$

$$T_i = min\{T, 4(T_c + L)\} \tag{50}$$

Consider controlling the plant in example 1 using an on/off actuator. Based on the desired closed loop time constant and the delay of the plant, we set T_s = 0.02 sec and T_{cycle}=0.3 sec.

Compute the desired closed-loop time constant:

$$T_c = max \ (L + 0.5T_{cycle}, \ 0.5T) = 0.65$$

Compute the proportional gain:

$$K_p = \frac{T}{K\left(T_c + L + 0.5T_{cycle}\right)} = 0.385$$

Compute the integral time constant:

$$T_i = min(T, 4(T_c + L)) = 1$$

The resulting PI controller is:

$$C(s) = 0.385\left(1 + \frac{1}{s}\right).$$

Figure 30, given in example 1, but this is expected since the cycle period introduces an extra effective delay into the closed loop and the PI controller is tuned to be less aggressive accounting for this extra delay.

MIMO CONTROL SYSTEM DESIGN EXAMPLE

At this point, it is beneficial to present a concrete control design problem demonstrating the application of the methods presented in this chapter. A MIMO control system will be used as a control design example. We will follow the controls design process: defining control requirements, identifying plant models, controllability analysis, PI controller tuning, and model in the loop

Figure 30. Step response of the closed loop with on/off actuator

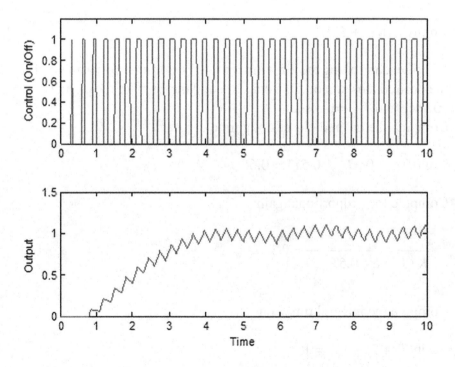

simulation and verification. Readers should be able to perform a complete controls design process for a simple control system following instructions given in this chapter after some practice.

Control Design Steps

Control Requirements

The control system example is constructed after a real control system. The system has two control variables and two controlled variables.

Pressure operating limits for a key system component include inlet pressure limit and outlet pressure limit. Minimal allowed inlet pressure is 1.3bar. Maximal allowed outlet pressure is described by a pressure profile, as plotted in Figure 31.

The control requirements, at the algorithm level, for the controlled variables are:

1. No overshoot during set point change,
2. 0.2C steady state error band,
3. Reach the temperature set point as fast as possible.

Figure 31. Envelope of max allowed outlet pressure

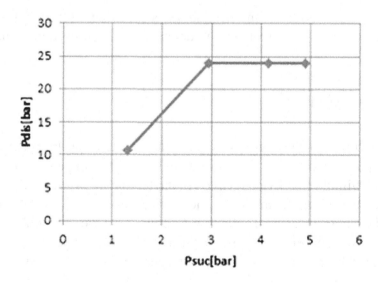

These control objectives can be translated into specific control loop requirements. Non-overshooting requires a critical damped or over damped closed loop system assuming a second order plant. Approximately, damping is related to the phase margin, so non-overshooting requires adequate phase margin. 0.2C error requires integral action. Reaching set point quickly requires high bandwidth. So, in terms of control loop properties, it is required that

1. Phase margin greater than 70 degree,
2. Control has integral action,
3. Highest possible bandwidth.

Keep in mind that these requirements are for demonstration purposes only. Other requirements are also possible in real applications; the list here is not intended to be complete.

Model Identification

The controllers used for industrial applications are primarily PI controllers. PI controllers work well when the plant dynamics is first order or approximately first order. When a plant possesses second order dynamics, typically it requires a PID controller because phase compensation is needed. Under a step input change, if the plant output response is primarily monotonic, the plant dynamics can be modelled using a first order plus time delay (FOPTD) model, $G_p(s) = \dfrac{K}{TS+1} e^{-LS}$. We typically use a FOTD model for control design. We can identify such models from the plant physical model using step response data. We are going to find a linear model around an equilibrium point:

$$\begin{pmatrix} y_1 \\ y_2 \end{pmatrix} = \begin{bmatrix} G_{11} & G_{12} \\ G_{21} & G_{22} \end{bmatrix} \begin{pmatrix} u_1 \\ u_2 \end{pmatrix}$$

There exist various techniques for obtaining a linear model from a nonlinear physical plant model. Numerical (and analytical) techniques exist in both MATLAB/Simulink and Modelica (Dymola) for linearizing a dynamic model at an operating point. Examples of such techniques are the Linear Analysis tool in the Control Design Toolbox in Simulink and the "linmod" function in MATLAB. The effectiveness of these techniques depends greatly on properties of the model and quality of initial guesses for the steady state points.

An alternative technique is to treat the physical plant model as a black box model and exercise it with test inputs around an operating point, record input and output data, and then use system identification techniques, such as the System Identification Toolbox in MATLAB to obtain a linear model. While this technique may be less accurate than "exact" linearization methods it is relatively straightforward to use for an open loop stable system. A Simulink model is built for the open loop step test on the plant model. You will run this model to obtain the step response data and save it for model identification. The step test is conducted around a selected point in the operation envelope where we want to establish a model. The plant is usually brought to this point under a closed-loop controller and maintained there to reach a steady state. A step change in one input channel is introduced, usually in an open loop fashion. The step size should be chosen such that the plant response is basically linear. Start to collect both input and output at a fixed sampling rate. Allow the response to reach the steady state for a sufficient period of time then stop the test and data collection.

Following these steps for a step response test:

1. Fix input variables (including control variables and boundary conditions) constant, let the plant reach a steady state (equilibrium point).
2. Introduce step changes in control variables one at a time, let the outputs reach their new steady state. The step size should not be too large to cause nonlinear response.
3. Record the time history of both input and outputs.

Identify G_{22} first Plot and examine step response. It is possible the data includes some initial transient, so remove the transient part. Now, use an identification method to get the model, and the linear model step response fits the data very well (Figure 32).

Repeat this to get G_{12}, G_{21} and G_{11}. For G_{11}, the procedure is different. The dynamics from input #1 to output #1 is not of first order; it has an extra pole and an extra zero (Figure 33). So it is not a good idea to try to fit the data using a FOTD model directly. Instead, in this case, we first used MATLAB Sysid toolbox to get a second order model from the data, then using model reduction to get a first order model:

$$G_{11} = -\frac{0.105}{5.08s+1}e^{-2.5s}$$

Figure 32. Identify G_{22}

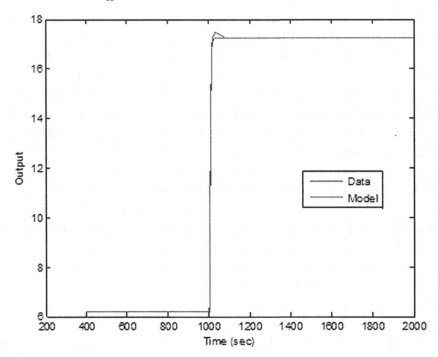

After this step, we have all four FOTD models.

Variation of Plant Dynamics

The linear model obtained so far is only valid around the equilibrium we choose. Under various application conditions, the system could be operating in other states. Will the dynamics stay the same at other operating points? If not, how much does the plant dynamics vary? A rigorous investigation involves creating a grid of points covering the entire operating envelope, obtaining linear model at each point and comparing the models. The conclusions of this analysis decide whether to use a single controller or gaining scheduling control. For our purpose, we will only look at the dynamics at another point.

Consider another equilibrium point which is closer to the limit of the operating range. The relative position of the two equilibrium points is shown in the operating envelop below in Figure 34. the triangle represents the first operating point and the rectangle represents the second operating point.

Let's look at G_{22} again at this new operating point. The identified model from step test, shown in Figure 35. Figure 35 is very different from the model

Figure 33. Step response for G_{11}

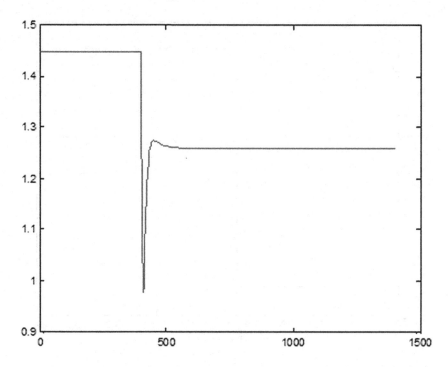

Figure 34. Pressure profile and operating points

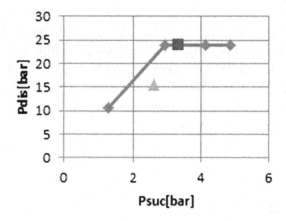

identified earlier in Figure 32. So, it may be necessary to use gain scheduling control depending on the control requirements. In this exercise, we will not show how to design a gain scheduling controller.

Figure 35. Step response and model response for another operating point for G_{22}

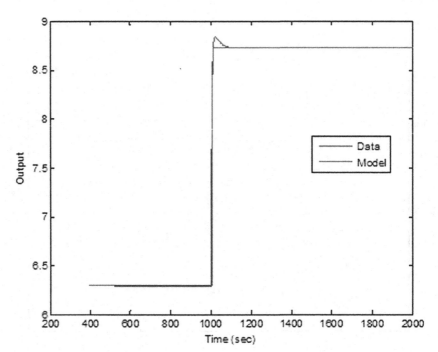

Controllability Analysis

We have a two-input-two-output plant, in the controllability analysis we will look at the input-output pairing, singular values, condition number, relative gain array (RGA), and RGA-number to find out the interaction level in the plant and how difficult it is to control the plant. This step will give a good indication whether a diagonal control design can work or a multivariable control design needs to be applied.

We first get the steady state RGA:

$$RGA(0) = \begin{bmatrix} 0.6778 & 0.3222 \\ 0.3222 & 0.6778 \end{bmatrix}$$

which shows that diagonal elements are closer to 1, so our original pairing of the inputs and outputs is the correct choice.

Figure 36. MIMO controllability analysis results

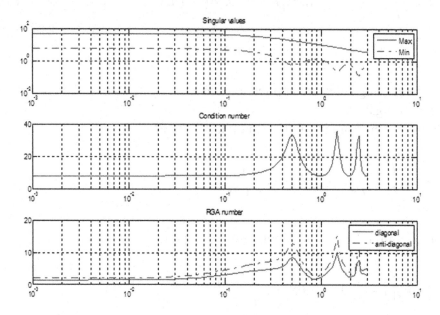

Next, look at the plots for singular values, condition number, and RGA-numbers in Figure 36. The minimal singular value drops under 1 at 0.4rad/sec and beyond, thus causing the sharp increase in the condition number, so the control bandwidth should stay below 0.4rad/sec. The RGA-numbers become larger 0.1rad/sec, which indicates stronger interactions between control loops. So, bandwidth staying below 0.4rad/sec and close to 0.1rad/sec, will maintain diagonal dominance, and the diagonal control design approach is then valid.

PI Tuning

Now, it is justified that we can design diagonal controllers for the plant. We conduct the diagonal controller design one loop at a time, just like designing the controller for a single-input-single-output plant. Many tuning rules can be applied, referring to earlier section for various tuning methods, and serve as a starting point of the controller design and verification process. The SIMC tuning rules is one among the best tuning methods and we use them for this example, see Equations 51 and 52 below.

$$K_p = \frac{1}{k}\frac{T_1 + L/3}{T_c + L}, \quad T_i = \min\left\{T_1 + L/3, \; 4(T_c + L)\right\}. \tag{51}$$

$$T_c = L. \tag{52}$$

The PI tuning rules are applied to each single loop to find the proportion and integral gains.

For the loop from input #1 to output #1, the PI obtained is:

$$C(s) = k_p\left(1 + \frac{1}{T_i s}\right) = -9.68\left(1 + \frac{1}{5.08s}\right).$$

Next, for the loop from input #2 to output #2, the PI obtained is:

$$C(s) = k_p\left(1 + \frac{1}{T_i s}\right) = -1.05\left(1 + \frac{1}{4.65s}\right).$$

Figure 37. Open loop Bode plot for output #1 and input #1

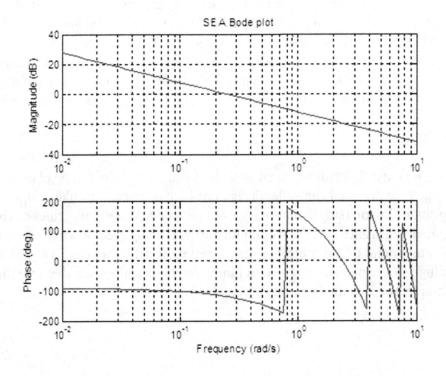

Open Loop Analysis

Now, we have identified plant models, designed PI controllers for each loop. We can plot the Bode plot of the open loop transfer function which is the product of the FOTD plant model and corresponding PI controller.

The open loop Bode plot from input #1 to output #1 is shown in Figure 37, the crossover frequency is 0.25rad/sec, the phase margin is close to 70degree, and the gain margin is close to 10dB. Recall the control loop requirements and the controllability analysis conclusions, the bandwidth should stay below 0.4rad/sec. The controller is acceptable at this point.

For this loop from input #2 to output #2 shown in Figure 38, the crossover frequency is 0.2rad/sec, and the phase margin and the gain margin look adequate. The controller also seems acceptable.

Figure 38. Open loop Bode plot for output #2 and input #2

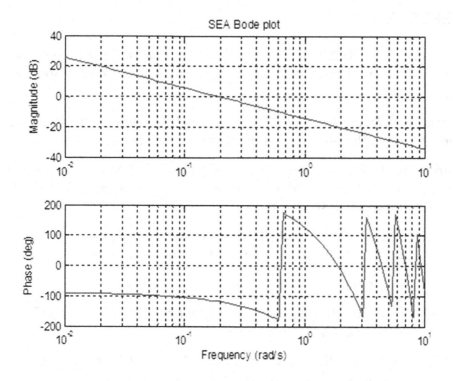

Simulation and Testing

After obtaining the controller, the control system performance is analyzed through computer simulations. At this step, the physical plant model is used together with the controller model to compute the closed-loop response. The control system is tested under various operating conditions to evaluate the controller performance against the controls requirements. The controllers usually are adjusted according to the simulation results on the nonlinear plant model. It may become necessary to use a gain scheduling controller due to variations in plant dynamics over the operating range, as pointed out earlier. In that case, the steps illustrated earlier are repeated for each operating points at which the controller is designed.

How to construct the test model and use the model-in-the-loop (MIL) technique to formally test against requirements will be discussed in detail in a later chapter on testing, where the example will be continued.

REFERENCES

Astrom, K. J., & Hagglund, T. (1995). *PID controllers: Theory, Design and Tuning* (2nd ed.). Research Triangle Park, NC: The Instrument Society of America.

Astrom, K. J., & Hagglund, T. (2005). *Advanced PID control*. Research Triangle Park, NC: ISA-The Instrumentation, Systems, and Automation Society.

Astrom, K. J., Panagopoulos, H., & Hagglund, T. (1998). Design of PI Controllers Based on Non-Convex Optimization. *Automatica, 34*(5), 585–601. doi:10.1016/S0005-1098(98)00011-9

Astrom, K. J., & Wittenmark, B. (1997). *Computer Controlled Systems: Theory and Design* (2nd ed.). Prentice-Hall International, Inc.

Brogan, W. L. (1990). *Modern Control Theory*. Prentice Hall.

Franklin, G. F., Powell, J. D., & Emami-Naeini, A. (1986). *Feedback Control of Dynamic Systems*. Addison-Wesley.

Franklin, G. F., Powell, J. D., & Workman, M. L. (1990). *Digital Control of Dynamic Systems* (2nd ed.). Reading, MA: Addison-Wesley.

Grimholt, C., & Skogestad, S. (2012) Optimal PI-Control and Verification of the SIMC Tuning Rule.*Proceedings of the IFAC conference on Advance in PID Control PID'12*. doi:10.3182/20120328-3-IT-3014.00003

Guzman, J. L., Hagglund, T., Astrom, K. J., Dormido, S., Berenguel, M., & Piguet, Y. (2014). Understanding PID Design Through Interactive Tools. *Proceedings of IFAC World Conference*.

Hagglund, T., & Astrom, K. J. (2002). Revisiting the Ziegler-Nichols Tuning Rules for PI Control. *Asian Journal of Control*, *4*(4), 364–380. doi:10.1111/j.1934-6093.2002.tb00076.x

Horowitz, I. (1993). *Quantitative Feedback Design Theory (QFT)*. Boulder, CO: QFT Pub.

Rivera, D. E., Morari, M., & Skogestad, S. (1986). Internal Model Control for PID Controller Design. *Industrial & Engineering Chemistry Research*, *25*(1), 252–265.

Seborg, D. E., Edgar, T. F., & Mellichamp, D. A. (1989). *Process Dynamics and Control*. New York: John Wiley & Sons.

Skogestad, S. (2003). Simple Analytic Rules for Model Reduction and PID Controller Tuning. *Journal of Process Control*, *13*(4), 291–309. doi:10.1016/S0959-1524(02)00062-8

Skogestad, S., & Postlethwaite, I. (1996). *Multivariable Feedback Control: Analysis and Design*. New York: John Wiley & Sons Ltd.

Smith, C. A., & Corripio, A. B. (1985). *Principle and Practices of Automatic Process Control*. New York: John Wiley & Sons.

Wu, W. (2000). A New QFT Design Method for SISO Cascaded-loop Design. *Proc. American Control Conference*. doi:10.1109/ACC.2000.876938

Wu, W. (2001). A QFT Design Methodology for Feedback System with Input Rate or Amplitude and Rate Saturation.*Proc. American Control Conference*. doi:10.1109/ACC.2001.945575

Wu, W. (2009). A Cogging Torque Compensating Disturbance Estimator for DC Motor Speed Regulation: Design and Experimentation.*Proceedings of International Symposium on Industrial Electronics*. doi:10.1109/ISIE.2009.5222732

Wu, W. (2015). Disturbance Compensation using Feedforward and Feedback for DC Motor Mechanism Low Speed Regulation. *Journal of Dynamic Systems, Measurement, and Control, 138*(4).

Younklin, G. W. (2003). *Industrial Servo Control System: fundamentals and applications* (2nd ed.). New York, NY: Marcel Dekker.

Ziegler, J., & Nichols, N. (1942). Optimum Settings for Automatic Controllers, *Transactions of ASME, 64*, 759-768.

KEY TERMS AND DEFINITIONS

Anti-Windup for PI Controller: When the integral part is included in a PI controller, an anti-windup method must be considered and implemented. Integral windup refers to the phenomena where the discrepancy between the PI controller command and the actuator output due to the limit on the actuator output, causes the integrator output to grow large and stay beyond the physical limits of the actuator. Windup can cause large overshoot, oscillations or instability. The back-calculation (also known as external-reset feedback) technique is used to avoid integral windup.

Closed Loop Test: Testing with the feedback control in place regulating the process variables. A closed loop test is usually carried out after controller is developed and tuned. Closed loop test results are used to verify the control performance against its requirements.

FOPTD: First-Order-Plus-Time-Delay Dynamics (also call FOPDT, First-Order-Plus-Dead-Time). The transient response of a system with FOPTD dynamics to a step input is a transport delay followed by a monotonous, exponential rise/decay towards its new operating point. FOPTD dynamics is represented in transfer function, $G_p(s) = \dfrac{K}{Ts+1} e^{-Ls}$, where K is the process gain, T is the process time constant, and L is the time delay.

Kp: Proportional gain in PI controller. The bigger the gain, the more aggressive the actuator movement is.

Open Loop Test: Testing with directly changing the system actuators as opposed to using feedback (closed loop) control (e.g., with a PID). Open loop test is usually carried out ahead of controls algorithm design to understand the operating envelope and the dynamic behavior of the system. Open loop test results are used for model verification, controller design and tuning.

Overshoot: The maximum amount the closed loop system overshoots its final value divided by its final value for a step response, often expressed as a percentage.

Peak Time: The time it takes for the closed loop system to reach the maximum overshoot point.

PI Controller: Proportional-Integral Controller. A PI controller is represented in transfer function, $C(s) = K_p(1 + \dfrac{1}{T_i s})$. Kp is the proportional gain, and Kp/Ti is the integral gain. The proportional part makes the movement of the actuator proportional to the response error (how far away the controlled response is from its set point). The integral part makes the movement of the actuator proportional to the accumulated (integral) response error.

Rise Time: The time it takes for the closed loop system to reach the vicinity of its new set point.

Set Point: The desired process output (reference) that a control system will aim to reach.

Settling Time: The time it takes for the closed loop system to enter and stay in a prescribed band around the new set point for a set point change.

SOPTD: Second-Order-Plus-Time-Delay Dynamics (also call SOPDT, Second-Order-Plus-Dead-Time). The transient response of a SOPTD system to a step input is a transport delay followed by a decaying/rising oscillation towards its new operating point. SOPTD dynamics is represented in transfer function, $G_p(s) = \dfrac{K}{(T_1 s + 1)(T_2 s + 1)} e^{-Ls}$, where K is the process gain, $T1$ and $T2$ are the time constants, and L is the time delay. In time domain, $T1 > T2$ and is referred to as the dominant/slow time constant.

Step Response: For open loop test, the step response refers to the response of the sensor reading upon a step change of the actuator. For closed loop test, the step response refers to the response of the actuator and the sensor reading after a step change of the reference input. Step test can be used for either open loop test or closed loop test: in open loop test, the step change is introduced to the input to the unit (example, change the indoor fan speed from 30% to 50%). In closed loop test, the step change is introduced to either the disturbance to the system (such as cooling load) or the set point that the PI controller is regulating to (such as supply air temperature set point).

Step Response Test: A test for obtaining the step response. It has the following steps: 1) get the system under test to reach a steady state condition under fixed inputs; 2) change one input to the system to a different set point value; 3) wait till the system goes through the transience and reaches its new steady state condition.

Ti: Integral time in PI controller. The longer the integral time, the slower the feedback error is accumulated, the more sluggish the controlled response is.

Transfer Function: A mathematical representation of system dynamics in the Laplace or s-domain (as opposed to the time-domain).

Ts: Control update interval for PI(D) controller – this refers to the time interval at which the PI(D) controller output gets updated.

Chapter 5
Control Algorithm Development:
A Real Control Problem Example

INTRODUCTION

In this chapter, we will show a real life control design example. This real motion control example covers several steps of the entire control algorithm development process from the beginning to the end. This problem is to control the scan speeds of a scanner in a multifunction printer. A low quality, cheap direct current (DC) motor is used to move the scan bar. The reason for using this low quality motor is cost savings as it is common for product development. For higher scan resolutions, the scan speeds are very low. At these low scan speeds, disturbances due to torque ripples and friction in the motor begin to have a major impact on the speed response and disturbance rejection becomes challenging. To begin with the control algorithm design, we need a model of the plant or the dynamic system under control. Modelling is the first step of control design. Physics based models can be developed such as nonlinear or linear differential equations. In industrial control development, usually simple low order models at some operating points of the product are derived for control algorithm design and simulation in the design phase. If it is too difficult or too expensive to build a physics based model, system identification methods can be applied to identify a model from data. We will begin the example with an approach to identify motor parameters using a speed step test data. A disturbance observer design is presented to show how

DOI: 10.4018/978-1-5225-2303-1.ch005

disturbance can be estimated based on an observer using state space control techniques. This disturbance estimator in effect introduces notch filter actions at disturbance natural frequencies, where notch filter is a familiar method used by industrial engineers to deal with resonances in motion control. An online disturbance estimation and feedforward compensation scheme is also given after this, showing a simple and effective way to attenuate disturbances. This idea is extended in a combined feedforward and feedback implementation of disturbance estimation and compensation, which is the solution for the speed regulation problem we considered here. At the end, it is shown how we can identify the drive mechanism dynamics which also affects the speed response of the scan bar, and how including this drive dynamics can further improve the closed-loop control speed performance at the scan bar.

All approaches presented were developed by the author while working on scanner speed control problem. System identification, physical modeling, algorithm design, rapid prototyping and experimental testing were applied to develop the control solutions. This example shows that many skills are required for developing a successful control algorithm. It is hoped that this real control problem example gives readers some insight on how to solve a real world control problem and benefits their learning and careers.

SYSTEM IDENTIFICATION

DC motors have wide applications in industrial control systems because they are easy to control and model. For analytical control system design and optimization, sometimes, a precise model of the DC motor used in a control system may be needed. In this case, the values of the motor parameters given in the motor specifications for reference, usually provided by the motor manufacturer may not be considered precise enough, especially for cheaper DC motors which tend to have relatively large tolerances in their electrical and mechanical parameters. General system identification methods proposed by Ljung (1999), Unbehauen and Rao (1998), Franklin, Powell, and Workman (1990), Basilio and Moreira (2004) can be alied to DC motor model identification. In particular, various methods have been applied to DC motor parameter identification, i.e., Mamani, Becedas, Sira-Ramirez, and Feliu-Batlle (2007), Mamani, Becedas, and Feliu-Batlle (2008), used the algebraic identification method, Krneta, Antic, and Stojanoviv (2005) used the recursive least square method, Hadef and Mekideche (2009) applied the inverse theory, Ruderman, Krettek, Hoffman, and Betran (2008) used the least square method, Hadef, Bourouina, and Mekideche (2009) applied the moments method. Identified DC motor models are often subsequently used for controller design and/or optimization, e.g. Ruderman, Krettek, Hoffman, and Betran (2008), Rubaai and Kotaru (2000), Mamani, Becedas, and Feliu-Batlle (2008).

Without expensive testing apparatus and a long testing cycle, a quick and effective system identification approach based on the motor input and output is desirable and valuable, especially for the field applications and quick controller prototyping. In this section, a DC motor parameter identification approach based on the Taylor series expansion of the motor speed response under a constant voltage input is presented (Wu, 2012). The relationships between the motor parameters and the coefficients of the Taylor series are established. In the implementation, the motor speed response under a constant voltage is sampled, then curve fit the samples to obtain the coefficients of power terms in the Taylor series. Then, the DC motor mechanical and electrical time constants, Back-emf and the friction can be computed using these coefficients. With the knowledge of these parameters, a precise motor model is obtained for the subsequent controller design.

For application point of view, this approach requires only a speed/position sensor, such as an optical encoder, and a voltage power supply, no current measurement is needed and the motor is run in open loop, thus it is practical and cost effective. The curve fitting can be performed using many existing methods, such as the least square method, and these optimization methods are widely available in commercial computing packages such as MATLAB and LabVIEW.

Identification Algorithms

Consider the DC motor governing equations given below

$$L\frac{di}{dt} + iR + k_b\omega = V,$$

$$J\frac{d\omega}{dt} = k_t i + T_d, \tag{1}$$

where ω is the motor angular speed, V. is the motor terminal voltage, i is the winding current, k_b is the back-EMF constant of the motor, k_t is the torque constant, R is the terminal resistance, L is the terminal inductance, J is the motor and reflected load inertia, and T_d is the disturbance torque acting on the motor. T_d is a combination of the cogging torque, T_{cog}, the kinetic friction, T_f, and the viscous friction(viscous damping force)

$$T_d = T_{cog} + T_f + c\dot{\omega}, \tag{2}$$

where c is the viscous damping coefficient.

According to Equations 1 and 2, the velocity response in the Laplace domain is

$$\omega(s) = \frac{1/k_b}{t_m t_e s^2 + t_m s + 1} V(s) + \frac{1/J(t_e s + 1)t_m}{t_m t_e s^2 + t_m s + 1} T_d(s), \tag{3}$$

where $t_e = L/R$ is the electrical time constant, $t_m = RJ/k_t k_b$ is the mechanical time constant, and s is the Laplace variable.

Based on these equations, we would like to know motor parameters t_m, t_e, T_d, J, and so forth, by measuring the velocity response under a known, controlled voltage input. Let us consider two distinct application situations: The first situation is that the disturbance torque is negligible; while in the second one, the disturbance torque is relatively large and needs to be considered.

Estimation Without the Disturbance Torque

When the speed response part due to voltage input dominates, e.g. the input voltage is large, we can ignore the effect of the disturbance torque on the speed response, see Equation 4. In this case, we can consider the following DC motor model

$$\frac{\omega(s)}{V(s)} = \frac{1/k_b}{t_m t_e s^2 + t_m s + 1}, \tag{4}$$

The transfer function can be factorized into

$$\frac{\omega(s)}{V(s)} = \frac{1/k_b}{t_m t_e (s+a)(s+b)},$$

(5)

With roots

$$a, b = \frac{1 \mp \sqrt{1 - 4t_e / t_m}}{2t_e}.$$

(6)

Usually the mechanical time constant, t_m, is much bigger than the electrical time constant t_e, so we assume here that there are two distinct real roots; that is the following condition holds $t_m > 4t_e$.

For a constant voltage input V_0, the Laplace transform is $V(s) = V_0/s$, and the motor speed response in the Laplace domain is

$$\omega(s) = \frac{V_0/k_b}{t_m t_e s (s+a)(s+b)} = \frac{\alpha_1}{s} + \frac{\alpha_2}{s+a} + \frac{\alpha_3}{s+b}$$

(7)

with constants

$$\alpha_1 = \frac{V_0}{k_b}, \qquad \alpha_2 = \frac{V_0}{k_b}\frac{b}{a-b}, \qquad \alpha_3 = \frac{V_0}{k_b}\frac{a}{b-a}.$$

(8)

Let us consider the three terms in the step response in Equation 7 one at a time. α_1/s is a step function in the time domain, both $\alpha_2/(s+a)$ and $\alpha_3/(s+b)$ are exponential functions in the time domain and can be expanded using Taylor series. First expand the term $\alpha_2/(s+a)$, we get

$$\frac{V_0}{k_b}\frac{b}{a-b}\left(1 - at + \frac{1}{2}a^2 t^2 - \frac{1}{6}a^3 t^3 + \dots\right).$$

(9)

Then expand the term $\alpha_3/(s+b)$, we get

$$\frac{V_0}{k_b}\frac{a}{b-a}\left(1 - bt + \frac{1}{2}b^2 t^2 - \frac{1}{6}b^3 t^3 + \dots\right).$$

(10)

When we combine the three terms together, we have the total speed response in the time domain

$$\omega(t) = \frac{V_0}{k_b}\left(\frac{1}{2}\beta_0 t^2 + \frac{1}{6}\beta_1 t^3 + \frac{1}{24}\beta_2 t^4 + \cdots\right) \tag{11}$$

where $\beta_0 = ab, \beta_1 = -ab(a+b),$ and $\beta_2 = ab(a^2 + ab + b^2).$

According to Equation 6

$$ab = \frac{1}{t_m t_e}, \qquad a + b = \frac{1}{t_e}. \tag{12}$$

Thus, we have

$$t_m = -\frac{\beta_1}{\beta_0^2}, \qquad t_e = -\frac{\beta_0}{\beta_1} \tag{13}$$

The above equation allows us to calculate the mechanical and electrical time constants t_m and t_e using the coefficients of the power series in Equation 11. These coefficients can be obtained by curve fitting the motor speed step response data using power functions during data analysis.

Estimation With the Disturbance Torque

We now consider the situation that the disturbance torque on the DC motor is not negligible. The disturbance transfer function is

$$\frac{\omega(s)}{T_d(s)} = \frac{(1/J)t_m(t_e s + 1)}{t_m t_e s^2 + t_m s + 1}. \tag{14}$$

Disturbance torque in general consists of the cogging torque and the friction torque. The cogging torque is quite complicated and is not addressed here. Both the kinetic friction and viscous friction are considered and they are assumed to be constant on average for a constant motor speed.

Given a constant motor terminal voltage $V(s)=V_0/s$ and a constant disturbance torque (ignore the cogging torque or consider the average cogging torque effect on speed over one revolution is zero) $T_d(s)=T_0/s$, the total speed response is

$$\omega(s) = \frac{1/k_b}{t_m t_e(s+a)(s+b)} \frac{V_0}{s} + \frac{(1/J)t_m(t_e s + 1)}{t_m t_e(s+a)(s+b)} \frac{T_d}{s}.$$
(15)

As for the previous case, applying the partial fraction expansion of the step response in the Laplace domain in Equation 15, then expanding the exponential terms in the time domain using Taylor series, we obtain the total step response in the time domain

$$\omega(t) = \beta_0 t + \beta_1 t^2 - \beta_2 t^3 + \beta_3 t^4 - \dots$$
(16)

Coefficients in Equation 16 are as follows

$$\beta_0 = \frac{T_0}{J}$$

$$\beta_1 = \frac{1}{2}\frac{V_0}{k_b} ab$$

$$\beta_2 = \frac{1}{6}\left[\frac{V_0}{k_b} ab(a+b) - \frac{T_0}{J}(a^2 + ab + b^2) + \frac{T_0}{J} ab(a+b)t_m\right]$$

$$\beta_3 = \frac{1}{24}\left[\frac{V_0}{k_b} ab(a^2 + ab + b^2) - \frac{T_0}{J}(a^3 + a^2 b + ab^2 + b^3) + \frac{T_0}{J} ab(a^2 + ab + b^2)t_m\right]$$
(17)

Based on these coefficients, we have

$$ab = \frac{18\beta_2^2 - 24\beta_1\beta_3}{3\beta_0\beta_2 + 2\beta_1^2}, \qquad a+b = \frac{6\beta_2 - \beta_0 ab}{2\beta_1},$$
(18)

and another equation for $a+b$,

$$a + b = \frac{12\beta_3 + \beta_1 ab}{2\beta_2}. \tag{19}$$

Based on equations 12 and 17, we can express the motor parameters as

$$t_m = \frac{a+b}{ab}, \quad t_e = \frac{1}{a+b}, \quad \frac{T_0}{J} = \beta_0, \quad k_b = \frac{ab}{2\beta_1} V_0. \tag{20}$$

In practice, fit the measured motor speed step response using power functions according to Equation 16 to get the coefficients β_0, β_1, β_2, β_3, then calculate the motor parameters using Equations 19 and 20.other relationship useful for checking the algorithm is based on the steady state response of Equation 15, expressed by the following equation

$$\frac{V_0}{k_b} + \beta_0 t_m = \omega_{ss}, \tag{21}$$

where ω_{ss} is the motor steady state angular speed.

Implementation and Results

The proposed approaches were first applied to a Mabuchi RK370CA motor, then a Mabuchi FC130 motor. To implement the algorithms, a LabVIEW program was written to send voltage command to a pulse width modulated (PWM) motor drive and receive the output signal of an optical encoder with quadrature digital outputs mounted on the motor shaft. The determinism of sampling was assured by using the LabVIEW real-time module. And, a National Instrument (NI) LabVIEW FPGA (field programmable gate array) card was utilized to process the digital quadrature encoder signals to obtain the motor speed and to control the motor PWM drive.

Values of the motor parameters given in the motor specifications provided by motor manufacturer for reference are presented in Table 1.

Note that the Back-emf and torque constant are not equal (although it should be theoretically). Terminal resistance and torque constant have a large varying range, making parameter identification important for modeling

Table 1. RK370CA motor parameter values

Parameters	Value	Unit
Terminal resistance	17 ± 15%	Ω
Terminal inductance	N/A	Henry
Torque constant	18.3 ± 18%	mNm/A
Mass moment of inertia	9.0	gcm²
Back electromotive force	0.0233	Volt/(rad/sec)

in this case. Inductance value is not given and was measured in the lab. as 20.25 Henry. The resistance was measured as 16.4Ω. Thus we calculated the electrical time constant $t_e = L/R = 0.00122$sec.

First, apply the algorithm for no disturbance torque. To apply this algorithm, the speed response part due to the voltage input is assumed to dominate. To meet this condition, e.g. the speed variation in the steady state is small compared to the average steady state speed, we sent a large voltage to the motor drive, V=20 volt. Next, we apply the approach for disturbance torque. The disturbance, that is, frictions, effects on the speed response are significant when the input voltage is small. To demonstrate the effectiveness of the algorithm, we sent two voltages, 2 volt and 10 volt, to the motor. Driving the motor at two different voltage levels can demonstrate that the viscous friction varies with the speed, also allow us to calculate the viscous damping coefficient of the motor.

Usually the electrical time constant t_e is very small compared to the mechanical time constant t_m, that is they are on different time scales, a good estimate of both t_e and t_m at the same time is difficult. Because t_m is usually much larger than t_e, t_m and t_e were estimated separately using different data collected with different sample rates and different time durations. For estimating t_m, the motor speed in both the transient state and the steady state was sampled at 1kHz for one second; for estimating t_e, the motor speed in the transient phase was sampled at 8kHz for 200 msec, since the electrical time constant affects the transient response, not the steady state response. In each test, the motor was driven multiple times, i.e. 10 times, and the estimated parameter values were averaged to obtain the final value.

Results are summarized in Table 2. Column two gives the values estimated using the algorithm for no disturbance, and column three gives the values obtained using the algorithm considering disturbance, values in the fourth column are computed using values from Table 1. Note R=17Ω, J=9gcm²,

Table 2. RK370CA test results

Parameter	w/o dist. 20v	w/dist. 2v/10v	Spec. (meas.)	Unit
k_t	0.0238	0.0207/0.0169	18.3 ± 18%	Nm/A
t_m	0.0407	0.0211/0.0203	0.0359	sec
t_e	0.00554	0.00122/0.00134	(0.00122)	sec
T_d/J	N/A	10.551/11.576	N/A	Nm/kgm²

k_b = 0.0233volt/(rad/sec). and k_t = 0.0183Nm/A are used to calculate t_m in the fourth column in the table. According to Table 2, the estimates of k_t, t_m and t_e are in good agreement with those given by the motor specifications.

Time responses sampled at 1kHz for 1sec are given in Figure 1, Figure 2, and Figure 3. In these figures, red curves represent the power series resulting from curve fitting the sampled motor speed responses. Compare these figures, it is obvious that the approach accounting for disturbance approximates the measurements much better, because of the existence of the linear term, $\beta_0 t$, in the power series due to the presence of the (average) constant disturbance torque in the motor.

To further demonstrate the effectiveness of the proposed algorithms, we compared to conventional identification approaches. First, we drove the motor using random voltage input (10volts maximum) and measured the motor

Figure 1. Approach considering disturbance under 2 volt input

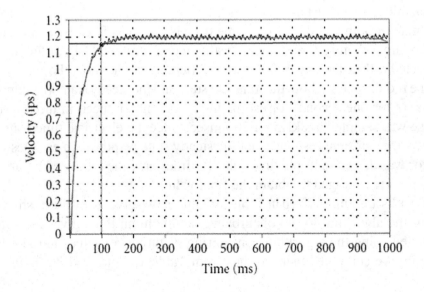

Figure 2. Approach without considering disturbance under 2volt input

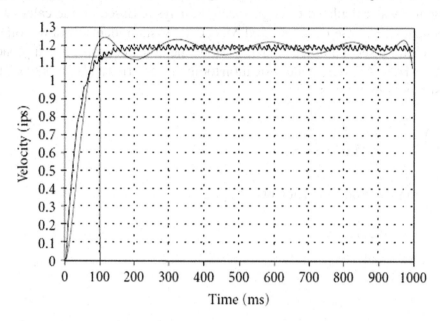

Figure 3. Approach without considering disturbance under 20volt input

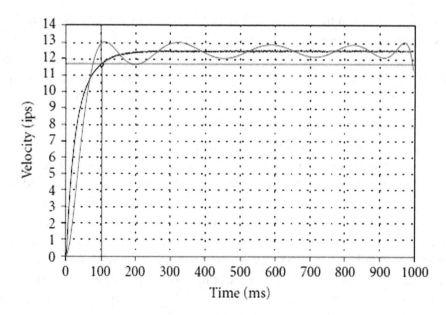

speed at a sampling rate of 10kHz. Then, the motor/drive frequency response function was calculated through spectral analysis. Based on the calculated frequency response data, we used MATLAB system identification toolbox to identify a second order model. Various methods, i.e. subspace approach in the MATLAB system identification toolbox were tried and compared. The best model found was

$$T(s) = \frac{9078}{s^2 + 334.6s + 18860}.$$

Using the model coefficients, we get

$$t_m = 0.0177 \text{sec},$$
$$t_e = 3 \text{msec},$$
$$k_t = 0.031 \text{volt}/(\text{rad}/\text{sec}).$$

These estimates are bad, especially the electrical time constant due to the very small time scale as alluded to earlier. The model identified using conventional approach will not be useful for control design and analysis in this case.

T_0/J can be used to calculate the friction (both kinetic and viscous) if the mass moment of inertia J is known. First, calculate the viscous friction coefficient using the estimated disturbance torques and measured motor steady state angular speeds under two different voltage inputs $c = (T_1 - T_0)/(\omega_1 - \omega_0)$. Then, calculate the dynamic friction, $T_f = T_0 - c\omega_0$. For example, $\omega_0 = 1.21ips$ under 2volt, $\omega_0 = 6.274ips$ under 10volt, J=9.0gcm^2, it renders c=0.0187 mNm/ips.

The number of terms included in the power series for curve fitting the data was determined through trial and error. When disturbance was not considered, twenty five terms were included; when disturbance was considered, including forty terms gave the best results during the experiment. Since the coefficients were calculated using the polynomial curve fitting function from the math library provided inside LabVIEW, it was not difficult and time consuming to try different number of terms. Including more terms does not necessarily improve the parameter estimation accuracy as it was observed in the experiment.

A Mabuchi FC130 motor was tested as well. It is a smaller motor compared to RK370. Good results were obtained again this time, see Table 3. Note the very small t_e in this small motor. The algorithm considering disturbance torque was applied because due to its small size, the disturbance torque cannot be ignored. In the testing, 10Volts was used as the motor drive input. For t_m estimation, the speed response was sampled at 1000Hz for 500 samples, while for t_e estimation, the motor speed response was sampled at 6000Hz for 850 samples. Again, good estimation was achieved by the algorithm.

Summary

A convenient, effective system identification approach is proposed to estimate the DC motor torque constant, mechanical time constant, electrical time constant, and friction. This approach was implemented on two Mabuchi motors, achieving great test results. This approach is implemented in open loop and requires little hardware, only a speed/position sensor and a voltage supply. The estimated motor parameters can be used to verify the DC motor performance against the motor specifications, or be used to build a model of the motor for the subsequent controller design or system optimization. This approach is especially suited to quick field applications.

A COGGING TORQUE COMPENSATING DISTURBANCE ESTIMATOR FOR DC MOTOR SPEED REGULATION: DESIGN AND EXPERIMENTATION

Introduction

DC motors are used in many control applications, because they are easy to model and control. However, cogging exists in DC motors, especially cheap ones. Due to the interaction between the DC motor stator magnet and armature winding, an amount of torque is generated by the magnetic field to hold the rotor at its equilibrium positions. This torque is the cogging torque. When

Table 3. FC130 motor test results

Parameter	w/dist.	Spec.	Unit
k_t	0.0137	$0.0127 \pm 10\%$	Nm/A
k_m	0.0208	0.024	sec
k_e	0.251	0.214	msec

a DC motors is used as the actuator in a control system, the cogging torque causes the torque ripples and subsequently the speed ripples in the system speed response, which may not be acceptable for some applications, especially for certain low speed regulation applications. The amount of cogging torque in a DC motor can be reduced or eliminated using better manufacturing techniques such as the skewed lamination armature described by Tatsuya & Takashi (1998), which increase the cost of the motor, or the cogging torque effect can be compensated using control techniques such as the feedforward control in Chung and Kang (2005), Kramer (2007), or the input and output based estimation in Nuninger, Balaud, and Kratz (1997).

A speed feedback control system was studied in this section. This system uses a DC motor as the actuator to move a linear load, a contact imaging sensor (CIS) through a transmission mechanism composed of gear, belt and pulley. The feedback control loop was closed using a proportional and integral (PI) controller. The speed of the linear load was the controlled variable, and the DC motor terminal voltage was the control variable. An optical digital encoder assembly mounted on the motor shaft was used as the speed sensor. The system operated at a range of speeds, and the system performance at low speeds such as 0.04 inch per second (ips) was especially critical. Speed ripples occurred in the speed output under constant speed commands. The speed ripples were largely attributed to the DC motor cogging torque. In this study, a feedback disturbance rejection scheme was used to attenuate the cogging torque effect. The scheme was presented by Wu (2009a). It was assumed that the cogging torque was equivalent to an input disturbance to the DC motor, or its effect can be caused by an equivalent disturbance at the motor input. An input disturbance estimator was designed to approximate this equivalent input disturbance. The estimated input disturbance was consequently used to counteract the cogging torque. The section is organized as follows. The disturbance estimator design is presented first. Experimental results are presented next. Finally, conclusions are given.

Input Disturbance Estimator Design

Consider the feedback system in Figure 4, where v_r is the reference speed or speed command, u is the controller output, and v is the speed output. The DC motor is driven by a pulse-width-modulation (PWM) motor driver, the PI controller output is the input of the PWM motor driver. The speed is detected by a digital encoder with the encoder wheel mounted on the motor shaft.

Figure 4. PI Controller speed feedback loop

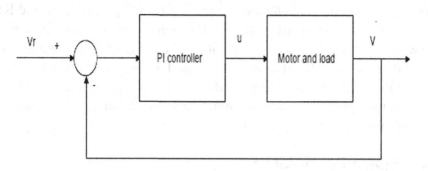

The plant of this control system is the combination of the PWM driver, the motor and the load. The linear speed of the load is the controlled variable, which is related to the motor shaft rotary speed through a gear ratio. When the speed reference is constant, there exists a periodic variation in the closed loop speed response. This periodic speed variation is largely due to the motor cogging torque. In this case, the cogging torque is considered as periodic and its period can be determined by the reference speed, the number of motor stator poles and the number of motor armature teeth. Since the existing PI controller is not effective in regulating the speed in the presence of this periodic cogging torque, an input disturbance estimator is augmented to the PI controller to suppress the cogging torque (Figure 5). The cogging torque is considered as a disturbance to the feedback system. Instead of modeling the cogging torque directly as in the feedforward approaches Chung and Kang (2005), Kramer(2007), the equivalent input disturbance estimation is applied

Figure 5. PI Controller speed feedback loop with the disturbance estimator

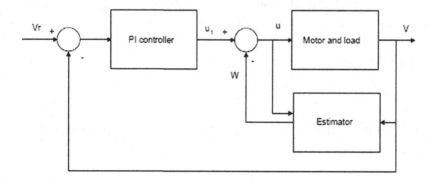

Franklin, Powell, and Emami-Naeimi (1994), Alvarez-Ramirez, Femat, and Barreiro (1997), She and Ohyama (2002), and Nuninger, Balaud, and Kratz (1997). As far as the steady state speed response is concerned, the cogging torque can be considered as equivalent to an input disturbance which enters the plant at the same point as the control and has the same dynamics as the cogging torque. In this specific speed control application, good steady state speed regulation is the goal. So applying input disturbance estimator for cogging torque attenuation is valid.

State Space Formulation

Suppose the plant is governed by the following state equations

$$
\begin{aligned}
\dot{x} &= Fx + Gu + G_1 w_1, \\
v &= Hx + J_1 w_1,
\end{aligned}
\tag{22}
$$

where x is the state vector, v is the linear speed of the load, u is the control input, and w_1 is the cogging torque, which is assumed to be periodic when the reference speed is constant. Assume the cogging torque satisfies the following equation

$$
\ddot{w}_1 + \omega^2 w_1 = 0,
\tag{23}
$$

where ω is the fundamental frequency of the cogging torque, which can be determined by measuring variations of the closed loop speed response. The above equation can be extended to consider the second and the third harmonics of the cogging torque and so on, to achieve better cogging torque rejection. See Appendix A for formula when including the second harmonic. Assume there is an input equivalent disturbance w that satisfies the same equation as w_1, Equation 23, we can replace Equation 22 with

$$
\begin{aligned}
\dot{x} &= Fx + G(u + w), \\
v &= Hx,
\end{aligned}
\tag{24}
$$

Note that in the above state equation we assume $G = w_1$, and in the output equation we assume $J_1 = 0$.

If we can estimate this equivalent disturbance, we can subtract the equivalent disturbance from the control signal to cancel out the cogging torque effects on the speed in the steady state. Combine Equation 23 and Equation 24 into a state space description to get

$$\dot{z} = Az + Bu,$$
$$v = Cz,$$

(25)

where the new state vector is $z = \begin{bmatrix} w & \dot{w} & x^T \end{bmatrix}^T$. The state, input and output matrices are

$$A = \begin{bmatrix} 0 & 1 & 0 \\ -\omega^2 & 0 & 0 \\ G & \underline{0} & F \end{bmatrix}, \quad B = \begin{bmatrix} 0 \\ 0 \\ G \end{bmatrix}, \quad C = \begin{bmatrix} 0 & 0 & H \end{bmatrix}.$$

(26)

when considering both the first and the second harmonics of the cogging torque, we have the following disturbance equation

$$\frac{d^4 w_1}{dt^4} + \left(\omega_1^2 + \omega_2^2 \right) \ddot{w}_1 + \omega_1^2 \omega_2^2 w_1 = 0,$$

(27)

where ω_1 is the first harmonic frequency and $\omega_2 = 2\omega_1$ is the second harmonic frequency. In the combined state space equations for the plant and the disturbance, Equation 25, the state vector is

$$z = \begin{bmatrix} w & \dot{w} & \ddot{w} & \omega & x^T \end{bmatrix}^T,$$

(28)

and the matrices are

$$A = \begin{bmatrix} 0 & 1 & 0 & 0 & 0 \\ 0 & 0 & 1 & 0 & 0 \\ 0 & 0 & 0 & 0 & 1 \\ -4\omega_1^4 & 0 & -5\omega_1^4 & 0 & 0 \\ G & \underline{0} & \underline{0} & \underline{0} & F \end{bmatrix}, \quad B = \begin{bmatrix} 0 \\ 0 \\ 0 \\ 0 \\ G \end{bmatrix}, \quad C = \begin{bmatrix} 0 & 0 & 0 & 0 & H \end{bmatrix}.$$

(29)

193

If F and G are observable and if the plant does not have a zero that is also a root of Equation 23, which prevents the input disturbance to appear in the output, then the system in Equation 25 will be observable and an estimator or observer can be constructed to estimate both the state of the plant and the disturbance w. The estimator equation is in a standard form

$$\dot{\hat{z}} = A\hat{z} + Bu + L\left(v - C\hat{z}\right),$$
$$\hat{w} = C_1\hat{z}, \tag{30}$$

where $C_1 = \begin{bmatrix} 1 & 0 \end{bmatrix}$, L is the estimator gain matrix, $\hat{z}$ and $\hat{w}$ are estimates of augmented state vector z and equivalent input disturbance w.

The control including the estimated cogging torque is

$$u = u_1 - F_r\hat{w}, \tag{31}$$

where u_1 is the PI controller output, and F_r is the robustness filter. As it will be presented in the next section, if we directly combine the disturbance estimate with the PI control, $u = u_1 - \hat{w}$, the stability robustness of the closed loop is degraded significantly, especially at mid and high frequencies where a larger amount of uncertainty is usually assumed to occur. The robustness filter F_r is introduced to deal with this issue. F_r is shaped in the frequency domain based on the dynamics of the expected disturbance and the associated uncertainty of the plant, e.g. it could be a low-pass or band-pass filter.

Robustness and Performance Analysis

With the addition of the disturbance estimator, the closed-loop system is more capable of rejecting the disturbances both at the plant input and at the plant output; meanwhile, the impact on stability robustness of the closed loop system can be minimized through shaping filter F_r.

Stability Robustness

For stability analysis, consider the plant additive uncertainty, $P' = P + \Delta$, where P' is the true plant model, P is the nominal plant model, and Δ is the perturbation. Consider the transfer function seen by the perturbation Δ, in another word connected to it, T_r. Without the estimator and filter,

$$T_r = -\frac{G_1}{1+G_1P} \tag{32}$$

where G_1 is the PI controller transfer function. With the estimator and filter,

$$T_r = -\frac{G_1 + F_r G_3}{1+G_1P + F_r G_2 + F_r G_3 P} \tag{33}$$

and G_2 and G_3 are estimator transfer functions such that $\hat{w} = G_2 u + G_3 v$. These transfer functions are given as follows

$$\begin{aligned} G_1\left(s\right) &= k_p + k_i s, \\ G_2\left(s\right) &= C_1\left(Is - A + LC\right)^{-1} B, \\ G_3\left(s\right) &= C_1\left(Is - A + LC\right)^{-1} L, \\ &\text{where}\, \hat{w} = C_1 \hat{z} \end{aligned} \tag{34}$$

It shows that T_r varies with F_r. When there is no filtering, that is $F_r=1$, T_r can be much larger in the mid-to-high frequency range, which means the allowable perturbation in the feedback loop is much less with the estimator. When F_r is properly designed, such as a low-pass filter, T_r is not affected at mid to high frequency range, which means the preservation of the robustness property of the existing loop. The impact of F_r on robustness is presented in the example section.

Reference Tracking

The estimator does not affect the reference tracking of the closed-loop. With the estimator, the equivalent controller of the estimator in the feedforward path for tracking is

$$G_{eq} = \frac{1}{1 + F_r G_2 + F_r G_3 P}$$

which is practically unity.

Disturbance Rejection

Here, we examine the disturbance rejection performance of the closed loop including the disturbance estimator.

Without the estimator the input disturbance transfer function is

$$v = \frac{P}{1 + PG_1} w \tag{35}$$

w is the input disturbance; with the estimator and the filter, the input disturbance transfer function is

$$v = \frac{P}{1 + \dfrac{F_r G_3 + G_1}{1 + F_r G_2} P} w \tag{36}$$

When $F_r = 1$, the inclusion of the estimator creates notches at the cogging torque fundamental frequencies according to the sensitivity function Equation 36, which is demonstrated in the example. When F_r is included and not equal to 1, the effectiveness of disturbance rejection is compromised to a certain extent for preserving the robust stability, which is expected.

Implementation and Results

Setup of the Experiment

The estimator design was digitally implemented and experimentally verified. The experimental system used a Mabuchi RK370CA motor whose parameters given in the motor specifications are presented in Table 1. RK370CA motor parameter values1. The same motor was used for motor parameter identification earlier to obtain the motor model. The digital controller which was implemented in LabVIEW, interfaced with a PWM driver circuitry and a digital optical encoder quadrature signals with 448x4 quadrature counts per revolution (cpr) through a National Instrument digital FPGA card. This FPGA card have multiple digital input/output channels, digital-to-analog converters (DAC) and analog-to-digital converters (ADC), hardware clock and counters, and configurable gates. The speed calculation from the encoder quadrature signals and the controllers (PI and PI with estimator) were programmed in LabVIEW using the LabVIEW real time module and the LabVIEW FPGA module. The control loop was updated every millisecond. PI controller has the proportional gain K_p=10volt/ips, and the integral gain K_I=500volt/in.

Design and Results

To design the estimator, a linear plant model was needed for Equation 22. The plant was excited by a random voltage to the PWM driver, the corresponding speed response was collected. The plant transfer function was calculated by spectrum analysis, shown in Figure 6. Based on this experimental transfer function, a linear model is obtained

$$P(s) = \frac{-2.73(s - 4540)}{(s + 73.95)(s + 430.6)}. \tag{37}$$

Note that the parameter identification algorithms introduced earlier in the chapter can also be applied to obtain a model. Realization of the transfer function Equation 37 gives the matrices in the state space model

$$F = \begin{bmatrix} -31.64 & -1291.5 \\ 13.07 & -472.93 \end{bmatrix}, \quad G = \begin{bmatrix} -11.62 \\ 12.62 \end{bmatrix}, \quad H = \begin{bmatrix} -0.578 & -0.749 \end{bmatrix}. \tag{38}$$

The cogging torque period was determined by measuring the speed response under a constant reference speed. The speed ripple has the same period as the torque ripple. Theoretically, this period can be calculated using the constant reference speed, the number of armature teeth and the number of magnetic poles. In reality, this period is different due to imperfection in motor manufacturing according to Tatsuya and Takashi (1998). The measured period is twice the calculated period. Figure 7 shows the frequency content of the speed response when the reference speed is 0.04ips. It shows that the fundamental frequency ω is 8.08 rad/sec or 1.29Hz, while the theoretical frequency is 16.16 rad/sec or 2.58Hz.

First, we designed the first estimator considering the first harmonic of the cogging torque, where ω_1=1.29Hz. The estimator gain was designed such that the estimator poles are three times faster than the dominant closed loop poles, which is indicated by the PI open loop bandwidth $\omega_b \cong 210 \text{rad/sec}$.

Figure 6. Plant transfer functions

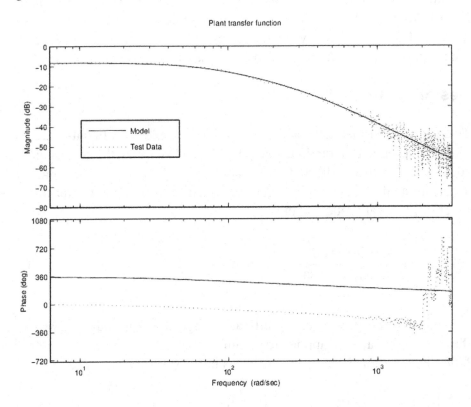

The four estimator poles are 600, 620, 640, 660 respectively. Then, the second estimator considering both the first and the second harmonic of the cogging torque was designed accordingly, where $\omega_1 = 1.29$Hz and $\omega_2 = 2.58$Hz. The estimated disturbance was filtered before being fed into the plant, because we do not want estimated disturbance to excite the plant at high frequencies. F_r was implemented as a digital low-pass Butterworth filter using a LabVIEW filter function. The pass band is chosen at 5Hz and the stop band at 8Hz for both estimators.

The control loop performance was tested using the reference speed $v_r = 0.04$ips. In the time domain, the standard deviation in ips of the speed response for the PI controller is 0.0078ips; while with the estimator, 0.0053ips. A 32% improvement in terms of speed variation was achieved. The performance improvement is more evident in the frequency domain. Figure 7 shows the frequency components of the speed responses of the PI controller and the PI controller with the estimators, respectively. It is clear the speed ripples due to the DC motor cogging torque had been significantly reduced by the

Figure 7. Frequency content of the speed responses

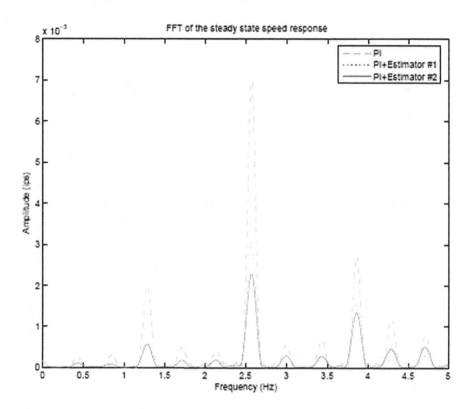

estimators with the second estimator being more effective by reducing the second harmonics of the speed response. The first estimator introduces a notch filter (see the sensitivity function Equation 36) at the cogging torque fundamental frequency to reject the cogging torque, Figure 8. while the second estimator introduces two notches at both the cogging torque first and second harmonic frequencies(Figure 9). In both Figure 8 and Figure 9, $F_r=1$, and the identified plant model was used to create the plots. The purpose of Figure 8 and Figure 9 is to show the notch action created by the disturbance estimators. When robust filter is introduced, the notch filter effect is reduced as a compromise for stability.

The estimator design is model based. The mismatch between the model and the real plant may cause instability and performance degradation. For plant additive uncertainty, T_r is considered in the analysis. As shown in Figure 10, the stability robustness level is largely reduced in the mid-to-high frequency range with the estimator without filtering. But, with the filter F_r proposed for the estimator, the stability robustness of the existing loop is basically

Figure 8. Input sensitivity functions with the first estimator

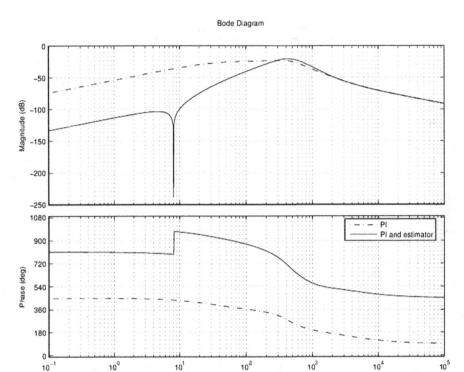

Bode Diagram

preserved by the augmented estimator loop. To test the performance robustness of this estimator, the same estimator was augmented to another unit of the same kind. Reference speed was 0.04ips again. The standard deviations of the speed responses are 0.0088ips with the PI controller and 0.0053ips with the PI and the estimator. A 40% improvement was obtained in this case. A better performance was achieved again. So it experimentally demonstrated the robustness of this scheme.

Because the period of the speed ripples is related to the reference speeds for a given DC motor, if the disturbance rejection is needed for several operating speeds, then a corresponding estimator is designed for each speed. We considered one speed in the implementation.

Summary

A disturbance estimator was designed and implemented for an existing PI speed control system to improve the speed regulation at the steady state.

Figure 9. Input sensitivity functions with the second estimator

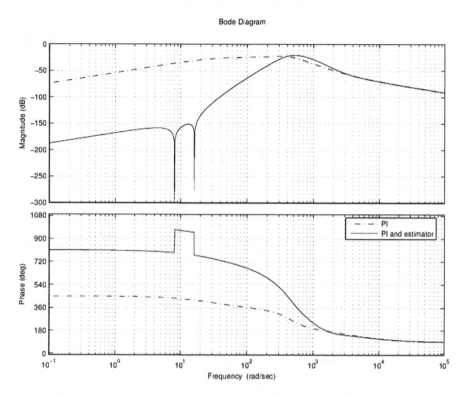

In this application, the low speed regulation is very critical. The DC motor cogging torque, especially that of a cheap motor, can cause a large amount of speed variation which is unacceptable for this application. From a disturbance rejection point of view, there exists a plant input disturbance equivalent to the motor cogging torque. When regulating the speed around a constant reference speed, an input disturbance estimator was designed. The combined PI and estimator design proves to be effective in regulating the speed by rejecting the DC motor cogging torque. Experimental results demonstrated the design and the effectiveness of the estimator. The stability robustness and performance robustness of this disturbance rejection scheme are also analyzed and experimentally proved.

Figure 10. Bode plot of Tr

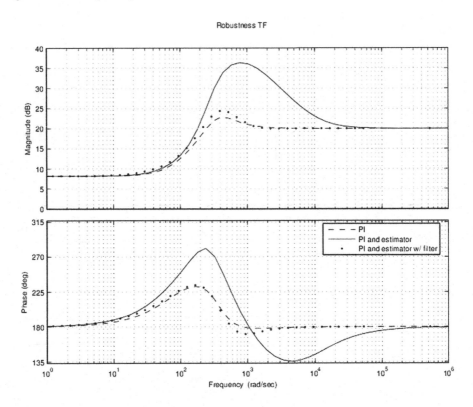

Robustness TF

DC MOTOR SPEED CONTROL IMPROVEMENT VIA ON-LINE DISTURBANCE COMPUTATION AND COMPENSATION

Introduction

DC motors are widely used in industrial control systems because they are well understood and easy to control. Usually, the cogging torque, commutation torque, and friction exist in DC motors, causing torque ripples in the motor output torque. For cost reduction reasons, cheaper DC motors are used in a lot of commercial products. For cheap DC motors, these disturbance torques can be quite large, causing performance issues, e.g. speed ripples as we already see earlier in this chapter. Usually, the closed and/or open-loop controls are used to suppress the disturbances, for example, we already discussed using a disturbance estimator for disturbance torque estimation and attenuation. In speed regulation, conventional industrial proportional, integral, and derivative (PID) controllers may not be very effective in eliminating the speed ripples, due to the periodic nature of the disturbance torque. In this case, the disturbance compensation is desirable. A feed-forward approach is to compute the disturbances off-line, then save them in a look-up table. Each time the control loop is updated, the controller output is calculated based on a value in the look-up table. This approach needs a large amount of memory space, and it needs information of the absolute position of the motor shaft because the disturbance torque could be position dependent, such as the cogging torque. Also, this approach may not be robust due to the large variation in motor parameters from motor to motor, especially for cheaper DC motors.

Here, we consider compensating the torque disturbance in a closed-loop DC motor speed regulation system. In this type of systems with a PID type controller, speed ripples are typically present in the speed outputs, and the performance gets worse at lower speeds. An on-line disturbance compensation scheme is proposed to eliminate the speed ripples at low speeds. This approach is applied readily to any existing DC motor closed or open-loop speed regulation systems. In this approach, first the disturbance torque is computed on-line using the physical model of the DC motor; then, the computed disturbance torque is used on-line to generate the additional motor terminal voltage required to counteract the effect of the disturbance torque on the speed output via a simple control law.

This approach does not require any extra sensing. It needs the information on the motor terminal voltage and the motor speed, which is usually available for a closed-loop speed regulation system. The on-line feature makes it suitable for direct digital implementation. The effectiveness of the approach is demonstrated through experiments. Both the open loop and the closed-loop control case are presented. Experimental results show that the performances were largely improved using the proposed disturbance compensation.

Off-Line Disturbance Computation

Consider the following DC motor physical equations

$$L\frac{di}{dt} + iR + k_b\omega = V,$$

$$J\frac{d\omega}{dt} = k_t i - T_d, \tag{39}$$

where ω is the motor angular speed, V is the motor terminal voltage, i is the winding current, k_b is the back-EMF constant of the motor, k_t is the torque constant, R is the terminal resistance, L is the terminal inductance, J is the motor and reflected load inertia, and T_d is the disturbance torque acting on the motor. T_d is a combination of the cogging torque, T_{cog}, the kinetic friction, T_f, and the viscous friction(viscous damping force).

Discretize the above two differential equations using the backward Euler's method to have the difference equation for the motor winding current

$$i(k) = \left[\frac{L}{\Delta t} + R\right]^{-1}\left[\frac{L}{\Delta t}i(k-1) - k_b\omega(k) + V(k)\right], \tag{40}$$

where Δt is the sample time interval, and k is the step number. The disturbance equation is

$$T_d(k) = k_t i(k) - J\dot\omega(k) \tag{41}$$

In practice, apply a known voltage to the motor at rest, measure the speed of the motor through an optical encoder. Then, the acceleration $\dot\omega(k)$ can be computed using the speed measurement. Then, Equations 40 and 41 are used to computer the disturbance with the following initial condition $\omega(0)=0$ and $i(0)=0$.

Here, motor parameters are assumed known or measured. Otherwise, system identification methods can be applied to obtain the motor parameters as the algorithms we introduced at the beginning of the chapter. The disturbance consists of the cogging torque which is periodical and positon dependent (that is dependent on the rotor angular position) and the static and dynamic frictions. The static friction is assumed to be constant on average, and the dynamic friction (viscous damping) is constant for a constant motor speed.

On-Line Disturbance Compensation

In the application of motor speed regulation, especially at the steady state, the periodical disturbance torque can cause the speed ripples. If the disturbance is known by the controller, a voltage can be applied to the motor to counteract the disturbance, eliminating the torque ripples, thus the speed ripples. To accomplish this, an on-line estimation of the disturbance and a control law that generates the counteracting voltage need to be designed. The discrete time disturbance estimation presented earlier is applied. Next, we present the disturbance controller.

The motor speed response is due to both the terminal voltage manipulated by a controller and the disturbances in the motor. Besides the voltage output of the existing controller in the loop, consider applying an additional voltage at the motor terminal required to cancel off the disturbance effect on the speed output, V_{ff}. The speed response is

$$\omega = \frac{1/k_b}{t_m t_e s^2 + t_m s + 1}\left(V + V_{ff}\right) + \frac{t_e t_m s/J + t_m/J}{t_m t_e s^2 + t_m s + 1} T_d(s), \tag{42}$$

where $t_m = \dfrac{RJ}{k_b k_t}$ is the mechanical time constant, $t_e = L/R$ the electrical time constant.

Choosing V_{ff} to eliminate the effect of T_d on, it leads to

$$V_{ff} = \frac{t_e t_m}{J}\left(t_e s + 1\right)T_d, \tag{43}$$

If using original motor parameters, the above equation is

$$V_{ff} = \left(\frac{L}{k_t}s + \frac{R}{k_t}\right)T_d. \tag{44}$$

Adding the disturbance compensating voltage to the controller output, the overall terminal voltage V_T is

$$V_T = V + V_{ff} \tag{45}$$

where V is the output of the existing controller.

Computation of Disturbance Compensation Voltage V_{ff}

Now, we consider the implementation of the compensation scheme in digital form.

Equation 44 can be discretized using the Euler's backward method to have

$$V_{ff}(k) = \left(\frac{L}{k_t \Delta t} + \frac{R}{k_t}\right) T_d(k) - \frac{L}{k_t \Delta t} T_d(k-1). \tag{46}$$

$V_{ff}(k)$ can be computed if $T_d(k)$ and $T_d(k-1)$ are known.

According to the current Equation 47 and the disturbance Equation 48, we have

$$i(k) = \left(\frac{L}{\Delta t} + R\right)^{-1} \left[\frac{L}{\Delta t} i(k-1) - k_b \omega(k) + V_T(k)\right], \tag{47}$$

$$T_d(k) = k_t i(k) - J\dot{\omega}(k). \tag{48}$$

Equations 46, 47, and 48 are used together to compute the disturbance compensating voltage on-line. When updating the total terminal voltage to the motor at each time instance, $V_{ff}(k)$ is to be computed. According to Equation 47, $V_T(k)$ needs to be know in order to compute $V_{ff}(k)$. This is not possible because $V_T(k)$ is dependent on $V_{ff}(k)$. To overcome this difficulty in implementation, we compute $V_{ff}(k)$ in the following way. At step k, $\omega(k-1)$ and $V_T(k-1)$ are known, so $i(k-1)$ can be computed according to Equation 47. Then, $T_d(k-1)$ can be computed based on Equation 48. Note that acceleration $\dot{\omega}(k)$ is computed using the speed measurement. $T_d(k-2)$ can be computed in the same way. Then $T_d(k)$ is approximated at the current time step using linear extrapolation as

$$T_d(k) \approx 2T_d(k-1) - T_d(k-2). \tag{49}$$

Using Equation 49, Equation 46 becomes

$$V_{ff}(k) = \left(\frac{L}{k_t \Delta t} + \frac{2R}{k_t}\right) T_d(k-1) - \left(\frac{L}{k_t \Delta t} + \frac{R}{k_t}\right) T_d(k-2). \tag{50}$$

Finally, using the disturbance compensation voltage computed using Equation 50, the total motor terminal voltage is computed according to Equation 49, giving $V_T(k)$. The same steps are repeated at each time step during the closed-loop operation.

Stability and Performance

The disturbance control presented assumes the knowledge of the motor parameters, e.g. the winding inductance and resistance L and R. In reality, the true values of these parameters may not be known and may be identified using various system identification techniques. Because of the feedback nature of this method, that is the disturbance torque is estimated online, the closed-loop may not be stable, if there are significant uncertainties in these parameters. In order to prevent against the instability in the local feedback loop around the motor introduced by the torque estimation, we introduce a stability gain in the computation of the torque compensation voltage

$$\tilde{V}_{ff}\left(k\right) = k_r \left(\frac{L}{k_t \Delta t} + \frac{2R}{k_t} \right) T_d \left(k - 1 \right) - \left(\frac{L}{k_t \Delta t} + \frac{R}{k_t} \right) T_d \left(k - 2 \right), \tag{51}$$

where $0 < k_r < 1$ is the stability gain. And, the total terminal voltage implemented is

$$V_T\left(k\right) = V\left(k\right) + \tilde{V}_{ff}\left(k\right). \tag{52}$$

The online disturbance torque computation introduces a local feedback loop around the motor described by Equations 52, 53, and 51(see Figure 11). According to the stability analysis conducted by Wu (2009b), this local feedback loop is stable as long as the stability gain k_r is kept sufficiently small.

The smaller k_r is, the smaller the disturbance compensation effect because of less disturbance torque compensating voltage is applied. Consider the sampled data system consisting of the motor and the digital disturbance compensator (Figure 11). The motor output speed ω is a function of the controller voltage V and the motor intrinsic disturbance torque T_d. From Equation 51, the DC gain of the motor for the control voltage and the disturbance torque is $1/k_b$ and t_m/J, respectively. Under the online disturbance compensation method, the DC gain for the control voltage is unchanged. The DC gain for the disturbance torque is

Figure 11. Local feedback loop due to disturbance torque computation

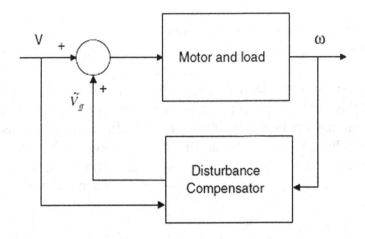

$$\frac{1-\left(\dfrac{L}{\Delta t}+R\right)^{-1}\left[\left(1+k_r\right)\dfrac{L}{\Delta t}+2k_r R\right]+k_r}{1-\left(\dfrac{L}{\Delta t}+R\right)^{-1}\dfrac{L}{\Delta t}}\cdot\frac{t_m}{J}.$$

This gain equals zero when $k_r=1$ and it is equal to t_m/J when $k_r=0$. Thus disturbance rejection performance is compromised in exchange for robust stability in application if we keep the stability gain small such as $k_r<1$. Also, due to less disturbance effect under the disturbance compensation since the friction torques are canceled as a fact of disturbance compensation, for a constant input voltage to the motor, the average motor speed is higher than the average speed under the same input voltage without the disturbance compensation. This higher motor gain increases the loop gain in the forward path between the motor voltage input and the motor speed output consequently, which may not be desirable for an originally optimal controller because an increased gain in the motor can lead to the closed-loop instability due to feedback. Thus, the gain of the original controller may need to be lowered to make the loop gain unchanged when implementing this scheme inside an existing control loop.

Implementation and Results

We implement our methods to a Mabuchi RK370-14420 motor, the same motor used earlier in this chapter for parameter identification and disturbance compensation using estimator. The parameters of the motor given in the motor specifications for reference are summarized in Table 4.

Note the inductance is not given by the specifications. The inductance of the motor for experiment was measured as L=20.25mH. Also note that the values given in the above table is for reference only. A large amount of variations in the parameters exist from motor to motor, e.g. the resistance of the motor under test is 16.4ohm. To test the robustness of our methods, we use resistance, torque constant, mass moment of inertia in the specifications and the measured inductance for disturbance calculation and control.

To calculate the disturbance torque using the proposed method, we sent a voltage of 2volt to the motor PWM driver. We measured motor shaft speed and position using an optical encoder with a resolution of 448 counts per revolution. The speed and angular position of the rotor over five revolutions were measured. The calculated torque versus time is shown in Figure 12.

Figure 12 was broken when the motor started to move from rest. When the rotor was moving, the cogging torque and dynamic friction dominated and the total disturbance appears periodic. To eliminate the transient effect on the speed in the calculation of the cogging torque, we calculated the torque for the last four revolutions respectively, then took the average of the disturbance torques for the four revolutions as the disturbance torque estimate. The mean of the disturbance torque over one revolution gives the value of the friction. And the calculated friction is 0.333mNm. Removing the mean from the disturbance torque gives the cogging torque. The calculated cogging torque versus the angular position is shown in Figure 13. Calculated average 3 shows that the calculated cogging torque is periodic and has peak to peak values in agreement with the specifications (see Table 4).

Table 4. Mabuchi motor parameters

Parameters	Value	Unit
Terminal resistance	$17 \pm 15\%$	Ω
Terminal inductance	N/A	Henry
Torque constant	$18.3 \pm 18\%$	mNm/A
Mass moment of inertia	9.0	gcm^2
Cogging torque	1.57 p-p (max.)	mNm

Figure 12. Computed Disturbance Torque

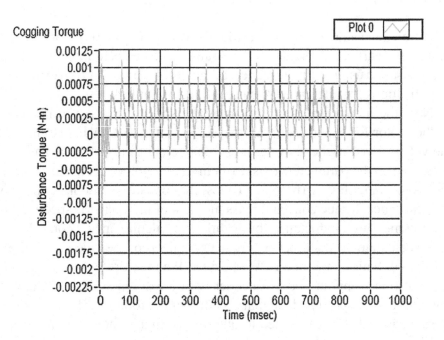

Figure 13. Calculated average cogging torque

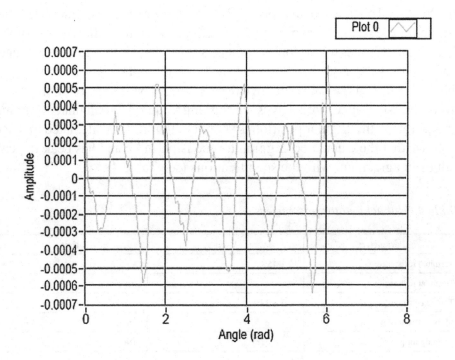

Next, we applied the on-line disturbance estimation and compensation for motor speed regulation. Speed ripples exist in motor speed due to the existence of the cogging torque. It may be harmful for some speed regulation applications, especially at low speeds. This on-line disturbance compensation scheme proves to be effective in reducing the speed ripples through experimentation. In this experiment, a 1volt command voltage was sent into the motor driver. The speeds with and without the disturbance cancellation are shown in Figure 14 and Figure 15 respectively. The standard deviation of the speed at steady state is 0.02ips without compensation, and 0.01ips with disturbance cancellation, respectively. A 50% improvement in the steady state speed response was achieved. Also, the steady speed is faster with compensation because an extra terminal voltage is applied to overcome the friction, leading to a higher speed gain in the motor. The terminal voltage with compensation is shown in Figure 16, which is the sum of the 1volt command voltage and the computed disturbance compensation voltage $\tilde{V}_{ff}$.

The first experiment is an open loop test. The application of this scheme to a closed-loop feedback control system has also been investigated. A DC motor driven speed control system with an existing proportional and integral (PI) controller was used for testing. For the existing PI controller, the proportional gain is 10, and the integral gain is 500. At the reference speed, ω_r=0.04 ips, the standard deviation of the speed of the load at the steady state is 0.0075ips, which is not satisfactory. When applying the proposed scheme, reference values for the motor parameters in the motor specifications were used to compute the disturbance compensation voltage command. Also, reflected load inertia on the motor was ignored. Both served to test the robustness of the proposed scheme. After applying the disturbance compensation, the standard deviation is 0.0052ips. A significant performance improvement was achieved. To maintain the open loop gain under the disturbance compensation unchanged, the proportional gain was lowered, k_p=8 to maintain the closed-loop stability.

In both the open loop and the closed-loop experiments, k_r=0.3, which rendered both the stability and the performance improvements.

Conclusion

Another on-line DC motor disturbance torque compensation scheme is proposed for speed regulation. Based on the motor equations, the disturbance torque is computed at each instance the controller in the closed-loop is updated, then the terminal voltage required to eliminate the speed ripples is updated

Figure 14. Speed without disturbance compensation

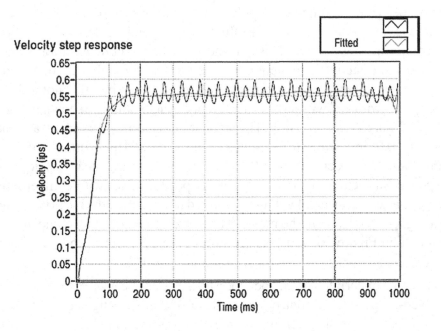

Figure 15. Speed with disturbance compensation

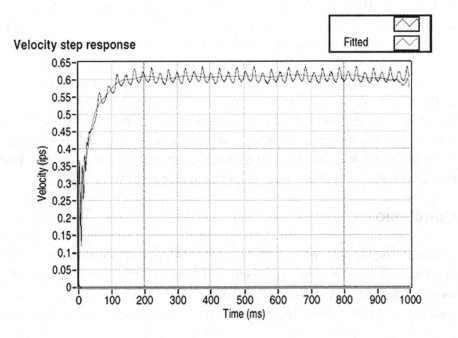

Figure 16. Motor terminal voltage applied

Terminal voltage

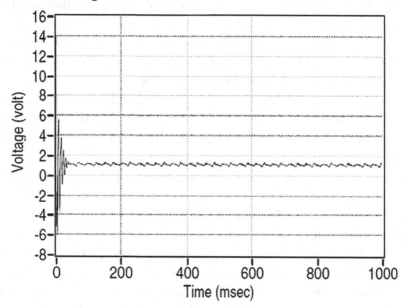

via a simple control law. Robust stability condition and performance index are analyzed for this approach. Experimental results on both the open loop and closed-loop control system are presented. These results prove the effectiveness of the scheme. In both cases, the performances were significantly improved. This approach is simply to apply, especially suitable for improving an existing speed control system and can be easily implemented in the digital form.

DISTURBANCE COMPENSATION USING FEEDFORWARD AND FEEDBACK

Introduction

Here, we continue to consider compensation of the torque disturbance in a closed-loop DC motor feedback speed regulation system. PID controllers are widely used for motion control in the printer industry. When a PID controller was used in the speed closed-loop feedback control system, speed ripples were present in the speed output and the performance got worse for lower speeds. However, increased scan resolutions in new products, such as 1200 pixels-per-inch (ppi), demanded the scan speeds of a contact imaging sensor (CIS) to be 0.1 inch-per-second (ips) or lower. Speed regulation in this low speed range using an existing PID controller could not meet the scan quality requirements. A new disturbance compensation approach needed to be developed to meet the motion quality requirements. This problem has been treated by using a disturbance observer Wu (2009a) and the online disturbance estimation Wu (2009b), presented in previous sections in this chapter, but was not fully solved by these methods to meet the scan quality requirements. The approach proposed by Wu (2015) and presented in this section solved the speed regulation issue, meeting scan quality requirements. It was the first time an advanced control solution, beyond PID, was implemented in a scanner at the company. In this approach, besides using the disturbance estimated off-line, the disturbance is also estimated on-line to eliminate the speed ripples at low speeds, thus resulting in a combined feedforward and feedback disturbance compensation structure. First the disturbance torque is computed off-line every time before a scan move is made based on a physical model of the DC motor, from which a voltage to the motor drive is generated as the feedforward control signal; then, for the feedforward compensated motor drive, the disturbance torque not cancelled in the scan mechanism, such as friction variation, is computed on-line to generate, via a simple control law, an additional voltage signal in the feedback path to counteract the effect of the un-canceled disturbance torque on the speed output.

This approach does not require any extra sensing. It needs the information on the motor terminal voltage and the motor speed, which is usually available for a closed-loop speed regulation system. The discrete form makes it suitable for direct digital implementation. The effectiveness of the approach was proved through extensive experiments on prototype scanner units. Experimental results demonstrated that the speed performances have been largely improved using the proposed disturbance compensation.

Off-Line Disturbance Computation and Compensation

Off-Line Disturbance Computation

Recall from last section, the disturbance torque can be computed using Equation 40

$$i(k) = \left[\frac{L}{\Delta t} + R\right]^{-1} \left[\frac{L}{\Delta t} i(k-1) - k_b \omega(k) + V(k)\right],$$

and Equation 41

$$T_d(k) = k_t i(k) - J\dot{\omega}(k)$$

with the known terminal voltage to a motor at rest, the speed of the motor measured through an optical encoder, and the acceleration computed using the speed measurement.

Off-Line Disturbance Compensation

For motor speed regulation applications, especially at the steady state, the periodical disturbance torque can cause the speed ripples. If the disturbance is known to the controller, a voltage can be applied to the motor to counteract the disturbance, eliminating the torque ripples, thus the speed ripples. To accomplish this, an off-line estimation of the disturbance and a feedforward control law that generates the counteracting voltage may be desired. The discrete time disturbance estimation presented earlier can be applied to calculate the disturbance. Next, we present the feedforward disturbance controller given by Equation 46

$$V_{ff}(k) = \left(\frac{L}{k_t \Delta t} + \frac{R}{k_t}\right) T_d(k) - \frac{L}{k_t \Delta t} T_d(k-1).$$

Add the disturbance compensating voltage, the overall terminal voltage is

$$V_T = V + V_{ff},$$

where V is the output of the existing controller.

On-Line Disturbance Compensation Scheme

We have presented an off-line disturbance torque calculation approach and a feedforward control law. However, since the torque is calculated *a priori*, it may not represent the actual disturbance torque in a real operation due to changes in system parameters and operating conditions, i.e. the scan bar moves from one end of the scanner to the other end along a guide. Also, any unexpected disturbances that occur in an operation will not be accounted for. For these reasons, we would like to develop a feedback compensation approach based on the equations we have derived so far.

According to the previous results in the last section for online disturbance estimation and compensation, the disturbance compensation voltage is given by

$$\tilde{V}_{ff}(k) = k_r \left(\frac{L}{k_t \Delta t} + \frac{2R}{k_t} \right) T_d(k-1) - \left(\frac{L}{k_t \Delta t} + \frac{R}{k_t} \right) T_d(k-2),$$

The disturbance torque at previous steps is computed using the off-line torque computation method, Equation 40 and Equation 41.

A Combined Feedforward and Feedback Compensation Implementation

We have presented a feedforward and feedback disturbance compensation approach, respectively. It is natural and also practical to combine the two approaches together to obtain a combined feedback and feedforward compensation structure, shown in Figure 17.

The feedforward disturbance compensation is expected to reject most of the disturbance in the motor, where V_{ff} in Figure 17 is calculated using

Figure 17. Combined feedforward and feedback structure

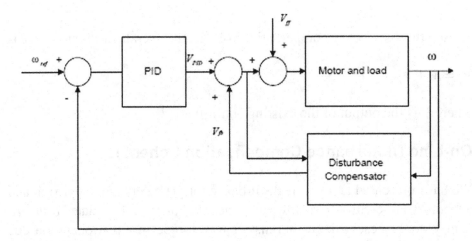

Equation 51 based on the off-line disturbance torque obtained. For the feedforward compensated motor drive mechanism, there will still be some amount of disturbance left in the system. The feedback on-line disturbance compensation we developed earlier can be subsequently applied around this system to cancel the remaining disturbance in the system, where V_{fb} is computed as $\tilde{V}_{ff}(k)$ is in Equation 51. This feedback loop around the feedforward compensated motor mechanism provides further performance improvement against these disturbances unaccounted for in the off-line computation.

The online disturbance compensation adds another local feedback loop around the motor within the existing PID feedback control loop (see Figure 17). This local feedback can cause stability problems, a stability gain k_r is introduced to ensure closed-loop stability for the over feedback system. This gain affects the disturbance rejection performance as a compromise for stability. The analysis of stability and performance with addition of this local loop has been done in the last section where the online disturbance compensation is discussed.

Implementation and Results

We will present the application of the combined feedforward plus feedback disturbance compensation to real commercial scan units. Extensive reliability testing conducted on engineering sample units and large amount of statistical data collected on production units built from the various manufacturing lines validated the effectiveness and robustness of this control scheme. These scan units are currently on the consumer markets.

The application of the combined scheme to a closed-loop DC motor system has been implemented. A DC motor driven mechanism carrying a CIS scan bar in a flatbed scan unit had a proportional, integral and derivative (PID) controller to regulate the scan speed. The mechanism consisted of a pulley, gear, and belt transmission which moves the scan bar. A Mabuchi FC130 motor, which was driven by a pulse-width-modulated (PWM) drive, was used to drive the transmission. A 112 CPR quadrature digital output encoder mounted on the motor shaft was the position and speed sensor. The combined disturbance compensation was implemented in the firmware using integer arithmetic. The control loop updates every one milli-second (msec). For the PID controller in the speed loop, the proportional gain is 5, and the integral gain is 1000, and the derivative gain is 5, all in its appropriate unit respectively. For 600 pixel per inch (PPI) scan, the required speed is 0.2ips.

The speed response with the PID controller was shown in Figure 18., with motor terminal voltage shown in Figure 19. From Figure 18, the speed response was very poor, and the corresponding scan image test failed. Tuning the PID gains has proved to be ineffective in this case after many trials.

The combined disturbance compensation strategy was applied to the PID loop. Nominal motor parameter values from the manufacturer's motor specifications were used for the model, and the reflected load inertia on the motor was ignored in purpose. This serves to test the robustness of the proposed scheme. When a scan command is issued, the scanner will first make a short move, then return to the home position, before it makes the actual scan move. The off-line disturbance computation was done based on the collected speed and voltage data after the pre-move, during which the system was controlled by the PID controller. The actual 600ppi (pixel per inch) scan move took place after the pre-move, during which both the feedforward and the feedback disturbance compensation were turned on in addition to the PID controller. The disturbance torque computed off-line after the pre-move was obtained by averaging over several shaft revolutions and was mapped to the 448 quadrature encoder edges (notice that the cogging torque is rotor position dependent). Note that there are 448 quadrature edges per shaft revolution. The encoder edge counts which increase or decrease during an actual scan operation when the motor rotates, and which include both the pre-move and the scan move, were saved in a register in the ASIC which was reset to zero before every scan operation. At each sample instant, based on the overall counts in the register, the corresponding disturbance torque value at the current shaft position was found from ASIC register. Knowing the current and the previous disturbance torque values, the feedforward voltage can be generated. For the feedback disturbance rejection, letting k_r=0.15 gave the best results in this case through several trials. Based on the experimental results, the feedback disturbance compensation further improved the performance of the feedforward compensated PID closed-loop by 10%-15%. Figure 20 and Figure 21, show the speed response and the voltages, respectively, under the combined disturbance compensation scheme. From Figure 20, it is evident that a significant performance improvement was achieved at the steady state. Under the current scheme, there were larger errors and more oscillations in the transient responses compared to the PID control. However, in our application, scan occurs only after the speed reaches the steady state. Steady state speed regulation was our focus. Thus, this application of the proposed disturbance compensation scheme for low speed regulation was considered very successful.

Figure 18. PID control steady state speed

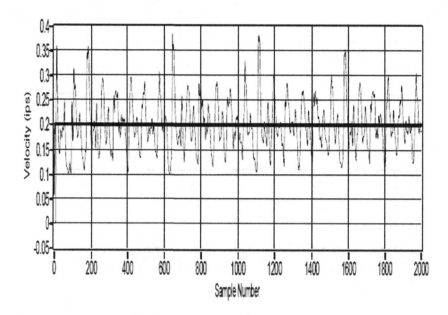

Figure 19. PID control terminal voltage

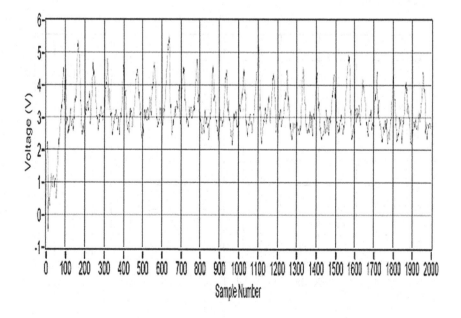

Figure 20. Speed under the combined scheme: actual speed (thin), reference speed (bold)

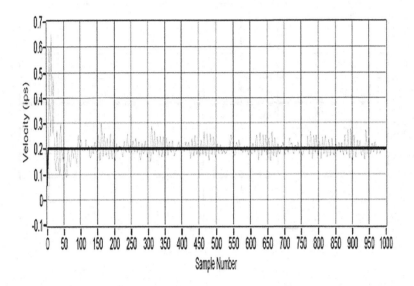

Figure 21. Voltages under the combined scheme: total voltage (solid), feedforward disturbance compensation voltage (dashed), and feedback disturbance compensation voltage (dash-dotted)

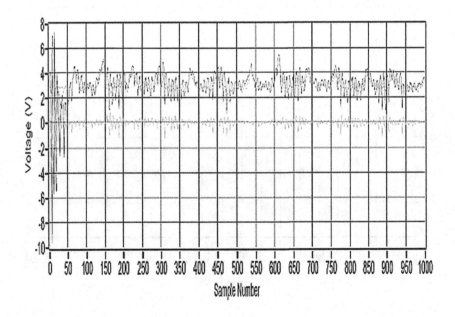

Conclusion

Based on the DC motor equations, the disturbance torque in a mechanism can be computed in either the off-line or the on-line fashion. Consequently, control laws can be derived to reject the disturbance utilizing the computed disturbance torque. Robust stability condition and performance index are discussed for the on-line disturbance compensation. A combined online and off-line (feedback and feedforward) disturbance rejection scheme is presented. Experimental results proved the effectiveness of the scheme, including a real application example of consumer scan units. Results showed the steady state speed performances were significantly improved. This approach is especially suitable for improving an existing speed regulation system and can be easily implemented due to its digital form. No extra sensing is required for implementing this approach and the computation load is small. Despite its apparent simplicity, this scheme was prove to be very effective and solved a real control application problem.

IMPROVING SCAN BAR SPEED REGULATION BY INCLUDING IDENTIFIED DRIVE DYNAMICS IN THE FEEDBACK DESIGN

Introduction

In a consumer scanner, a brushed DC motor drives the CIS scan bar in Wu (2012a). A drive mechanism connects the motor to the scan bar, which usually comprises gears, pulleys, timing belt, and a guide rail. The drive mechanism transfers the motor rotational motion to the scan bar translational motion while adding the effect of its own dynamics on the scan bar motion. Scan bar speed and position are important variables for scan quality. However, they are not measured in current scanners. Instead, motor speed and position are measured using a shaft mounted optical encoder and subsequently used for feedback control. Thus, the scan bar speed is not directly controlled since the scan bar speed is different from the motor speed due to the presence of the drive mechanism dynamics.

To meet increasing scan quality requirements and controller performance, the drive mechanism dynamics should be considered in the controller design. Thus a model of the drive mechanism needs to be established. Besides improving the controller performance via including the drive dynamics in the feedback loop, it can be used for diagnosing and improving the drive mechanism mechanical design, and predicting the scan bar motion using the motor encoder data. System identification techniques as Ljung(1999), Unbehauen,and Rao(1998), Chen, Juang, and Lee (1992), and Horta, Juang, and Chen (1993) can be used to establish a drive model. Having established this model and the estimated scan bar speed based on the encoder measurement, the model is used for the controller design. Compared to the controller designed using the motor speed measurement, the controller designed using the estimated scan bar speed improves the scan bar speed response.

Next, we will first describe the data acquisition and the system identification; then presents the controller design and the experiment. Conclusions and future work are given in the end.

System Identification

Obtaining the drive mechanism dynamic model is considered here. The scan bar was controlled by a proportional and integral (PI) feedback controller running at 1000Hz sample rate. During the closed-loop data acquisition, the scan bar was regulated using the PI controller at several speeds in the scan speed range. The motor motion was measured by the shaft mounted optical encoder which output quadrature signals with 448 counts per revolution (CPR) resolution. The LabVIEW field programmable gate array (FPGA) module was used to process the encoder signals based on edge counting. The scan bar motion was measured using a laser interferometer with quadrature outputs and a 79nm resolution. The laser interferometer output was sampled at 1000Hz sample rate using a national instrument NI 6602 DAQ card. The eigensystem realization algorithm with data correlation (ERADC) in Horta, Juang, and Chen (1993), Chen, Juang, and Lee (1992) was used to identify the drive mechanism model. ERADC took the motor speed and the scan bar speed as input and output respectively, and identified a fourth order discrete time state-space model. Figure 22 shows the frequency responses of the identified models for each scan speed. The identified models can be used to estimate the scan bar speed using the motor speed as an input. Figure 23 shows the estimated scan speed for three command speeds, 0.2 inch per second(ips), 0.8ips, and 3.2ips, where the identified model at each scan command speed was used respectively. It is clear from Figure 23 that the estimated scan speeds match the measured scan speeds very well. To require a model for every command speed may not be efficient and practical. It may be feasible to use one drive model for all command speeds if the drive dynamics is not strongly dependent on the scan speed. The drive model at 0.8ips was selected and Figure 24 shows the estimated scan speeds at 0.2ips, 0.8ips, and 3.2ips using this model. According to Figure 24, the estimated scan speeds for 0.2ips and 3.2ips using the model identified under the command speed of 0.8ips are worse, compared to corresponding ones in Figure 23, but may still be considered adequate depending on performance criteria and applications.

With the drive models identified, there are several applications of the identified model. The drive mechanism natural frequencies and damping ratios are obtained from the models, which can be used to improve the drive mechanism design, see Table 5. The models can be used to predict the true scan bar motion. The models can be included in the feedback loop, by using the estimated scan speed as feedback signal, to improve the control of the scan bar motion, which is the true control objective in this design.

Figure 22. Transfer functions identified for various speeds

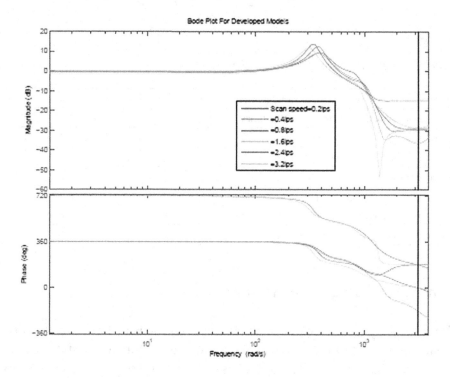

Figure 23. Estimated speeds using one model for each speed

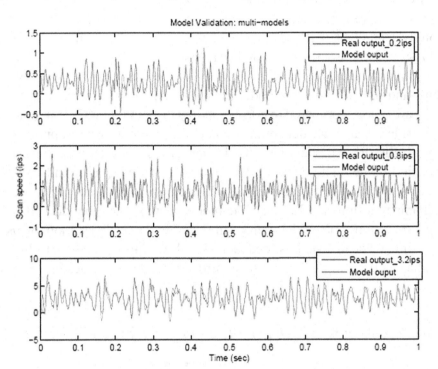

Table 5. Identified Drive mechanism dynamics

Fundamental Natural frequency (rad/sec) @0.2ips	396
Damping ratio for fundamental frequency (%) @0.2ips	19.8
Second Natural frequency (rad/sec) @0.2ips	839
Damping ratio for second harmonic (%) @0.2ips	20.2
Fundamental Natural frequency (rad/sec) @3.2ips	311
Damping ratio for fundamental frequency (%) @3.2ips	14.9
Second Natural frequency (rad/sec) @3.2ips	856
Damping ratio for second harmonic (%) @3.2ips	17.6

Controller Design and Testing

Motor cogging torque (Wu, 2012b; Tatsuya, & Takashi, 1998) and the drive dynamics have been identified as the major causes for steady state scan bar speed variations. Controller tuned based on the motor speed does not give good scan bar speed response if the drive dynamics is significant. However,

Figure 24. Estimated speeds using one model for all speeds

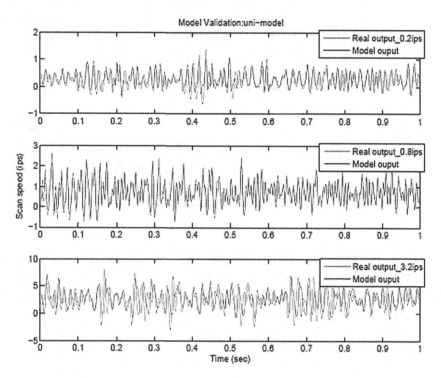

controller tuned based on the model predicted scan bar speed can improve the speed response. After identifying a drive mechanism dynamic model, the controller design was shifted from being based on the motor speed to being based on the predicted scan bar speed (see Figure 25). The controller parameters are determined based on the estimated scan speed response instead of the motor speed response. The controller was originally designed using a motor model and then tested and tuned using LabView real time module and FPGA module. A new PI controller was designed by utilizing the scan speed estimated using the drive model output as the feedback signal. This new controller was implemented and tested in a LabVIEW program. Again, the motor speed was measured using the optical encoder and the scan speed measured using the laser interferometer. The motor and scan bar speed response for the existing controller, when the command speed was 0.8ips, are shown in Figure 26. The speed responses for the new controller tuned including the drive model for the same command speed are shown in Figure 27. Steady state speed responses for the two controllers are compared in Figure 28 where it is quite clear that the new controller regulates both the motor speed and scan

Figure 25. Control loop feedback signal change

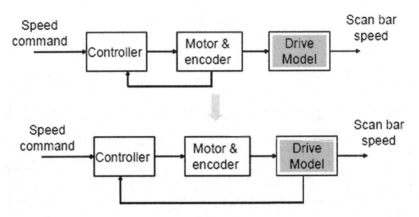

speed well. The new controller, which may not be optimal, was already better than any controller tuned earlier using the motor speed as the feedback signal. Testing results confirm that including the drive dynamics in the controller design improved the controller performance.

Figure 26. Existing controller performance

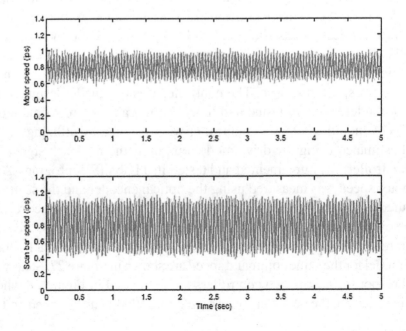

Figure 27. New controller performance

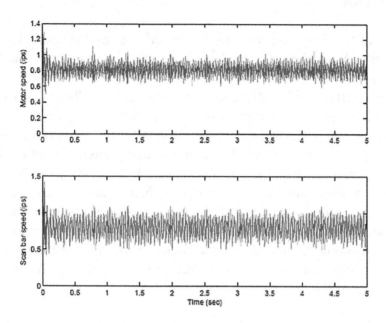

Figure 28. Comparison of steady state speed responses

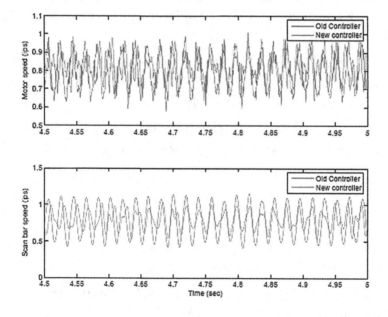

Conclusion

In order to truly regulate the scan bar speed, we need the scan bar speed information. Since the scan speed is not measured, it can be estimated using a dynamic model of the drive mechanism and the motor speed measurement. We improved the scan speed regulation by closing the feedback loop using the drive model output as the feedback signal. This solution requires no hardware cost and the computational complexity is small using a low order dynamic model for the drive mechanism. It is demonstrated in this design example that, in general, knowledge on the true motion variables gained through applying the system identification theory enables product quality improvement.

In the future, the variability of the drive mechanism dynamics, that is how the models vary from one scanner to another, needs to be investigated. When the drive dynamics is included in the controller design, the robust stability and robust performance of this controller will need to be investigated due to products variations and wear and tear with time.

REFERENCES

Alvarez-Ramirez, J., Femat, R., & Barreiro, A. (1997). A PI Controller with Disturbance Estimation. *Industrial & Engineering Chemistry Research*, *36*(9), 3668–3675. doi:10.1021/ie970230v

Basilio, J. C., & Moreira, M. V. (2004). State-space Parameter Identification in a Second Control Laboratory. *IEEE Transactions on Education*, *47*(2), 204–210. doi:10.1109/TE.2004.824846

Chen, C.-W., Juang, J.-N., & Lee, G. (1992). *Frequency Domain State-Space System Identification*. NASA Technical Memorandum 107659.

Chung, M., & Kang, D. (2005). Nono Positioning System using Trajectory Following Control Method with Cogging Force Model. *The 3rd International Symposium on Nanomanufacturing*.

Franklin, G. F., Powell, J. D., & Emami-Naeini, A. (1994). *Feedback Control of Dynamic systems* (3rd ed.). Addison Wesley.

Franklin, G. F., Powell, J. D., & Workman, M. L. (1990). Digital Control of Dynamic Systems (2nd ed.). Addison Wesley.

Hadef, M., Bourouina, A., & Mekideche, M. R. (2007). Parameter Identification of a DC Motor Using Moments Method. *Int. J. Electrical and Power Engineering*, *1*(2), 210–214.

Hadef, M., & Mekideche, M. R. (2009). *Parameter Identification of a Separately Excited DC Motor via Inverse Problem Methodology*. Monaco: Ecologic Vehicles and Renewable Energies.

Horta, L., Juang, J.-N., & Chen, C.-W. (1993). *Frequency Domain Identification Toolbox*. NASA Technical Memorandum 109039.

Liu, C., & Peng, H. (1997). Disturbance Estimation Based Tracking Control For A Robotic Manipulator. *Proceedings of ACC*.

Ljung, L. (1999). *System Identification: Theory for the User* (2nd ed.). Prentice Hall.

Kramer, B. (2007, Jan.). Smooth Rotation: An Adaptive Algorithm Kills Jerky Motions in Motors. *Machine Design*.

Krneta, R., Antic, S., & Stojanovic, D. (2005). Recursive Least Square method in Parameters Identification of DC Motors Models. *Facta Universitatis. Ser.: Elec. Energ*, *18*(3), 467–478.

Mamani, G., Becedas, J., Sira-Ramirez, H., & Feliu Batlle, V. (2007). Open-loop Algebraic Identification Method for DC Motors. *European Control Conference*.

Mamani, G., Becedas, J., & Feliu Batlle, V. (2008). On-line Fast Algebraic Parameter and State Estimation for a DC Motor Applied to Adaptive Control. *Proc. of the World Congress on Engineering*.

Nuninger, W., Balaud, B., & Kratz, F. (1997). Disturbance Rejection Using Output and Input Estimation. Application to the Friction Compensation of A DC Motor. *Control Engineering Practice*, *5*(4), 477–483. doi:10.1016/S0967-0661(97)00027-0

Rubaai, A., & Kotaru, R. (2000). Online identification and Control of A DC Motor Using Learning Adaptation of Neural Networks. *IEEE Trans. Ind. Application*, *36*(3), 935–942. doi:10.1109/28.845075

Ruderman, M., Krettek, J., Hoffman, F., & Betran, T. (2008). Optimal State Space Control of DC Motor. In *Proceedings of the 17th World Congress IFAC*. doi:10.3182/20080706-5-KR-1001.00977

She, J., & Ohyama, Y. (2002). Estimation and Rejection of Disturbances in Servo Systems. *The 15th IFAC World Congress*. doi:10.3182/20020721-6-ES-1901.01479

Tatsuya, K., & Takashi, K. (1998, November). In-depth Learning of Cogging/Detenting Torque through Experiments and Simulations. *IEEE Transactions on Education*.

Unbehauen, H., & Rao, G.P. (1998). A Review of Identification In Continuous-time Systems. *Annual Review in Control, 22*, 145-17.

Wu, W. (2009a). A Cogging Torque Compensating Disturbance Estimator for DC Motor Speed Regulation: Design and Experimentation.*Proceedings of International Symposium on Industrial Electronics*. doi:10.1109/ISIE.2009.5222732

Wu, W. (2012a). DC Motor Drive Speed Regulation: Using a Repetitive Control Application in a Flatbed Scanner. *Industry Applications Magazine, IEEE, 18*(2), 38–46. doi:10.1109/MIAS.2011.2175569

Wu, W. (2012b). DC Motor Parameter Identification Using Speed Step Responses. *Modelling and Simulation in Engineering, 2012*, 1–5. doi:10.1155/2012/189757

Wu, W. (2009b). DC Motor Speed control Improvement Via Online Disturbance Computation And Compensation.*Proceedings of Joint 48th IEEE Conference on Decision and Control and 28th Chinese Control Conference*.

Wu, W. (2015). Disturbance compensation Using Feedforward and Feedback for Scanner direct Current Motor Mechanism Low Speed Regulation. *Journal of Dynamic Systems, Measurement, and Control, 138*(4).

Chapter 6
Control Analysis and Simulation

INTRODUCTION

So far, we have talked about control requirement derivation, control structure design and control algorithm design steps in the model-based control development process. After the initial control algorithm design is completed, the resulted control system needs to be carefully examined to make sure that the control system behaviors and performances meet the initial control requirements.

In the control architecture and algorithm design stage, a linearized plant model around an operating point or a set of linearized plant models at different operating points within the operation range are first obtained and usually used for design and analysis such as for PID controller tuning, open and closed-loop analysis instead of the nonlinear, full order plant model developed based on physical principles. Once the control law designed based on the linear plant model(s) is considered adequate by meeting predefined control performance criteria, the evaluation of the control performance on the nonlinear, full order plant model is started. In this detailed system analysis, compared to conceptual control design and analysis, control implementation details are included in the controller model including actuator saturation (magnitude, rate or both), sensor noise and delay, bumpless transfer (controller switching or parameter change), control modes and mode change, etc. to fully characterize the actual control system.

DOI: 10.4018/978-1-5225-2303-1.ch006

Control performances are evaluated in terms of four areas: set point tracking, disturbance rejection, noise reduction, and robustness against process variation and model uncertainty. The four aspects can be investigated both in the time domain and the frequency domain. In the time domain, step responses for set point change and disturbance change are generated, indexes relating to a step response such as the rise time, the settling time, the percentage overshoot, and the steady state error are used to compare against control performance requirements. In the frequency domain, the open/closed loop bandwidth, the gain margin and phase margin, the sensitivity function peak, and the complementary sensitivity function peak are used to compare against predefined control requirements. Pole and zero positions, the resonance frequency and damping ratio of complex pole pairs, singular values of multivariable system are also used to evaluate the system performance. Bode plots of open and closed-loop transfer functions are very useful for the frequency domain control performance evaluation. Similarly, for multi-input-multi-output control systems, singular value plots of open and closed-loop transfer function matrices are very helpful. Commercial control design software available is now very mature and has made the types of control analyses just mentioned earlier simple and easy, for example MATLAB control toolbox and MATLAB robust control toolbox. Using software control design tools, you can easily create plots such as Bode plot, Nyquist plot, Nicole's chart, and step response plot for visual examination, or you can also compute and plot poles and zeros, the gain margin and phase margin, the natural frequency and damping ratio of complex poles, etc. for stability and performance assessment. Powerful control analysis capabilities are built into the available modeling and simulation environments such as MATLAB/Simulink through both command line interface and graphical user interface (GUI), which is very efficient and user friendly for performing control system analysis in a modeling and simulation environment.

MIMO Control System Analysis Example

In chapter 4, we introduced a two-inputs-two-outputs plant control design example. In that example, the plant transfer functions were first identified from step responses generated from the detailed physical model of the plant using simulation by introducing step changes in the plant inputs one at a time. The plant model is given by

$$\begin{pmatrix} y_1 \\ y_2 \end{pmatrix} = \begin{bmatrix} G_{11} & G_{12} \\ G_{21} & G_{22} \end{bmatrix} \begin{pmatrix} u_1 \\ u_2 \end{pmatrix}$$

where the individual transfer functions are

$$G_{12} = -\frac{0.144}{4.67s + 1} e^{-9s}$$

$$G_{21} = \frac{0.384}{3.85s + 1} e^{-1s}$$

and

$$G_{22} = -\frac{1.105}{4.65s + 1} e^{-2s}.$$

Input and output pairing was first checked to make sure that plant inputs have the most effect on their corresponding plant outputs: that is the plant is diagonal dominant. Then, a diagonal controller was designed for the two-inputs-two-outputs plant by ignoring the plant interaction. The two PI controllers for the diagonal controller were obtained by applying one of the best PI controller tuning rules to the diagonal transfer functions of the plant transfer function matrix G_{11} and G_{22}. The transfer functions of the two PI controllers of the diagonal controller obtained using SIMC tuning rules are given by

$$C_1(s) = k_p \left(1 + \frac{1}{T_i S} \right) = -9.68 \left(1 + \frac{1}{5.08S} \right).$$

for the loop from plant input one to plant output one and

$$C_2(s) = k_p \left(1 + \frac{1}{T_i s} \right) = -1.05 \left(1 + \frac{1}{4.65s} \right)$$

for the loop from plant input two to plant output two.

For the open loop formed by $C_1(s)$ and G_{11}, the control performance was analyzed using the Bode plot. The Bode plot for $C_1(s)G_{11}$ was given in chapter 4, shown in Figure 1.

According to the Bode plot, the crossover frequency for this loop is 0.25rad/sec, the phase margin is close to 70degree, and the gain margin is close to 10dB. Recall the control loop requirements and the controllability analysis conclusions (see chapter 4), the bandwidth should stay below 0.4rad/sec for a diagonal control design. The closed-loop step response for a set point change for this loop is shown in Figure 2, where it can be seen that there is some amount of overshoot. However, no overshoot is allowed according to the control requirements. This suggests that some adjustment of the controller will be needed to meet the control performance requirements.

For the open loop formed by $C_2(s)$ and G_{22}, the Bode plot was also given in chapter 4, shown in Figure 3.

For this loop $C_2(s)G_{22}$, based on the Bode plot, the crossover frequency is 0.2rad/sec, and the phase margin and the gain margin look adequate. The controller seems acceptable. Next the time response is checked. The closed-loop response for a step change in the set point is shown in Figure 4, again an

Figure 1. Open loop Bode plot for output #1 and input #1

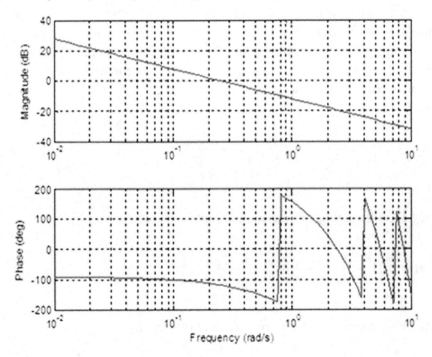

Figure 2. Closed-loop step response for a set point change

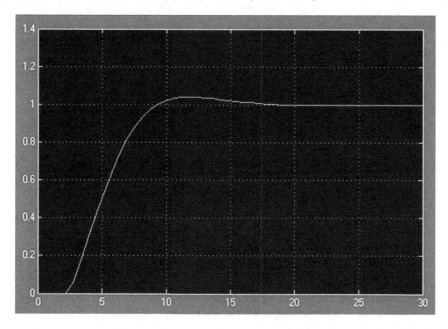

Figure 3. Open loop Bode plot for output #2 and input #2

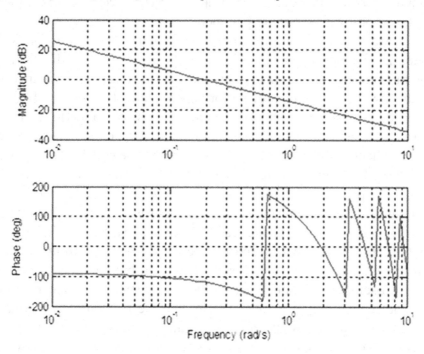

Figure 4. Closed-loop step response for a set point change for the second loop

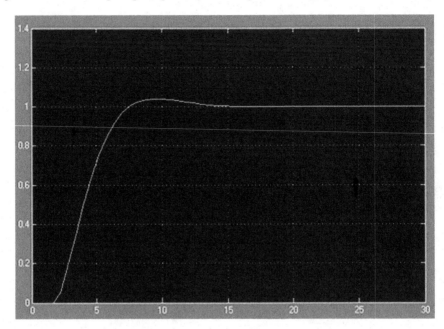

amount of overshoot is observed and fine tuning of the controller is required to meet the non-overshooting requirement.

So far, we have analyzed the control performance for each single loop, considering only the diagonal transfer functions of the plant and disregarding the interaction between the plant inputs and outputs. It is not precise in terms of predicting the actual control performance. Next step is to look at the effect of interaction in the plant on the closed-loop control performance by considering the dynamics of whole plant including the off-diagonal transfer functions. The linear plant model identified around a selected operating point (see Chapter 4 for details) is used together with the diagonal controller for the closed-loop simulation. A unit step change is introduced to the two set point commands at the same time and the responses of the two plant outputs under feedback control were obtained in Simulink and are shown in Figure 5. From the plots, we can see the responses are greatly degraded from the single loop responses due to the interactions in the plant: both outputs show large overshoot, oscillations before entering the steady state, and longer settling times. The second output is much worse than the first output in terms of overshoot and it also shows the non-minimum phase response (the response initially goes in the opposite direction before it reverses course and moves in the correct direction towards the set point). The coupling effect between the second plant output and the first plant input is particularly strong and there is more performance loss when including the plant interactions in analysis.

We have found from simulation using the full plant model that the set point step responses of the closed-loop showed strong interactions, the first plant output is affected by the second plant input and the second plant output is affected by the first plant input. Our diagonal controller designed based on the decoupling of the plant does not work very well when it actually deals with the interactions in the plant. In some industrial control applications, a simpler controller is preferred because it is easier to design, implement and maintain or because the control requirements are not very tight. In the case that a simpler controller such as a diagonal controller does not work well then the controls engineer has to resort to a more complex controller and more advanced control design techniques, for example using a multivariate controller instead of a diagonal controller in this case. We will not discuss advanced multivariable controller design problems, readers interested in this topic can easily find many technical books and literature dealing with multivariable control design.

We have used the full linear plant model to evaluate the control design. To truly understand and predict the control system performance before running test on the physical system, we can run the closed-loop simulations using the nonlinear physical plant model. Predicting a system performance using a system model in a virtual environment is a technique called the model in the loop (MIL) testing.

CLOSED-LOOP SIMULATION: MIL, SIL, AND HIL SIMULATION

One of the model-based control design advantages is to allow testing the control design and system performance early in the development cycle using models of the plants. In terms of testing this means to test functionality in the controller model before the control software is implemented and integrated into the target hardware. For embedded control system development, between the initial control model and the final integration of the application software into the target hardware, there are different levels of integration during the control development process, and consequently the control design and control implementation at different stages of the development are tested by using

Figure 5. Set point responses for the two-inputs-two-outputs plant with interactions

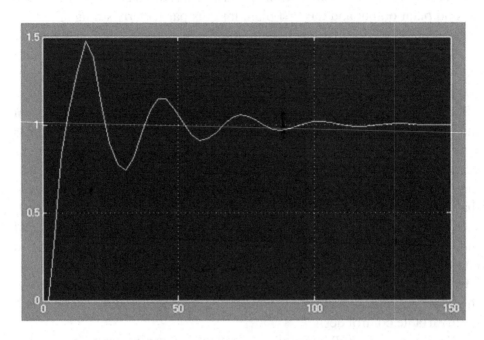

(a) First output

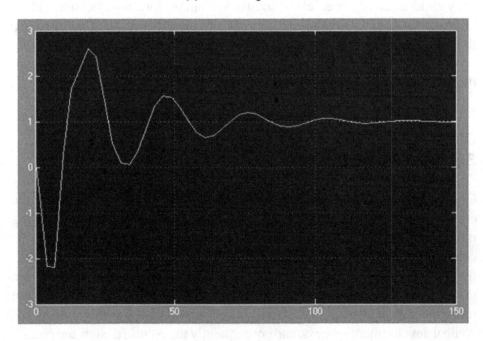

(b) Second output

different simulation techniques: model-in-the-loop (MIL), software-in-the-loop, and hardware-in-the-loop simulations.

- Model-in-the-Loop (MIL) verification is a form of model-based testing of controls algorithm where a model representing the physics of the plant (for example mechanical equipment) is used to test a model of the control algorithm. Testing occurs via a series of simulations representing use cases of the system under control. The purpose of MIL is to evaluate, down-select, and tune control algorithms before control implementation and before testing it on the real physical plant.
- Software-in-the-loop (SIL) verification is a form of model-based testing of controls algorithm where a model representing the physics of the plant (for example mechanical equipment) is used to test production software code of the control algorithm. Testing occurs via a series of simulations representing use cases of the system under control. The purpose of the SIL is to verify and test the production software code of the controller. SIL can be done at different levels of the software architecture.
- Hardware-in-the-loop (HIL) verification is a form of model-based testing of controls algorithm where a model representing the physics of the plant (for example mechanical equipment) is used to test the embedded control system (control software code integrated with the hardware target). Testing occurs via a series of simulations representing use cases of the system under control. The purpose of HIL is to verify and test the behavior of fully implemented embedded control system when connected to a virtual plant as if it were the real physical plant.

Model-in-the Loop Simulation

The first integration level is based on the model of the control system itself. Testing an embedded control system on MIL level means that the plant model and the control algorithm model connected through feedback in the closed-loop configuration are simulated in the modeling framework without any physical hardware components. This virtual testing technique allows testing control design at early stages of the development cycle before implementing it. It is much cheaper and quicker to fix issues that are found at this step compared to discovering them at later stages of the development cycle, thus saving cost and schedule. In the model-based control development projects, there are different kinds of control algorithm models. Functional models have a higher level of abstraction and do not consider all aspects such as robustness and performance. They are mainly used during early control design and verification. In the course of the development these functional abstract models of control algorithms are transformed into control algorithm implementation models. Aspects such as encapsulation, abstraction, robustness, performance, fixed-point scaling, readability and reuse are treated in implementation models. These models are designed to meet the requirements from a software engineering point of view. Control algorithm implementation models are often used together with a code generator to automatically generate production code from the models. Both control algorithm functional and implementation models can be tested using MIL. MIL testing can be done on a system level or on the component level. When testing the model of a complex controller it makes sense to conduct both component tests (testing subsystems of the controller model that handles particular function areas) and system tests.

Control algorithms models are tested using model-in-the-loop simulation to verify that they meet functional requirements and model structural coverage requirements. Control algorithms must meet functional requirements and predetermined model structural coverage standards before generating production code from the control model and proceeding to the next step of verification: software-in-the-loop simulation. Based on the control requirements, test cases are designed and used to test the functionalities and performances of the designed control algorithm. Test inputs of a test case are used as stimuli for the closed-loop control simulation and the simulated results are compared with the desired output of the test case or evaluated against the control requirements. Extra coverage oriented test cases are introduced if the first set of functional requirement oriented test cases does not lead to satisfactory model coverage. Test cases can be implemented in models and combined with the closed-loop control system model to form the test harness models. The test harness models generate pass/fail result after running the simulations. In practice, it is desirable that test case execution can be automated and pass/fail results are recorded in a test report after test case execution. Automated test case execution and reporting is beneficial for regression testing and continuous integration.

The model-in-the-loop simulation was run for the example used in the previous section for control analysis (this example was first introduced in Chapter 4 for controller development process). The detailed physical plant model was used for MIL simulation. Note that the linear plant model used for controller design and analysis was derived from step responses generated using the detailed physical model. The controller includes a state machine for implementing operation modes: start-up mode and automatic control mode. In the start-up model, the feedback control is not used and inputs to the plant are set at a constant value to bring the plant to a stable operating point. When the control model is activated after the plant reaching the steady state, the feedback controller regulates the outputs of the plant to make them to move to and stay close to the set points. The integrator anti-windup and the bumpless transfer for mode switching were implemented for the two PI controllers and included in the controller model for MIL simulation.

The system output responses are shown in Figure 6. In MIL simulation, the system started in the start-up mode with constant inputs and reached a steady state. The automatic control model was enabled when the time was equal to 350 second. In this mode, the PI controllers manipulated the plant inputs to bring the plant outputs to the set points and eventually settle at the set points. The set point responses were nonlinear, showing large overshoot, lightly damped oscillations, and large settling times. The MIL simulations results are consistent with the linear control analysis results done earlier, shown in Figure 5, especially the non-minimum phase step response of the second output was found in both the control analysis and the MIL simulation.

Based on the MIL simulation results shown in Figure 6, the original controller performance is not satisfactory in terms of meeting the control requirements such as overshoot and settling time. The reason for unsatisfactory performance is the presence of interactions in the plant: each plant output is affected by all plant inputs. Our control design used a diagonal controller and a PI controller was tuned by considering an individual loop one at a time ignoring interactions in the plant. To improve the performance of the diagonal controller, we need to adjust the PI controller parameters. Because of the interaction, the first PI controller output which is the first plant input, acts as a disturbance to the second plant output; the second PI controller output which is the second plant input, acts a disturbance to the first plant output. It was found that the first PI controller has more impact on the second plant output than the impact of the second PI controller on the first plant output. One thing you can do is to tune down the PI controller in the first loop to filter out the disturbance to the second loop. Change the proportional gain from -9.6762 to -6, and the integral time constant from 5.08 to 10 to get the new controller for the first loop as follows

$$C_1(s) = k_p \left(1 + \frac{1}{T_i s}\right) = 6\left(1 + \frac{1}{10s}\right).$$

Figure 6. MIL simulation results with original controller

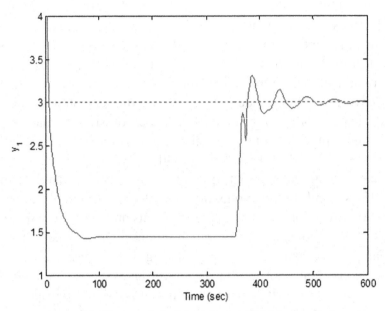

(a) First output(solid: response; dashed: set point)

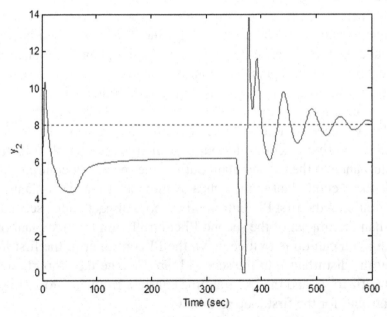

(b) Second output(solid: response; dashed: set point)

This adjusted PI controller gives a lower loop bandwidth with more phase margin. It also helps to reduce the disturbance effect from the first loop on the second loop. With this new first loop PI controller, the responses of both plant outputs were significantly improved, shown in Figure 7. There is no overshoot and oscillations in the response and the outputs settle into set points quickly. In this example, tweaking the original controller results in good control performance so the diagonal control strategy works out in the end. If the controller requirements cannot be met by tweaking the PI controller parameters of the diagonal controller, one may have to design a multivariable controller using more advanced control techniques.

Software-in-the Loop Simulation

After the production source code of a control algorithm is hand written or automatically generated from the control algorithm model which passed MIL testing, the next step of testing is the software-in-the-loop simulation. Testing an embedded control system on SIL level means that a control software component or the entire control software is tested within a simulated environment model but without any hardware (i.e. no mechanical or hydraulic components, no sensors, and no actuators). Usually the embedded control software and the simulated environment model run on the same machine. The virtual simulation environment is used and a real-time simulation environment is not necessary. Usually SIL tests are performed on Windows or Linux based desktop machines.

The aim of this step is to assess that the quality of the control software is satisfactory, or find the reasons why it is not. The concept of coverage is used, both in MIL and SIL, to make this satisfactory notion measurable. Practically, coverage is used as a termination condition to stop the iterative process of definition of new tests. To clarify the different purpose of MIL and SIL, let's stress the difference between the different kinds of coverage:

1. Coverage of the Requirements.
2. Coverage of the model (as provided by the Simulink toolbox *Verification & Validation*).
3. Coverage of the code.

MIL targets items 1 and 2, whereas SIL targets items 1 and 3. SIL targets integration tests, specifically, by running the code generated from a control model (e.g. in Simulink) with the middleware (e.g. data dictionaries or other

Figure 7. MIL simulation results with new controller

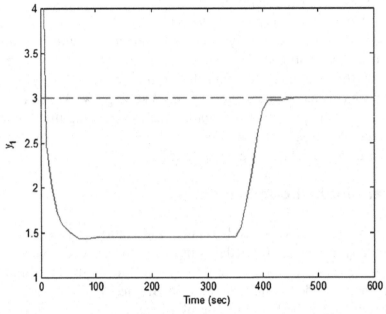

(a) First output(solid: response; dashed: set point)

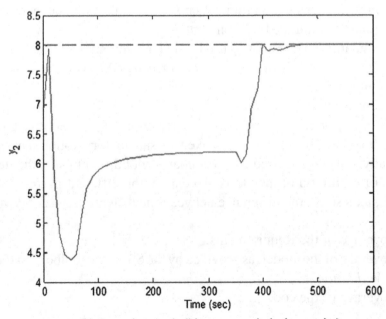

(b) Second output(solid: response; dashed: set point)

communication services) or with other application software components. The reuse of MIL functional test cases in SIL simulation guarantees item 1. The reuse of MIL model coverage targeted tests provides a good starting point for item 3. For SIL, the quality of the integrated control software is said to be satisfactory if minimum standards are reached, with the following priority, for:

1. **Requirements Coverage:** The SIL testing checks the software behavior against the functional requirements. Requirement checking provides the percentage of requirements effectively satisfied, or trace the subset ofrequirements satisfied. To this extent, the suggested approach is to reuse, or adapt the MIL validation tests. If the available SIL technology enables performance evaluation (computation time, memory usage, etc.) also performance requirements can be targeted by the SIL testing.

2. **Software Code Coverage:** Code coverage is part of the current industrial practice. It allows the identification of unexecuted statements and unevaluated expressions during the tests. This prevents the deployment of never tested software code on the hardware. In practice, requirement coverage is not enough to guarantee high code quality. Extra effort is required to explicilty target those implementation artifacts not properly exercised during the logically antecedent phase of requirement oriented tests. This is the motivation behind the introduction of model coverage analysis already in the MIL validation phase. As MIL model coverage addresses the gaps left behind by requirement oriented tests, SIL code coverage addresses behavior not yet existent in MIL testing. Specifically, SIL coverage testing addresses:
   ○ The code that bridges the automatically generated code to the embeded software system.
   ○ The consequences of behavior-affecting autocoder parameters and configuration.
   ○ Middleware software.
   ○ Hand written application software.
   ○ Formal certification standards that explicitly address the C code.

The role of model/code coverage to assess the *requirement completeness* shall be considered too. The test engineer may in this way identify a set of use cases relevant to the application, which however are not covered by the existing requirement specification. A requirement refinement is then performed. Requirement completeness is often not feasible in practice. However, model/ code coverage is a valuable tool to systematically identify the control system response discontinuities (e.g. those introduced by an if-then-else) or other abnormal behaviors, which is essential to:

- Get a good sample of the system possible behaviors.
- Get a good confidence of the completeness of the requirements.

Minimum standards for software code coverage and functional requirement coverage vary from case to case and must be previously discussed and agreed on by the project team. For example, it may be requested for a specific software subsystem to reach at least a 90% of code coverage and an 80% of requirement coverage. It may happen that running the curret tests (e.g. MIL test cases) once is not sufficient to reach the minimum standards for code coverage. An iterative process is put in place for new tests definition to eventually lead to the agreed coverage threshold. The standard approach to increase the code coverage is to create more use cases to represent more scenarios the controller software may be subjected to, and run the enlarged set of tests again.

The embedded control system software architecture becomes relevant during the automatic code generation and SIL steps. Specifically, the software architecture drives the automatic code generation configuration, also affects validation of the software integration in the SIL step. The Control software developed entirely or partially using model in Simulink is typically only one among many other software components that compose the whole embedded software. The purpose of the software functional architecture is to define these software components and their interactions. The functional architecture is the result of an iterative, top-down, refinement and partitioning of the functional requirements. The functional architecture specifies the application software component interactions dictated by the functional requirements. Both the behavioral and API details are included. The functional architecture is refined into the software architecture. The software architecture specifies how the component interactions from the functional architecture are implemented. The software architecture distinguishes between the application software and the software platform:

- The (software) platform is the set of SW layers between the hardware board and the application software. Roughly speaking, it includes the device drivers, the operating system, and other general-purpose services (the middleware).

- The application software implements the domain specific product design which meets the product's functional requirements. The application software is structured as a set of interacting application software components. The partitioning of the functionality, as specified by requirements, in application software components is documented by the functional architecture.

In Figure 8, the product's software architecture specifies that:

- All *application components* use the *DataDictionaryInterface* to access the *setpoint, sensor,* and *actuator* data. The *platform* provides this data dictionary service.
- The *UI* and *Remote Configurator* use the *IOccupancySched* interface to interact with the *OccupancyScheduler* component.
- The *DataDictionaryInterface* and *IOccupancySched* interfaces are defined as a list of methods that constrain the component interactions. How these methods are used to realize the component behavior will not be discussed here.

Figure 8. The software architecture of an example product

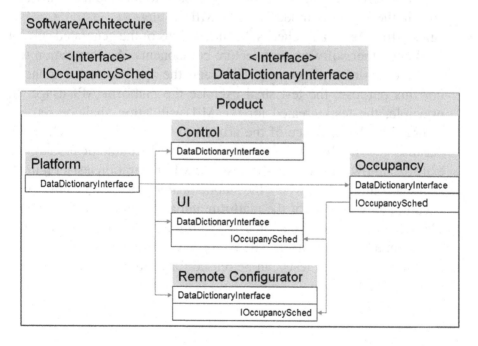

Application software components are later implemented independently, possibly by means of different technologies and tools. For example, the control component is realized in Simulink, whereas other application components are hand-written. The Simulink model interface matches the interface as specified in the software architecture. After MIL validation, by means of the code generation process, the control model is translated to C code and interfaced with the rest of the embedded software. The software architecture is the specification of the model retargeting required by the code generation, i.e. how the platform independent signals of the Simulink model are mapped on the embedded system's services API. After code generation, each component, already independently tested, shall be tested upon integration in the embedded controller. Unlike MIL, SIL simulation runs the production C code. SIL addresses production code validation in several ways:

- **Unit Test:** This checks that the generated code matches the model. The same test cases and test environment model are reused for this test. The simulated results from the model and the generated code are compared. In this step, you are detecting whether your controller as implemented in a model such as in Simulink is suitable for code generation (data types, sample times, etc...) and whether there are any bugs/issues with the code generation process. This step now can be easily done in Simulink environment: an S-function is used to include the generated code in the Simulink model used for MIL testing.

- **Integration Test:** This checks the interactions of the generated control code and other software architecture components. An integration test runs the involved platform services and the application component. For this purpose, the test shall exercise the platform API usage. In principle, the tests created for the MIL validation shall be reused. In practice, the interface of the artifact to be tested is now changed, because now it's based on the platform API. Technological solutions exits that allow reusing the MIL tests for SIL integration tests. Figure 9 shows a configuration where the automatically generated Control code is compiled with part of the platform and a custom Simulink bridge. The resulting binary functional mockup unit (FMU) is wired to the signals of a Simulink block, SIL Wrapped Control in the figure, so that the MIL models and tests can be reused for testing against the model generated code.

Figure 9. The reuse of MIL infrastructure for SIL.

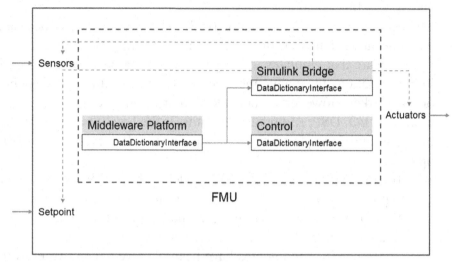

SIL Wrapped Control

- **System Test:** This logically follows the integration test. It includes the platform and the complete application software. The purpose of this phase is:
  - To functionally validate the complete system against the functional requirements.
  - To evaluate the performances of the embedded system.

MIL tests cannot be reused because the interface changed: the system test targets the complete embedded system, not the Control component.

Integration and system tests require the execution of the platform. In the SIL validation step, the platform is executed on a host computer. The unabridged platform code contains, however, HW specific code that cannot be run by the host machine CPU. A properly layered platform enables different trade-offs in order to overcome this limitation (Figure 10). The more platform layers are included in the SIL, the more the simulation is accurate, but also the complexity of the SIL simulation increases. Two main SIL technologies can be utilized:

- SIL by recompilation. No HW specific code is included in the SIL-trimmed platform. The code is compiled with a host compiler and executed natively on the host computer. This solution can include up-to the middleware layer (Figure 10). This SIL is capable of integration and system functional tests.

- SIL by Instruction Set Simulator (ISS). The code is cross-compiled with the target hardware tool chain. The resulting binary is run by ISS software that emulates the target CPU on the host computer. ISS implementations for many embedded CPU architectures are available on the market. However, an embedded board usually comes with a set of custom I/O, DSP, and other HW units. If the functionality provided by these units is required by the test plan, the SIL developer has two options:
  - To augment the ISS with a SW model of these HW units in order to provide a complete execution environment.
  - To replace the device driver in the platform code with a stub that simulates the unit behavior of interest in testing.
    Different ISS technologies have been observed. The two ends of the spectrum with respect to accuracy are:
  - Instruction accurate ISS, which ensures a functional equivalence of the executed code but no timing guarantees.
  - Cycle accurate ISS, which typically exploit a model of the CPU registers, pipelines, and caches. These emulators can provide performance measurements that are accurate at the clock level.

System performance evaluations, such as average latencies or average CPU load, require an ISS kind of SIL or are deferred to HIL step. The implementation of the SIL technology is dependent on the target hardware platform.

In summary: SIL runs production code, not a model of the functionality. SIL includes other application components and parts of the platform. It enables the testing of the interactions that occur between these components. SIL runs on a common host computer, it doesn't require any hardware equipment. SIL can be done at unit, integration and system levels. SIL enables debugging capabilities that may not be available in HIL. SIL enables quicker design-to-integration iterations. SIL enables the simulation of complex scenarios with the hardware.

Hardware-in-the Loop Simulation

After SIL simulation, the next step is testing using hardware-in-the-loop simulation (HIL). When testing the embedded control system on HIL level the control software runs on the final hardware controller, for example an

Figure 10. A summary of SIL technology tradeoffs

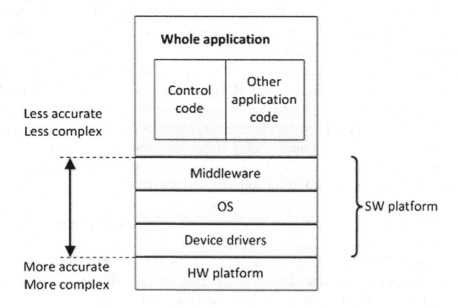

electronic control unit (ECU). However the environment around the control hardware is still a simulated one. Hardware controller and environment interact via the digital and analogue connectors of the hardware controller. The objective of testing on HIL level is to reveal faults in the low-level services of the hardware controller and in the I/O services. HIL testing requires real time behavior of the environment model (plant model) to ensure that the communication with the hardware controller is the same as in real application.

Hardware-in-the-loop simulation is a form of real time simulation. The HIL simulation includes a mathematical model of the process under control, the plant model, and a hardware device, e.g. an ECU or an industrial PID controller, you want to test. The hardware device is normally an embedded control system. In HIL simulation, the plant model provides all of the electrical signals needed to fully exercise the hardware device. In this way, the hardware device thinks that it is indeed connected to a real plant. The purpose of HIL simulation is to provide an effective platform for developing and testing real-time embedded systems, often in close parallel with the development of the hardware. Software development no longer needs to wait for a physical plant in order to test an embedded controller.

The roots of HIL are found in the Aviation industry. HIL simulation is widely used in developing embedded control systems for medical devices, industrial machines, power generation systems, aircrafts, automotive, and process control. The reason the use of HIL simulation is becoming more and more popular in more industries is driven by two major factors: time to market and complexity. As the complexity of the hardware being controlled increases, so does the complexity of the embedded control system that is designed to control the hardware. HIL simulation is a technique that is used increasingly in the development and testing of complex real-time embedded system. The complexity of the plant under control is included in testing and development by adding a mathematical representation (model) of all related dynamics in the plant. With HIL simulation cost and risk of testing are reduced. Other merits of HIL include:

- **No Real Plant:** Tests can be carried out even when there are no real plants;
- **Reproducibility:** Even complicated malfunctions can be reproduced;
- **Complete Coverage:** Improved coverage of test with at will changes of environmental conditions and operating conditions;
- **Safety:** Tests can be done without damaging equipment or endangering lives;
- **Reusability:** Test scenarios and evaluation functions can be reused once made;
- **Training:** It is also very useful for training purposes, i.e., the process operator may learn how the system works and operate by using the HIL simulation.

Figure 11 presents a typical HIL simulation testing system. Real-Time Windows Target and xPC Windows Target provided by MathWorks can be used for real-time simulation and testing. The Real-Time Windows Target is a PC solution for prototyping and testing real-time systems. It is an environment where you use a single computer as a host and target. xPC Target is a solution for prototyping, testing, and deploying real-time systems using standard PC hardware. It is an environment that uses a target

PC, separate from a host PC, for running real-time applications. Also, third-party software and hardware provide interfaces to MathWorks Simulink. These products include dSPACE with its Control Desk and Quanser QUARC real-time control software. MATLAB and Simulink support many products from well-known hardware manufacturers such as Texas Instruments and can directly generate executable code for them from Simulink models. National Instruments also offers a HIL platform. The NI hardware-in-the-loop (HIL)

Figure 11. A typical HIL test system

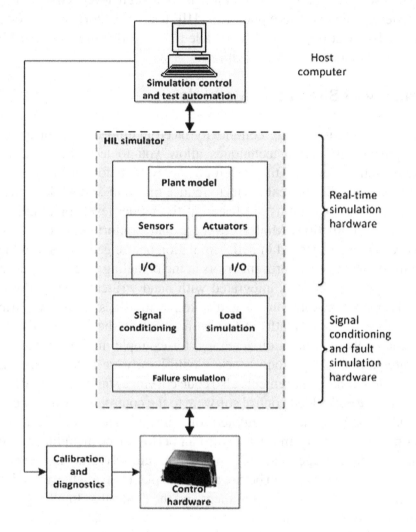

test platform uses open hardware and software technologies to reduce the time, cost, and risk associated with embedded software test. Because its modular architecture, the NI HIL platform can be easily upgraded with additional functionality. In addition to the widest range of I/O on market, National Instruments offers software tools that enable to automate your HIL tests, perform post processing and report generation, and map test results to requirements. These tools help you perform a wider range of tests earlier in the software development process, which reduces overall development cost while improving product quality.

The discussion of HIL simulation is at a high level. Given different embedded system hardware platforms, HIL testing platforms and tools, and different HIL test objectives, the detailed HIL workflows can be different for different engineering organizations.

Summary of Simulation Methods

To deal with the increasing complexity faced in embedded control system development, simulation techniques allow you to test your design and implementation early in the development cycle before testing the final embedded controller on real plants to reduce time and cost while improving quality. Control algorithms are tested at the model level for functionality using MIL simulation. Model coverage and conformance to modeling standards are also checked in MIL simulation before generating production code from the models to prevent errors at the modeling level. The generated control algorithm code is integrated with hand written code and/or other control application components and tested using SIL simulation. Different layers of the software platform can be included in the SIL simulation for different levels of simulation accuracy, for example, middleware, OS, I/O software stacks, and protocol stack. Control software is tested in SIL for meeting functional requirements also code coverage standards. Finally, after deploying the embedded control software to the control hardware, the entire embedded control system (integrated software and hardware) is tested using HIL simulation in real-time. The controller performance including execution timing, memory usage, and CPU usage etc., are tested at this level. HIL simulation can be performed before the actual plant is available, allowing the parallel development of the equipment and the controller. In all there levels of simulations, it is desirable that the same set of test cases is used and tests are automated.

Chapter 7
Validation and Verification

INTRODUCTION

In last chapter, we introduced simulation techniques that are used in testing. In this chapter we will talk about verification and validation for which we apply these simulation techniques along with other methods to test requirements, design and implementation.

Verification is the process of evaluating design artifacts of a development phase to determine whether they meet the specified requirements for that phase. Verification is performed to ensure that the design artifacts meet their specified requirements. Design artifacts include requirement specifications, design documents, code, and test cases. It asks the question: "Are we building the product right?"

Validation is the process of evaluating final product, system or system component during or at the end of the development cycle to determine whether it meets specified business requirements. It is performed to ensure that the product actually meets the user's needs and that the specifications were correct in the first place; in other words, to demonstrate that the product fulfills its intended use when placed in its intended environment. It asks the question: "Are we building the right product?" It is performed on actual product or software by testing. It is entirely possible that a product passes verification but fails validation. This happens when a product is built as per the specifications but the specifications themselves fail to address the user's needs.

DOI: 10.4018/978-1-5225-2303-1.ch007

Verification and validation is applied throughout the development process and enables you to find errors before they can find a way into the next development phase or the final product. Most system design errors are introduced in the original specification, but aren't found until the test phase. When engineering teams use models to perform virtual testing or real-time testing early in the development cycle, they discover and eliminate problems and reduce development time by as much as 50%. Verification and validation should be systematically performed across all design artifacts including requirements, model, code, and the final embedded system (Figure 1).

Early Requirements Validation

You can uncover incorrect, inconsistent, and missing requirements and design flaws early by simulating system behavior to validate requirements and by specifying system design properties that guarantee functional behavior. This

Figure 1. Model-based control design verification and validation workflow

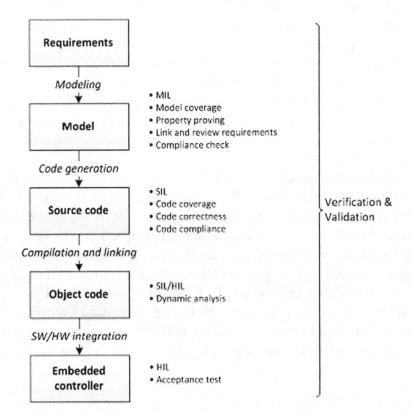

can be done by creating high-level system models and running simulations. A high-level system model is a functional model without implementation details. You can gain further insight into system behavior through simulation by creating a system model that includes the control algorithm or software model and the physical plant and environmental models of your system. This system model is associated with system requirements to analyze and validate requirements early in the development process.

You write system-level tests and link them to requirements. You define key test scenarios and document and systematically analyze system behavior captured in the system model simulation. Analysis results provide early feedback on the completeness and integrity of requirements and can be used to define expected behavior of the algorithm or software model for further design refinement. You explore the entire design parameter space in simulation to help select those tests that are critical to run on real-time targets or real-world hardware. Requirements traceability to design helps manage change and reduce waste in the design lifecycle.

Through requirement validation you can iteratively refine requirements and refine design properties. Formal methods can be applied to analyze models to improve your designs and reveal unanticipated functionality that would be difficult to uncover by simulation alone.

Design Verification

Model-based design incorporates simulation and testing to streamline the design verification process. Design verification is performed through iterative testing and analysis. You refine your design through rapid iterations and verification cycles in an interactive test environment. Early in the development process, you can:

- Detect design errors such as integer overflow, division by zero, and dead logic in models
- Generate reusable unit tests that satisfy model coverage and meet specific user-defined design
- Verification objectives
- Expose design flaws and inconsistencies in requirements using the model coverage test

In Model-based design you create a system model that serves as an executable specification for component design and verification. Previously developed system-level tests can be reused to verify detailed component designs against the executable specification in simulation. You can also apply model coverage analysis tools e.g. Simulink Verification and Validation to pinpoint untested elements of your design or missing requirements.

You can adopt or develop modeling standards and check your model for compliance. By applying modeling standards to your design verification process you can reduce the number of errors introduced early in the development process. You can create custom model checks or use modeling checks in model-based design tools that help you comply with industry standards, such as DO-178B, IEC 61508, and ISO 26262.

Embedded Software Test and Verification

Two standard approaches are used for verifying embedded software: model-to-software verification and run-time error detection in the source code. With model-to-software verification, a fully verified model of your embedded software serves as a golden reference for comparing the model's behavior with your handwritten or model-generated software. With run-time error detection, tools for run-time analysis apply formal methods on handwritten or automatically generated source code to verify that the code does not have run-time errors. These verification processes are especially important for high-integrity embedded systems.

With Model-based control design, you first develop a model of your embedded control software. After verifying the control model against requirements or expected behavior, you can generate code automatically from the model to reduce the chance of errors being introduced through hand coding. Model-to-software verification techniques like software-in-the-loop (SIL) testing and processor-in-the-loop (PIL) (by running the object code on real target hardware or an instruction set simulator) testing can be applied to handwritten or model-generated code to confirm that the behavior of the software matches the behavior of the model.

Code verification tools which apply formal methods are used to ensure code correctness and detect run-time errors. For example, MathWorks Polyspace® code verification products detect run-time errors and prove the absence of specific errors in C/C++ and Ada source code, whether handwritten, model-generated, or a combination of the two. Mathematical analysis techniques in Polyspace® products prove the absence of overflow, divide-by-zero, out-of-bounds array access, and other run-time errors in source code, without requiring program execution, code instrumentation, or test cases.

Industry Standards for High-Integrity Systems, including DO-178B, IEC-61508, and ISO-26262, are sometimes applied as part of the verification process for safety related software or for software certification.

Hardware-in-the-Loop Simulation for Embedded Systems

Hardware-in-the-loop (HIL) simulation minimizes costs and risks in embedded system development by enabling you to test your embedded system before deploying it in a production environment. You test your embedded system in real time by connecting it to a simulation of the environment. This approach enables you to use the same system-level models throughout the development process, from requirement analysis to design to real-time HIL simulation.

HIL simulation begins with a system-level model that includes the control algorithm, the plant and its operating environment. You can automatically generate C code and HDL code from the plant and environment models to run on a real-time simulator that delivers inputs and receives outputs from the embedded control system (actual hardware product) as the real physical system would. As a result, you obtain greater value from the system-level model for testing and verifying the real-time performance of your embedded system.

HIL simulation is especially valuable when:

- The plant under control is not yet built.
- Safety and performance concerns dictate testing the embedded system prior to human involvement.
- You need to minimize expensive downtime for the real plant.
- You need to test operation and failure conditions that are difficult to physically replicate.

TESTING AGAINST FUNCTIONAL REQUIREMENTS

Since functional requirements specify behavior in response to particular conditions, you can build test cases (test inputs, expected outputs, and assessments) from the system functional requirements. Test cases reproduce specific test conditions using test inputs, and assess the actual system model outputs against the expected outputs. As you develop the system model, you build test cases that check system behavior and link them to corresponding functional requirements. By defining these test cases in test files, you can periodically check your model and archive results to demonstrate that the design meets the requirements at different phases in the development lifecycle.

This section describes the process for control system requirements formalization. The outputs of this process are the executable models (for example, Simulink models) representing the test inputs (Test Generators) and representing the requirements (Test Monitors). These models are useful for automated verification, including MIL, SIL, and HIL testing. They are first created for MIL test and it is efficient they are reused for SIL and HIL test. Test Generators and Monitors are components of test harness models representing each test case. This process is a step of the model based control verification process.

This process applies to verification of a control model (for example developed using Simulink and Stateflow), a library of control models, or application software as implementation of control functions. This test definition process also extends to HIL test. Test case models generated through this process can be automatically executed with the aid of test management tools, e.g. IBM Rational Quality Manager (RQM) or a custom testing tool developed in MATLAB/Simulink. While the nature of tests and required infrastructure for MIL and SIL testing are different, the process for building tests from requirements and the modeling of tests is the same.

Formalize Requirements and Model Test Cases

In order to perform either formal verification or verification by simulation (run-time) of the control algorithm, the sentences representing the functional requirements are translated into an executable model (e.g. Simulink model), called Monitor model. This process is applicable for control algorithm/system models, a library of control models, or application software.

This section describes the formalization of functional requirements and then how to translate them into executable models (Monitor models) to be used in the formal verification test. During this process, a set of use cases (i.e. relevant input traces for the testing of the control algorithm) and the corresponding Test Generators shall be created.

To start this process, the control requirement document (SSRD or SRS) and the list of control system inputs and outputs provide by ICD (interface control document) are required. For example, the multivariable control example introduced in Chapter 4 has three control requirements, shown in Figure 2. Requirements are provided with an ID, name, rationale, and release attributes for better requirement management and traceability.

And the Inputs/Outputs of the example control system may be reported as in Figure 3 with all relevant information provided.

Refinement and Representation of Requirement Statements

The step of refining requirement statements into concise mathematical representation involves transforming functional requirements previously formulated into structured sentences with a well-defined logical interpretation (a pattern-based expression) with unambiguous meaning. This step ensures that the requirement can be either verified or not, without leaving margin to interpretations.

A pattern is a structured and formalized sentence containing free expressions for which the value is not specified. As soon as all the free expressions assume a Boolean truth value, the pattern is automatically verified or not (true or false) depending on the specific logic of the operators of which it is composed.

Figure 2. Example of definition of a requirement in the Control requirements document, with all the necessary information

ID	Name	Requirement	Rationale	Release
1.1	Overshoot	No overshoot during set point change.	Transient performance	First 8/12/2016
1.2	S.S. error	0.2C steady state error band.	Steady state performance	First 8/12/2016
1.3	Settling time	Reach the temperature set point as fast as possible.	Fast response time for set point change	First 8/12/2016

Figure 3. Example of input variable definition in the Control requirements document, with all the necessary information

Outputs							
Name	**Description**	**Type**	**Definition**	**Range**	**Units**	**Accuracy**	**ICD**
Y1	First output	Analog input, 0 to 5VDC Temperature sensor	Supply air temperature	-10 to 10	°C	0.1 °C over -10 to 10 °C	Controls ICD

For example, a pattern P may be defined as

P: (the temperature t is less than 50°C) AND (the temperature t is greater than 30°C)

The truthfulness of the pattern P depends on the truth values of the conditions "the temperature t is less than 50 °C" and "the temperature t is greater than 30°C" (i.e. on the values of the variables t), and on the logic operator AND. If the values of t are time varying, likewise is the truthfulness of the pattern.

The formalization step shall be applied to each functional requirement. Design team can decide what language to use for formalizing the natural language requirements. The test engineers shall ensure to master the language in which the requirements are translated in order to be able to recognize and transform sentences into the structured pattern of the specific language. After that, the natural language requirements specification is re-formulated using the patterns provided by the specific language of the team's choice. Once the requirements specification has been re-structured it is possible to obtain a logical/mathematical representation of each requirement (pattern-based expression). This step also helps find inconsistency, error, and missing requirements in the original requirements specification.

The formalization step is clarified with an example. Suppose a requirement present in the controls requirements document is formulated as follows:

REQ1: When the outside ambient temperature is greater than 30 °C for 30 seconds, the Control system must be operating

where the outside ambient temperature is described as a signal *OAT* with values from -273.15 to 100 and the state of the Control system (ON or OFF) is represented with a Boolean signal *cs*.

The main steps for formalizing the requirement are:

- Identify the "actors":
  - Define the two constants: *ThresholdTemp* as 30 °C, *ThresholdTime* as 30 seconds;
  - Define the condition *High Temperatures(HT) as* "the outside ambient temperature is greater than *ThresholdTemp*"
  - Define the condition *Operating (O) as* "the Control system must be operating".

The "actors" are the variables *OAT* and *cs*, the constants *ThresholdTime* and *ThresholdTemp*, and the conditions *HT* and *O*.

- Reformulate the specification with the help of the previous defined actors:
  - When *HighTemperatures* for *ThresholdTime, Operating*.
- Reformulate using predefined specific logic patterns (which depend on the specific semantic of the chosen language), for example:
  - If HighTemperatures hold for ThresholdTime then Operating hold

Translate Formalized Requirements into Test Monitors

In the previous step, statements representing functional requirements have been transformed into pattern-based expressions, thus they can be easily used to support either formal verification or verification by simulation (run-time). Indeed, pattern-based expressions are particularly suitable for the specification and modeling of a set of property checkers to implement a requirement satisfaction monitor for run-time verification. Moreover, the "actors" have been identified: variables, constants, events, conditions, etc.

Whatever is the language used to formalize the requirements in pattern-based expressions, these patterns can be transformed into Monitor models, for example Simulink models. The inputs of a Monitor model representing a pattern are typically actors (variables, events, or conditions) while the monitor model's output is the evaluation result of the pattern, e.g. Pass/Fail. A requirement pattern output signal represents the overall requirement evaluation result; its truthfulness depends on the values of the signals the Monitor model receives as inputs.

The engineer shall validate the Monitor model created, defining relevant input traces and checking the outputs are as expected, otherwise restart this process from the beginning. If the output is not what is expected, the formalization and modeling steps must be reviewed in order to detect the error.

Define Use Cases and Create Test Generators

In this step, use cases, which aim is to produce various operational conditions that the control systems are likely to encounter, are constructed. Use cases shall be created to represent the operation conditions described in the functional requirements. These use cases are defined, for example, as Simulink models or Excel files, called Test Generators. Test generator outputs are used to stimulate the control system and also serve as inputs to test monitors.

Test Monitor and Test Generator Example

Consider the control example used for control design process in Chapter 4 and control analysis and MIL simulation in Chapter 6. The example control requirements are given in Figure 2. Let's consider requirement 1.1: No overshoot during set point change. We will verify if the control design meets this requirement by designing a test case and creating test monitor and test generator for testing.

First the control requirement is formalized. The formalized requirement is: If the feedback control is enabled then the plant outputs shall not exceed their set points. This requirement statement is structured and verifiable. The test case is as follows. The system starts operation in open loop without feedback control and the plant inputs are fixed. After the plant outputs reaching their steady state, the feedback control is enabled and plant outputs begin to track their set points under the control action. The plant outputs are compared against the set points to check if there is overshoot or not. The test case inputs are generated by the test generator whose outputs are enable signals and the set points. The test generator is created in Simulink as a subsystem (see Figure 4). The formalized requirement is transformed into the test monitor model. The inputs to the monitor are the enable signals, the plant outputs, and the output set points. The test monitor for the first plant output is also implemented in Simulink, shown in Figure 5, which includes a state machine created using Stateflow. The state machine determines the output of the monitor which is a Boolean signal based on the monitor inputs. The states and transitions of the states of the state machine in the test monitor are shown in Figure 6. According to this state machine, the monitor output is true when the feedback control is not enabled (that is the there is no feedback control); when the feedback control is enabled and the output is less than the set point, the output is true; as soon as the output exceeds the set point, the output becomes false and remains false. Based on the monitor implementation, the requirement is met when the monitor output is always true during the testing; the requirement is not met if the monitor output becomes false at any instant during the test run. Recall that in Chapter 6 after the control adjustment, the first plant output tracks the set point without any overshoot (refer to Figure 7(a) in Chapter 6). It is verified by the monitor output which is true throughout the simulation

Figure 4. Test generator example

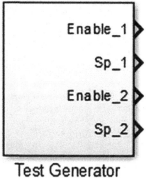

Figure 5. Test monitor example

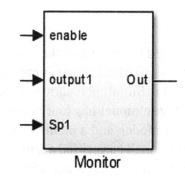

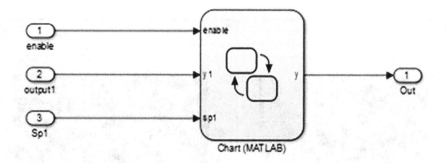

Figure 6. State machine in the example test monitor

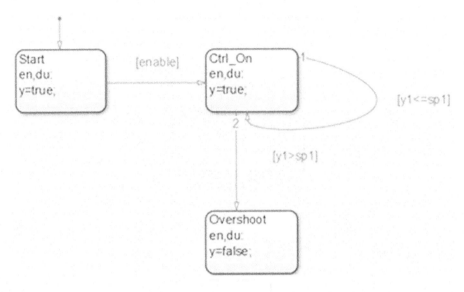

(see Figure 7). Thus, based on test result the non-overshooting requirement for the first plant output is satisfied by the control design. The complete test case model implemented in Simulink is shown in Figure 8. It can be seen that at a high level, the test case model has four components: a test generator, a controller model, a plant model, and a monitor model. Every functional and performance requirement shall be verified against the control design through test cases so that the both proper design and valid requirements are achieved.

Figure 7. Monitor output and the plant output during the test

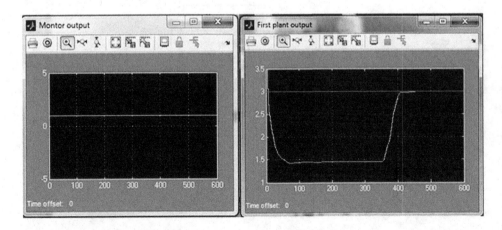

Figure 8. Test case model structure at a high level

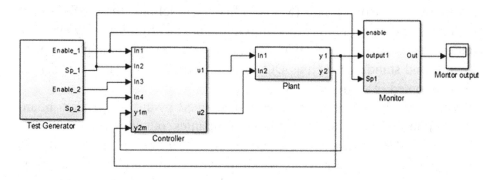

MODEL CHECKING

Model checking improves model quality by preventing design problems early in the design process: it enforces modeling best practices; it detects and troubleshoots modeling and code generation issues; it checks models for version related issues; it creates report useful for process audit. Modeling standards can be enforced as part of model checking. Static analysis of models is performed during model checking. Model checking is performed before automatic code generation from the model.

Modeling Standards Compliance

Engineering organizations in automotive, aerospace, and other industries can leverage the benefits of model-based design by implementing modeling standards across their teams. High-integrity guidelines, including IEC 61508-3(functional safety of electrical/electronic/programmable electronic safety-related systems-Part 3: software requirements) and MISRA-C (a set of software development guidelines for C programming language developed by MISRA (Motor Industry Software Reliability Association) aims to facilitate code safety, security, portability and reliability in embedded systems), strongly recommend the adoption and enforcement of modeling standards because of their numerous advantages. Models built with well-defined standards have a consistent visual presentation that makes them easier to read and understand. Such models have uniform interfaces, reducing integration problems and making it easier to share designs. Modeling standards also help ensure consistent code generation, model behavior, and traceability.

Primary existing guidelines for model-based design are the MathWorks Automotive Advisory Board (MAAB) Style Guidelines, the NASA Orion Guidelines, and the Simulink Modeling Guidelines for High-Integrity Systems. Guidelines cover efficient code generation, the design of high-integrity systems, and standards such as DO-178B and IEC 61508 (ISO 26262) are widely adopted in some industries.

While the MAAB guidelines were developed by an independent board of automotive OEMs and suppliers, companies outside the automotive industry use them to improve collaboration among internal teams and with partners. MAAB guidelines target to improve consistency, interoperability, error prevention and knowledge sharing. The Orion Guidance, Navigation, and Control MATLAB and Simulink standards were developed by a team of NASA engineers and contractors who updated and expanded the MAAB guidelines as needed for the NASA Orion program. The MAAB Style Guidelines version 3.0 incorporates a subset of the original Orion rules. Simulink Modeling Guidelines for High-Integrity Systems were developed to help engineers create Simulink® models that are complete, unambiguous, robust, and verifiable.

Once you have selected a basic set of guidelines, you can also modify and extend them to cover the specific needs of your organization. You can customize the MAAB guidelines by selecting specific implementations when the MAAB guideline provides options (as in rule NA_0005) or by adding specific detail when the rule provides general guidelines (for example, by specifying a compiler for rule NA_0026). Customization also involves defining basic standards, such as where labels should be displayed on signals (as covered by MAAB rule NA_0005). In addition, your organization can create new rules to address workflow issues not addressed by the industry standard.

Conformance to guidelines can be enforced more efficiently using an automated checking tool such as the Simulink Model Advisor. Enforcement is generally most effective if your organization requires mandatory guideline checks for certain projects in the development workflow—for example, if engineers are required to check their models for compliance before they check the models into a configuration management system or generate code. You may decide to relax enforcement of certain guidelines during initial development, requiring engineers to follow those guidelines only in later development stages. Enforcement of some guidelines may be stricter for fixed-point projects or high-integrity projects and more relaxed for projects that involve legacy modules.

Reports are the primary mechanism for enforcing guidelines. Reporting serves an immediate purpose in providing check feedback to the engineer and a long-term benefit in enabling the engineering team to determine which guidelines are causing the most modeling problems. On high-integrity projects, the reports may be checked into the configuration management system with the model and maintained as a development artifact.

As an example we apply MathWorks Model Advisor to check the test monitor model we developed. This tool allows you to apply different types of checks and industry standards. You can run individual or group checks with the Model Advisor tool. For demonstration purpose, we chose MAAB model guidelines (see Figure 9). The Model Advisor report was shown in Figure 10. To ensure your model complies with your own standards or guidelines, you can use the Model Advisor APIs and Configuration Editor to create your own Model Advisor checks. You can also modify the built-in modeling compliance and industry standards to create your own custom verification checks. Similar to the built-in checks, these custom checks permit you to specify what actions you want the Model Advisor to take, such as producing an error or automatically applying fixes to your model.

As another example for model checking, we apply Simulink Design Verifier tool to the same test monitor model for error detection. Design Verifier can be used to detect design errors in model including dead logic, integer overflow,

Figure 9. Model Advisor user interface

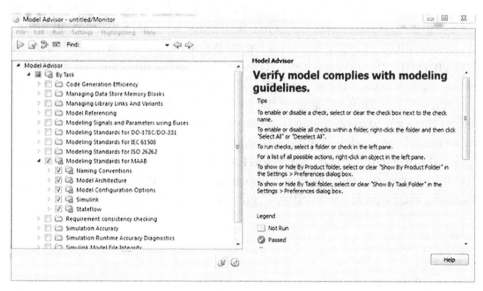

269

Figure 10. Model Advisor report

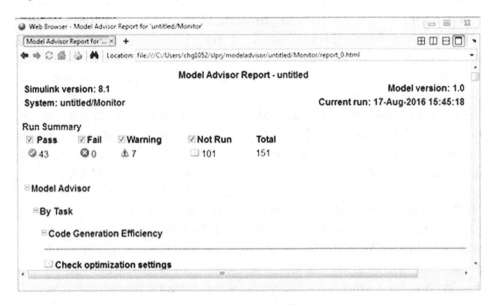

division by zero, and out of bound array access (see Figure 11). In this example, we selected to detect dead logic so other options were grayed out by the tool. After running the Design Verifier check on the test monitor model, dead logic was detected for one transition condition (highlighted in red in the model)(see Figure 12). In a state machine, multiple transition conditions are tested according to the assigned order. After the first transition condition was tested to be unsatisfied, this second transition condition is tested. Since y1 is always greater than the set point when testing the second transition condition, the condition of y1 being less than the set point will never happen. Although Design Verifier found dead logic, it does not affect the function of the monitor in this case. It means the second transition condition is unnecessary and you can remove it without changing the behavior of the monitor. This example shows that error detection can find error in the model for you and it becomes more useful for models of complex systems.

In addition to model checking, software tools exist for checking the source code through static analysis. For example, Mathworks PolySpace and Synopsis Coverity check code for MISRA-C guidelines conformance.

Figure 11. Design Verifier for model error detection

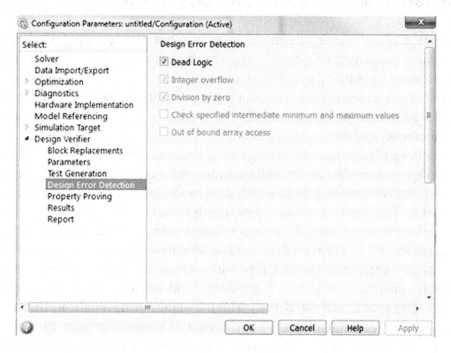

Figure 12. Dead logic detected by Design Verifier

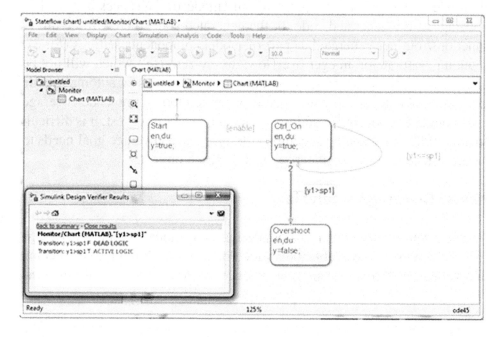

MEASURE MODEL AND CODE COVERAGE

Coverage is any metric of completeness of a test or a test suite. Coverage measures the quality of a set of tests; supplements functional requirements verification by pointing to untested areas; helps create regression test suites; provides a stopping criterion for unit testing. Coverage analysis can improve model and code quality. It can also be used as a tool to identify missing requirements and missing test cases.

Model and code coverage test identify untested elements of your design. Coverage test results can be collected for a test case or test suite. Coverage reports measure the degree to which your model is verified by a test case or test suite. The report determines how much a test case or test suite exercises execution pathways through the design. The percentage of pathways that a test case exercises is called its model coverage. Model coverage is a measure of how thoroughly a test tests a model. It provides a cumulative metric of executing logical conditions, switches, subsystems, and lookup table interpolation intervals in your model. Models with high coverage metrics indicate that they have been more thoroughly tested. You can use coverage information to traverse the model and identify which aspects of your design lack coverage. You can then determine whether you need to modify the requirements, test cases, or design to meet your coverage goals. The idea of code coverage is similar to the model coverage. However, coverage of a model doesn't necessarily reflect coverage of the generated code. In the generated code, there will be utility functions/routines generated as part of model components settings (for ex: rounding, saturate on integer overflow, div-by-zero etc.) which will not be covered using model coverage. Also optimization settings for automatic code generation play a part how the code is generated too. So the code coverage test should be conducted in addition to the model coverage test. It is difficult to have 100% coverage for a complex design, and a coverage goal needs to be pre-selected by the engineering team for each project.

Model Coverage Analysis

You detect untested elements of your design using model coverage. Coverage metrics provided by available tools vary. For example, Simulink Verification and Validation™ coverage analysis produces the following coverage metrics:

- Execution coverage is the most basic form of model coverage. For each block or subsystem, execution coverage determines whether or not the item is executed during simulation.

- Statement coverage is the basic form of code coverage for C S-functions and generated code. It identifies code statements that have been exercised.

- Cyclomatic complexity measures the structural complexity of a model, approximating the McCabe complexity measure for code generated from the model. In general, the McCabe complexity measure is slightly higher because of error checks that the model coverage analysis does not consider.

- Condition coverage examines blocks (or code) that output the logical combination of their inputs, such as the Logic block and Stateflow transitions. A test case achieves full coverage if it causes each input to each instance of a logic block in the model and each condition on a transition to be true at least once during the simulation and false at least once during the simulation. Condition coverage analysis reports for each block in the model whether the test case fully covered the block.

- Decision coverage examines items that represent decision points in a model, such as Simulink Switch blocks, Stateflow states, or conditional statements in code. For each item, decision coverage determines the percentage of the total number of simulation paths through the item that the simulation actually traversed.

- Lookup table coverage (LUT) records the frequency of usage for each interpolation interval. (A test case achieves full coverage if it executes each interpolation and extrapolation interval at least once.)

- Modified condition/decision coverage (MC/DC) analyzes safety-critical software, as defined by RTCA DO-178, and determines whether the logical inputs have independently changed the output (for models and code). MCDC check examines blocks that output the logical combination of their inputs (e.g., the Logic block) and Stateflow transitions to determine the extent to which the test case tests the independence of logical block inputs and transition conditions. A test case achieves full coverage for a block if, for every input, there is a pair of simulation times when changing that input alone causes a change in the block's output. A test case achieves full coverage for a transition if, for each condition on the transition, there is at least one time when a change in the condition triggers the transition.

- Relational boundary coverage examines Simulink blocks, Stateflow charts and MATLAB® function blocks that have an explicit or implicit relational operation.
- Saturate on integer overflow coverage records the number of times blocks such as the Abs block saturates on integer overflow.
- Signal range coverage indicates the minimum and maximum values generated during simulation by each block output and for all Stateflow data objects.
- Signal size coverage records the minimum, maximum, and allocated size for all variable-size signals in a model. Only blocks with variable-size output signals are included in the report.

We use the test monitor as an example here again for model coverage analysis. We used Simulink Design Verifier as the coverage tool in this case. Simulink Design Verifier coverage analysis records model coverage data for the Simulink blocks and functions in the model. After running coverage analysis, we got the report showing model complexity and decision coverage and we did not have full coverage (see Figure 13). The coverage report also

Figure 13. Monitor model coverage report

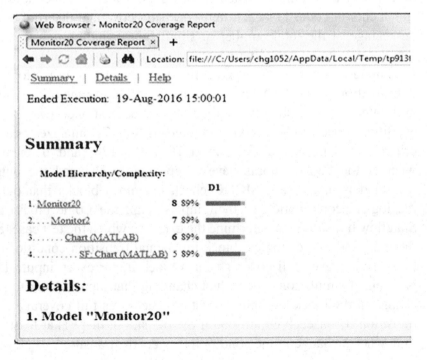

gave information about the uncovered model element which is the dead logic we found early during model error detection (see Figure 14). Since we know the uncovered transition statement is unnecessary, so we can remove it without affecting the function of the monitor (see Figure 15). Reran the coverage on the modified monitor model, we achieved full model coverage (see Figure 16). This example shows why and where coverage analysis is useful.

CONCLUSION

Validation makes sure the product developed meets user requirements and functions; verification makes sure that the design at each stage meets the requirements flowed down from the previous design stage. System requirements are modelled and analyzed to make sure that they are complete, consistent, and correct.

Figure 14. Coverage report showing uncovered model part

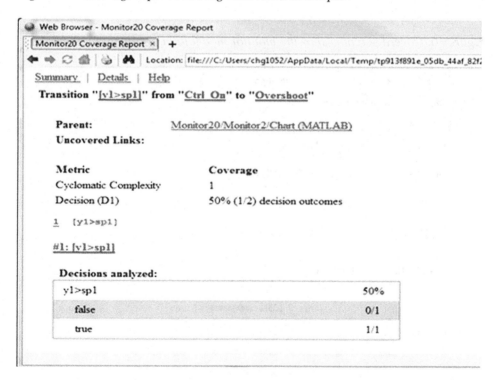

Figure 15. Monitor model with dead logic removed

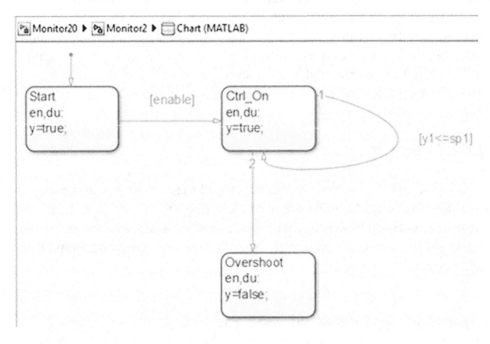

Figure 16. Coverage report showing monitor model full coverage

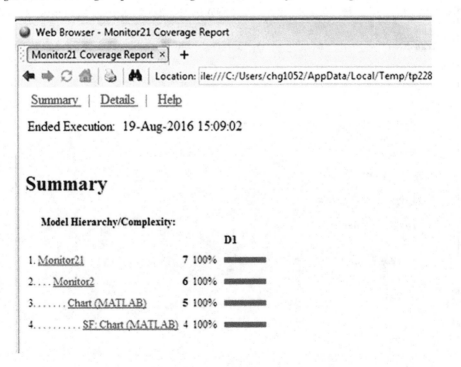

During the requirement decomposition process, subsystem and component requirements are derived and developed. They could be further refined at each step of testing and verification. With each level of decomposition, test plans for integration are developed to make sure the final product meets the custom requirements. For functional requirements testing, test cases are created and implemented in models. Simulation techniques are used to verify that the control design passes all test cases associated with requirements. The control model should also be checked for coding standards conformance and model coverage if it is used to auto generate the production code. The auto generated code, subsequently, should also be checked against coding standards and code coverage requirements.

Chapter 8

Configuration Management and Documentation

INTRODUCTION

Improving Communications of Complex Systems Projects

It is not just engineering alone that creates a successful product. It is shown that one third of all produced devices do not meet performance or functionality requirements, and that twenty four percent of all projects are cancelled due to schedule delays that could not be recovered (Shamieh, 2012). Quite often the reason for a fatal system failure is not due to the system's engineering design; rather, it is due to failures of communication. With ever increasing complexities in the systems and pressure for increased productivity from development teams, communication becomes the key for successful deployment of the model-based design process and ultimately successful product development.

Large, complex system development projects suffering from poor communications is not a surprise. Most large development teams are widely distributed across cities, countries, and even continents. Language and cultural barriers make communication more difficult, and time differences often make collaboration less productive. Even for employees within the same company, organizational divides can impede communication and reduce productivity. Poor communication can cause a lot of problems, including:

DOI: 10.4018/978-1-5225-2303-1.ch008

lack of clarity of system functions and use cases; multiple interpretations of system requirements; incomplete and overlooked requirements; time wasted gathering information manually from multiple sources; times wasted working with outdated documents; gaps and redundancies in responsibilities, etc. To make things worse, large, complex embedded systems development creates more documentation and design artifacts, uses tools from multiple vendors, and involves team members from multiple disciplinary areas. How to address these communication challenges is becoming more and more critical for achieving product development success.

The best way to overcome the communications difficulties inherent in a large team environment is to provide a common platform for development and maintenance and to establish a common language for communicating across the platform.

Today's embedded systems often contain multiple subsystems from various sources and millions of lines of code developed by engineering teams from multiple companies, countries, and cultures. To streamline the development and testing processes, it is essential to provide a unified systems development platform. Using a common development platform breaks down barriers between teams, enabling engineers to work together throughout the development lifecycle. A unified platform makes it easier for distributed teams to integrate their work and share knowledge, saving precious time off the development cycle. By reducing miscommunication and streamlining workflows, you can expect to see substantial improvements in quality and productivity and keep the project on track.

Based on this common platform, the overall development process can be managed and tracked. Using this platform, stakeholders and engineers process and create data that is shared, analyzed, and reported on efficiently and effectively throughout the systems development life cycle. Automation and federation tools that leverage technologies to streamline communication and automate workflows can help collaboration within a project team. System life cycle development tools need to be integrated to eliminate barriers between tools. Through tool integration, it makes it easier to use tools from different vendors for a system development project, while easily sharing system life cycle data, such as requirements, models, change requests, test cases, and code. Documentation often involves a lot of manual labor. Document automation tools can streamline the production of custom documents, while ensuring consistency of information across multiple documents.

Applying a model-based design approach is an effective way of uniting diverse development teams spanning multiple cultures and engineering disciplines. In this approach, a model is the common language used by all members in a design team throughout the development life cycle. Modeling breaks down communication barriers by providing models as visual representations of system specification and design, making it easier for every team member to understand the system and sharing cross-functional knowledge. A shared understanding leads directly into productivity improvements, since engineers are no longer wasting time resolving issues caused by misunderstanding and miscommunications.

Managing Changes During the Development Life Cycle

When designing a complex embedded system, critical information is constantly changing. The world around us is changing constantly and rapidly. Change is also the nature of the model-based design approach in response to the changing environment. Systems engineering involves iterative design and test processes: you design your system, develop models, test the models, redesign to fix defects, and the cycle repeats. So you are constantly updating models, test results, and other information. Requirements can change too as market and business needs vary or missing and inconsistent requirements are identified in the development process.

Traditionally, large engineering teams have relied on text-based documentation as the source of all project related information: requirements documents, architecture documents, design documents, and other related documents. But documents are limiting in the way that they simply record information and don't easily allow you to change the information and manage the information consistency across multiple documents. Documents are static and not organically connected. If you rely solely on documentation, documents will be obsolete before they have been shared. Systems development teams need a consistent, flexible mechanism for capturing critical information and facilitating updates while maintaining integrity.

In complex development environments of today, the number of requirements for complex systems is increasing, i.e. in the hundreds, or even thousands, managing changes become ever important in order to avoid chaos and confusion. Systems development teams need an approach that facilitates effective change management for large, complex systems. A robust mechanism for managing information is the only way to avoid problems that result when multiple versions of critical documents are floating around all over the place.

Configuration management can be applied to address this challenge, which is the topic discussed in the next section.

CONFIGURATION MANAGEMENT OF COMPLEX EMBEDDED SYSTEMS

What is Configuration Management?

Configuration management, as we know it today, started in the late 1960s. In the 1970s, the American government developed a number of military standards, which included configuration management. Later, especially in the 1990s, many other standards and publications discussing configuration management have emerged.

Configuration means "a relative arrangement of parts or elements." Configuration management therefore refers to managing a relative arrangement of parts or elements (Hass, 2003). There are many definitions of configuration management and many opinions on what is really its. We will not discuss them here for our purposes. It is perfectly alright for a company to use its own definition of configuration management, but it is advisable to investigate how that definition relates to other relevant definitions to make sure no activity constituting configuration management has been left out. "Configuration item" refers to an element of a configuration that is subject to configuration management or a component of a system requiring control over its development throughout the life cycle of the system. Configuration items that are different versions of the same original item are obviously strongly related, but each one is an individual item, which will be identified and may be extracted and used independently. This is one of the main points of configuration management: to be able to revert to an earlier version of an item. The major activity areas of configuration management include identification, storage, change control, and status reporting.

The identification activity is to uniquely identify a configuration item and specify its relations to the outside world and to other configuration items. Identification is one of the cornerstones of configuration management, because it is impossible to control something whose identity you don't know. Each organization must define its own conventions for unique identification. One general convention most often is not enough; typically, a number of conventions are necessary for various classes of configuration items, such as documents and code. These conventions may be difficult to define. You have to consider what purpose the unique identification serves and how to implement it in the easiest way. It will connect the registration and the physical configuration item in such a way that it's always possible to find the configuration item. This should be considered when defining conventions for unique identification. Furthermore, the procedures are tool dependent and often highly predefined in the tools available. The unique identification also registers the relations between configuration items, such as variations or parts of each other. It's important to define the conventions for unique identification so that the formation of new configuration items will not make it necessary to change or delete existing configuration items.

The storage is to ensure that a configuration item will not disappear or be damaged, that it can be found at any time and delivered in the condition in which you expect to receive it, and that a record is kept to indicate who has been given the item or a copy of it. Storage takes place in libraries. Traditionally, three types of libraries are mentioned in connection with software development: controlled, dynamic, and static libraries. The controlled or configuration management library is where configuration items are stored. The dynamic or development library is where items are kept while they are being developed. Typically, this will be in the developer's own area. In this library, it's possible to work with an item without bringing it into contact with other items or exposing it to the influence of other items. The static or user library is where items are used. When being used in the static library, items must under no circumstances be changed. The latter two libraries are not part of the configuration management system.

The purpose of change control is to be fully in control of all change requests for a product and of all implemented changes. For any configuration item, it must be possible to identify changes in it relative to its predecessor. Any change should be traceable to the item where the change was implemented. When developing and maintaining a product, changes are inevitable. People make mistakes, customers need changes, and the environment in which the product operates evolves. In addition, people constantly develop their knowledge of the problem and their ability to solve it, leading to design changes.

Status reporting makes available, in a useful and readable way, the information necessary to effectively manage a product's development and maintenance. Other activity areas in configuration management are the data sources for status reporting, providing metadata and change control data. Status reporting entails extraction, arrangement, and formation of data from various sources in response to demand.

Services Provided By Configuration Management

When focusing on software products, a typical configuration management system provides the following services (Estublier, 2001).

Managing a Repository of Components

There is a need for storing the different components of a software product and all their versions safely. This topic includes version management, product modeling and complex object management.

The idea of versioning is simple: each time a file is changed a revision is created. A file thus evolves as a succession of revisions, usually referred to by successive numbers. Then from any revision, a new line of change can be created, leading to a revision tree. Each line is called a branch. Services provided include: history, delta, multi user management, and merging facilities. History simply records when and who created a revision along with a comment. Because two successive revisions are often very similar, Delta is used to store only differences, vastly reducing the amount of required memory. Multi-user management consists in preventing concurrent changes from overlapping each other, for example using a lock/unlock mechanism. Merge is used to resolve the conflicts between copies modified by different users from the same revision.

A configuration is often defined as a set of files, which together constitute a valid software product. The question is twofold: (1) what is the real nature of a configuration, and (2) how to build it, prove its properties and so on. The traditional way to build a configuration is by changing an existing one. A baseline and change sets are combined to create a new configuration in this approach.

Engineers Support

Configuration management considers the developer or software programmer as a major target customer: helping him/her in the usual software engineering activity became a basic service. It includes rebuilding and building, workspace support, and cooperative work support.

The aim of rebuilding is to reduce compilation time after a change, i.e. to recompile, automatically, only what is needed.

A workspace is simply a part of a file system where the files of interest (w.r.t. a given task like debug, develop etc.) are located. The workspace acts as a sphere where the programmer can work, isolated from the outside world, for the task duration. The software configuration management system is responsible for providing the right files (often a configuration), in the right file system, to let users work almost independently, and to save the changes automatically when the job is done. It is this service that really helps practitioners.

A workspace also provides a support for concurrent engineering, since many concurrent workspaces may contain and change the same objects (files). Thus there is a need for (1) resynchronizing objects and (2) controlling concurrent work. Resynchronizing in this context means merging source files. Mergers found in tools of today simply compare (on a line by line basis) the two files to merge, and a file that is historically common to both (the common ancestor). Mergers proved to work fine, to be very useful and became almost unavoidable. Controlling concurrent work means defining who can perform a change, when, on which attribute of which object.

Process Support

Process support means (1) the formal definition of what is to be performed on what: a process model, and (2) the mechanisms to help/force reality to conform to this model. Process models can be based on a product-centered modeling like a State Transition Diagram (STD); the alternative way to model processes is the so-called activity centered modeling. Experience has demonstrated that both methods are needed. Both high level model (for concurrent activity, versioning etc.) and efficient engine for their execution are needed.

Software configuration management applies software process technology, and software configuration management processes include change control process, status accounting, configuration audit, and release management. For example change control is a process

- Submission of Change Request (CR)
- Technical and business evaluation and impact analysis
- Approval by Change Control Board (CCB)
- Engineering Change Order (ECO) is generated stating
  - Changes to be made
  - Criteria for reviewing the changed Configuration Item

- Configuration Item checked out
- Changes made and reviewed
- Configuration Items checked in

Configuration Management in Model-Based Design

Model-based design is centered on models. A robust configuration management process allows teams to manage the development and use of the models among distributed team members, including the various model files themselves; the configuration of a model built from many subsystems and components models; and the model data (parameters and signal specifications).

In addition to these model configuration management needs, within a production environment a configuration management tool is also used to store artifacts that document model-based design, including simulation results, test harnesses used to verify the design (both test inputs and test outputs), generated code and logs, and reports of formal coverage tests. To ensure reproducibility, the configuration management tool may catalogue the work environment – that is, the versions of the OS, modeling tools, compilers, etc.

Lastly, a configuration management tool can be used to manage the many model variants that are created to capture both the different systems being controlled, as well as the complexity of the controllers. For example, on a given vehicle program, engineers may need to develop controllers for luxury-, mid-, and base-level vehicles, with differing requirements for the North American, Asian, and European markets.

In this case, there are multiple related plant model and controller models to be managed.

Choose a Design Management Workflow

A well designed workflow integrating design, file and configuration management tasks across the entire team is critical for project success.

In Figure 1, we show a popular representative workflow used by many companies who have adopted Model-based design (Mahapatra et al., 2012). The development work starts off with the creation of a local copy on the design engineer's machine, checking out of required files to lock them, design with modeling, testing through simulation, and review by peers of the new changes. These changes are then submitted into the central repository where regression tests and additional tasks such as automatic code generation and builds are created.

Figure 1. A popular representative source code management workflow

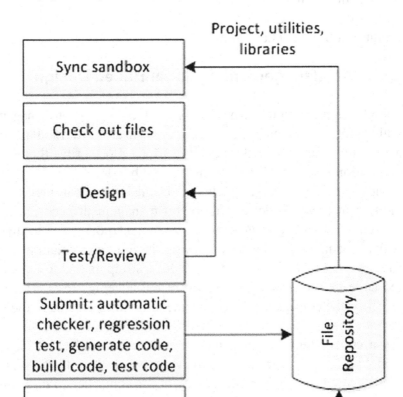

Artifacts such as reports containing design information, test pass/fail results are derived from the model files and checked into the repository. Although, the sequencing of the above steps seems logical, there are cases where it does not necessarily hold true and need to be modified to fit the specific needs of a project.

Setup Configuration Management Tool

To apply configuration management with model-based design, we need to set up a configuration management tool. The most straightforward way to put the files associated with model-based design under the control of configuration management software is to treat them as two separate tools (Walker, Friedman,

& Aberg, 2007). The user will have access to the full functionality of the configuration management software through its standard user interface.

Another approach is to connect a configuration management tool and a model-based design tool via an API. You can set up an interface from popular model-based design tools such as MATLAB and Simulink to a revision control tool. A tool called Simulink Projects offers an out-of-the-box connectivity to Subversion (an open source code management tool). It also provides a Java-based software development kit (SDK) that can be used to create connectivity to other source control tools. Such modular tool architecture where design and file management features can be decoupled from those of configuration management allows Subversion to be replaced with any desired software configuration management tool without disrupting the existing workflow. By providing flexibility to connect the design tool to various source control tools via an authoring API, the exposure of the latter tool's functionality for common tasks engineers perform can be managed, while other critical project management tasks still remain with the configuration management specialist.

Models, Data, and Artifacts

Not all information needs to be shared. What is the minimum information that should be shared to facilitate collaboration? The minimum requirement might be to store only the files required to ensure that a new user getting only these files from revision control would have a "fully functional" model. The definition of "fully functional" might change for a model as it progresses through a typical model-based design process. Initially it might be sufficient for the model to simulate. Later it might require additional files or libraries to support code generation.

To guarantee reproducibility at some point in the future, or for future root cause analysis or similar activities, it is common to additionally store "derived files" at specific points within the development process, such as the generated code, simulation or model validation results, linearized approximations to a non-linear model, etc. (Walker, Friedman, & Aberg, 2007) Other derivable files ("process artifacts") relating to the process, rather than the primary use of the models, that might be stored include model checking reports used to demonstrate review readiness, the code generation logs, coverage reports, etc. The decision about what files to store at what stages of the process will depend upon the working practices of individual groups, companies and industries.

In addition to the files we mention above, it is useful to also store "meta data" with the configuration. Such information is particularly useful for deciding which configuration to get from the repository without actually having to get it. Most revision control software automatically stores various items of metadata, such as who last modified a file, when they did it, and often a comment about what they did.

For a configuration management system to be relevant to model-based design we typically store more information than this. What is stored depends upon the task the models are being used for, the stage in the development cycle, and can vary from company to company. Some examples include:

- Project status (e.g. "current working", "release candidate", "delivered");
- Application suitability ("experimental", "robustness studies", "fixed-step solvers", "linearization", "Rapid-Prototyping", "Production Code", etc.);
- Classification ("internal use only", "suitable for export", or "imported from customer");
- The version of model-based design tools, for example the MathWorks tools, used to develop these files.

Creating Variants

For platform based product design or for product line design, you create product variants that need configuration management. A common workflow, especially in the automotive world, is to take a baseline configuration of a system, and to then create variants of it by swapping components for alternatives that implement the same type of functionality, but that are used for a different application (Walker, Friedman, & Aberg, 2007).

In reality, the creation of a variant may require a large number of components to be swapped.

One way to enable the creation of variants within the configuration management described is as follows (Walker, Friedman, & Aberg, 2007): The baseline model of the system is created. The various alternative implementations of a component are created and tested. All the models are stored within the same project. All the different models of a component which has alternatives are placed in a library under revision control, which is also placed in the same project if the component is project specific or in a utility folder if the component is a common part for the product line. The entire project is marked within the configuration management system as the baseline configuration. Part of the motivation of using a configuration management system is to be able to trace the development of a configuration, and to be able to reproduce its outputs, whether it is generated code, simulation results, linearized models, etc.

When a new team member creates a local copy of the project files to edit, often called a sandbox, from the baseline configuration, he or she has all the files need to create new variations (assuming that that team member has access to all common component libraries). This user can check-out the system model, replace a component with one of the alternatives from the revision controlled library, and hence create a new variation of the original model.

Parallel Development of Large Models

A large complex system is divided into subsystems, and subsystems are further divided into components based on system architecture. The decomposition allows parallel development and testing of subsystems and components, thus shortening the product development cycle. It is a best practice to discuss model architecture, criteria for componentization and file ownership early in the project. This would help establish contractual rules of engagement among the team members. In order to avoid later integration issues, the interfaces of subsystems and components need to be clearly defined early.

Defining the interface of a software component, whether it is a C code function, or a model subsystem, is a key first step for others being able to use it. There are a number of reasons for this (Walker, Friedman, & Aberg, 2007):

- Agreeing on interfaces is an important first step in deciding how to break down the functionality of a large system into subcomponents.
- Once component interfaces have been agreed upon they can be developed in parallel. If the interface remains stable then integrating those components into a larger system is straightforward.
- Changing the interface between components is expensive. To do so requires changes to at least two components (the source and receivers), and to their test harnesses. An interface change also makes all previous revisions of those components incompatible with the current and future configurations.

However, it does not imply that interfaces should be set in stone. If an interface change is required to support new design requirements, then the configuration management system can be used to support the interface change and minimize the impact on other team members or some tasks.

1. **Guidelines for Defining Interfaces:** The suggestions for defining the interfaces of subsystems for a new project are as follows (Walker, Friedman, & Aberg, 2007):
    o   Base the boundaries of the subsystems on those of the real systems.
    o   Keep model elaboration in mind. With the progression of the development, more and more details can be added to a model. For example, if the development process requires the addition of sensor models at a future step, one could start with an empty subsystem that either passes signals straight through, or performs a unit and/or name conversion so that the sensor interfaces are captured.
    o   Review the potential reuse of the component in support of the current design and future designs – some elements will have more common reuse than others.
    o   Define and use a signal naming convention.
2. **Define the Model Structure:** If it is possible, avoid to have a mix of implementation detail and subsystems or components in the same level of a model. This principle makes testing, and further subdivision into subcomponents, straightforward. Getting the right level of granularity for the components of a model is important. The following are some guidelines (Walker, Friedman, & Aberg, 2007):
    o   Pick granularity so that only one engineer is likely to need to edit each model at a time.
    o   For interface definition, consider the suggestions highlighted in the previous section.
    o   Group by rate of update.
    o   No decision should be set in stone. Components can and should be subdivided as they increase in size and complexity.
3. **Defining Component Interfaces:** There are many ways in which signals can be passed between different Simulink subsystems or components. The choice of which method is the most appropriate will vary from company to company, and project to project. Picking the most suitable method requires trading-off readability, robustness, and flexibility.

Walker, Friedman, & Aberg (2007) suggested the following. At the high levels of models, where components often either

- ○ Have a very large number of signals going into, and out of them; or
- ○ Do not use all the signals available, signal buses or similar model construct should be used. Should a change in the interface definition be required, one shall be able to avoid the need to make structural changes.

At the lower levels of a model, where the components are specifications or implementations of algorithms, the use of individual signal ports for example Simulink Inport and Outport can improve readability compared to the use of signal buses.

MODEL-BASED DESIGN DOCUMENTS

Role of Documents in Model-Based Design

Model-based design is centered on models. Models are used to represent the physical plant, the controller, requirements, and test cases, serving as the visualization layer between design and product. Models, when constructed, serve as the information sources of the objects they represent: ideally all information relevant to product development can be retrieved from models. Models serve as the common language among the project team. Models are understandable to domain experts, however, there are non-technical stakeholders involved in the product development. With the increase in complexity of systems and the associated models, it is becoming less likely that a non-specialist reviewer or stakeholder will be able to navigate the model, provide information for, check the information within and certify that the model is approved. However, the integrated use of documents produced as timely and consistent views on the model will facilitate stakeholder interaction. Consequently documents, as human readable reports on the model, will remain a key part of model-based design. While these information artifacts may be presented visually on screen – rather than paper-based – they remain an essential part of model-based engineering.

Engineers are comfortable interacting with information about a project in the form of a model or series of diagrams. However, the majority of stakeholders involved in a project are unlikely to be engineers. It is far more likely that these stakeholders will be more comfortable interacting with the project information using documents, whether they are in traditional paper format or in electronic format. Model-based design, with its links to stakeholders who provide input, review and approval and are far removed from the engineering world, has an even greater need to continue the effective use of documents (produced from the central model repository) to retain relevance. While use of models has been demonstrated advantageous throughout a system's life cycle, with those models being the 'source of truth', documents remain the primary means of examining, distributing and confirming that truth among broader audience.

Documents remain an essential part of model-based system definition, design, implementation and maintenance (Logan, Harvey & Spencer, 2012). By integrating documents as defined entities within a model-centric approach (Muranko & Drechsler, 2006), the content of the documents is timely, consistent and coherent and when validated provides verification that the model is "correct". Nonetheless, information in the form of a traditional document remains the principal means for most stakeholders to view and interpret the data contained within the model.

Document Generation in Model-Based Design

The essence of the systems engineering process, regardless of method (i.e. model-based), is progressive refinement of the description of a selected solution to a collection of system requirements and customer needs (Shamieh, 2012). In model-based design, this 'description', originally captured directly to paper-based documents in systems engineering process, now is captured, developed and maintained in a software data model. That data model can then be used to produce reports and documents of various kinds.

The model based design process represented by the V Model emphasizes the use and flow of data throughout the development process. Documents are generated at each stage as products or deliverables when the development team traverses the design process through it's every stage, shown in Figure 2. This model of the process shows that the initial 'design' arm of the V involves the progressive refinement of system definition data and associated validation and verification plans; the final 'test' arm of the V involves the test data and associated test reports.

During system definition and development, the outcome of each stage of refinement of the system description is a set of documents. The documents when finalized are the formal record of the output of activity at that level.

Figure 2. Document generation process in V model

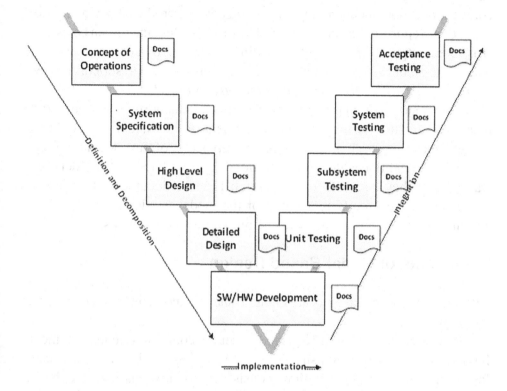

These documents are then the input for the next level of system definition – they provide requirements for the next level of activity in system definition and thus 'drive' the system definition. The documents also provide the criteria against which the system elements in the integration phase are verified and validated. For example, the system specification stage creates the system requirements specification and the system test plan, which are the inputs to the next stage of the high level design. The high level design stage creates the system architecture design document, the subsystems requirements documents, the subsystems interface control documents, and subsystem test plans. These documents subsequently become the inputs to the next stage of the detailed design.

Each set of documents is the product of the associated analysis and design activity at each level of system definition. Methods and techniques involved in developing document content can be very different, and model-based methods or techniques are used in the model-based design. Models range from spreadsheets to sophisticated computer simulations, which provide the data for document content when considered complete. Models of both the problem and solution spaces are used to enhance the validity and completeness of the content of the documents produced. Documents are produced when required to generate reports on the data captured by models. Documents can be used as structured output from a model, providing a snapshot of a chosen sub-set of data in the model at a given time. The documents are used to support review, approval and further development of the system model.

Model-centricity is maintained when the documents are used as a temporary means to validate and improve the refinement of the system model. And a model-centric approach provides a central repository of truth, the model, that is consistent and traceable while still interacting with the stakeholders in a way in which they are comfortable – though the use of documents. Documents can be created from different views of the model to address the needs of stakeholders who look at the system from various perspectives.

Documents of Model-Based Design

Different types of documents are created, shared, and maintained during the model-based design process.

These documents should be placed under the configuration management. It is a good practice to establish templates for model-based design documents for completeness of information, consistency of information, and better readability. There are several types of documents involved in model-based design.

- Regarding requirements, there are system requirement document, subsystem requirement document, software requirement specification, model requirement document, requirement traceability report.
- For design, there could be system description document, interface control document, architecture design document, controllability analysis report, and algorithm description document.
- For test, there are system, subsystem, component test plans and test reports, MIL, SIL, and HIL test plans and test reports, model check reports, model and code coverage test report, etc.
- For process, there are standard work documents, engineering guide documents, and modeling best practices etc.
- Other documents may include generated code and logs, the work environment (the versions of the OS, modeling tools, compilers, etc.) log, user manual, release notes.

Documentation Automation

Creating documentation often assumes a lot of manual labor, such as copying a diagram of a modeling tool and pasting it into a document. Also, engineers spend a lot of time collecting information from multiple sources, making sure they have the latest information, summarizing and reformatting information in order to create a customized report. It slows the development activities and is also error-prone.

Document automation tools can streamline the production of documents (Shamieh, 2012). Automation tools enables you to access a central repository of information, identify the types of information that you need, select it, and create a report. The process is simple and it also facilitates reuse and consistency of information. Not only it saves time producing the documents, but also it makes updating the documents easier. When something changes, make the necessary changes in the requirements and models, press a button and you will have the revised documents.

Many tools used in model-based design have reporting capabilities such as Simulink and IBM Rhapsody. Customization of reporting is also supported by some tools. For example Simulink Report Generator™ lets you customize and generate richly formatted Microsoft® Word, Microsoft PowerPoint®, HTML, and PDF reports from Simulink® models and simulations. The report generator lets you automatically create artifacts for model-based design, such as system design descriptions, generated code, requirements traceability reports, and model coverage reports. It can produce artifacts for DO-178, ISO 26262, IEC 61508, and related industry standards.

CONCLUSION

For complex embedded control systems development, configuration management and documentation are critically important. For a complex software project to be successful, communication among distributed development team members is critical and needs to be improved. The configuration management is applied to ensure timely and correct information sharing, is also used to manage changes during the development cycles. In model-based design approach, the plant and control system model serve as the executable specifications of the product. Models among other design artifacts are maintained by a configuration management system for version control, change management and other purposes. From the models, different design documents can be created, ideally using documentation automation tools, to maintain the consistency and timeliness of documentation. Documents are still an essential part of the model-based design process; they are used to record requirements, design, test plans and test results, etc. Textual documents are more effective for communication with non-technical stakeholders of the product. Documentation is used for many purposes including review, process improvement, and product certification.

REFERENCES

Estublier, J. (2001). Software Configuration Management A Road Map. *ICSE Proceedings of the Conference on The Future of Software Engineering*.

Hass, A. (2003). *Configuration management principles and practices*. Boston, MA: Pearson Education, Inc.

Logan, P., Harvey, D., & Spencer, D. (2012). Documents are an Essentail Part of Model Based Systems Engineering. *Proceedings of INCOSE International Symposium*. doi:10.1109/VLSISOC.2006.313244

Mahapatra, S., Schlosser, J., Roeder, S., & Segelken, M. (2012). Jumpstarting Team Collaboration in Model-based Design.*ASE Workshop on Comparison and Versioning of Software Models (CVSM 2012)*.

Muranko, B., & Drechsler, R. (2006). Technical Documentation of software and Hardware in Embedded Systems.*Proceedings of IFIP International Conference on Very Large Scale Integration*.

Shamieh, C. (2012). *System Engineering For Dummies*. Hoboken, NJ: John Wiley & Sons, Inc.

Walker, G., Friedman, J., & Aberg, R. (2007). *Configuration Management of the Model-based Design Process*. SAE Technical Paper 2007-01-1775. DOI: 10.4271/2007-01-1775

About the Author

Wei Wu is a model-based design technical lead at a global technology company. He has industrial controls experiences in semiconductor equipment, inkjet printer, unmanned aerial vehicle, and HVAC areas. His current research interests include model-based control design and novel controller synthesis strategies and applications. He graduated from Tongji University, Shanghai, China, with a B.E. and a M.E. degree in Bridge Engineering in 1992 and 1995, respectively. He received a M.S. degree in Civil Engineering from University of Missouri-Columbia, U.S.A. in 1996. He obtained a Ph.D. degree in System and Controls from the Mechanical Engineering department of Texas A&M University, U.S.A. in 2000. He has published thirty-seven journal and refereed conference papers, has one trade secret, was awarded the best session paper award twice at American Control Conference, and chaired or co-chaired four sessions at control conferences. He received Distinguished Graduate Student Award Doctoral from Texas A&M University in 2000. He was a Best Student Paper Award finalist at American Control Conference in 2001. He served as an Associated Editor for Dynamic System and Control Division, American Society of Mechanical Engineers, from 2010 to 2012. He is a member of American Society of Mechanical Engineers.

Index

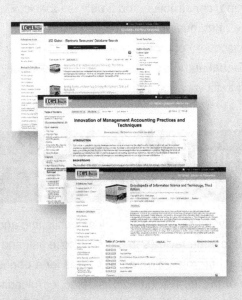

Printed in the United States
By Bookmasters